KNOWLEDGE-BASED VOCABULARY LISTS

British Council Monographs on Modern Language Testing

Series Editors: Karen Dunn, British Council; Tineke Brunfaut, University of Lancaster
Founding Co-editors: Vivien Berry and Barry O'Sullivan, both at the British Council

This series – published in cooperation with the British Council – provides short books in the area of language testing. These titles are written by well known language testing scholars from across the world including members of the British Council's Assessment Research Group (ARG). The books offer both a theoretical and a practical perspective to language testing and assessment – proposing, where required, models of development, which are reflected in actual test tasks. They are unique in that they are authored by individuals with considerable academic, teaching and assessment experience, thus offering the reader a unique insight into the link between theory and practice in the area. In many cases, the books illustrate their approach with reference to actual test items, from the British Council's Aptis test service.

Published:

Assessing the language of young learners
Angela Hasselgreen and Gwendydd Caudwell

Rethinking the second language listening test: From theory to practice
John Field

Scoring second language spoken and written performance: Issues, options and directions
Ute Knoch, Judith Fairbairn and Yan Jin

Validity: Theoretical development and integrated arguments
Micheline Chalhoub-Deville and Barry O'Sullivan

Forthcoming:

Assessing reading
Tineke Brunfaut and Jamie Dunlea

Assessing second language writing: Current and future perspectives
Anthony Green

Assessing speaking: Current and future perspectives
Fumiyo Nakatsuhara and Vivien Berry

Comprehensibility in language assessment: A broader perspective
Parvaneh Tavakoli and Sheryl Cooke

KNOWLEDGE-BASED VOCABULARY LISTS

Norbert Schmitt, Karen Dunn, Barry O'Sullivan,
Laurence Anthony, and Benjamin Kremmel

UNIVERSITY OF TORONTO PRESS

Toronto Buffalo London

Reprinted by University of Toronto Press 2024
Toronto Buffalo London
utorontopress.com
Printed in the USA

First published 2024 by Equinox Publishing Ltd

British Library Cataloguing-in-Publication Data
A catalogue record for this book is available from the British Library.

ISBN-13 978-1-8005-0413-4 (cloth)
          978-1-8005-0414-1 (paper)
          978-1-8005-0415-8 (PDF)
          978-1-8005-0454-7 (EPUB)

Library of Congress Cataloging-in-Publication Data

Names: Schmitt, Norbert, 1956- author. | Dunn, Karen, 1961- author. |
  O'Sullivan, Barry, author. | Anthony, Laurence, author. | Kremmel,
  Benjamin, author.
Title: Knowledge-based vocabulary lists / Norbert Schmitt, Karen Dunn,
  Barry O'Sullivan, Laurence Anthony and Benjamin Kremmel.
Description: Bristol, CT : Equinox Publishing Ltd., 2024. | Series: British
  Council Monograph on Modern Language Testing ; volume 5 | Includes
  bibliographical references and index. | Summary: "This volume explores
  the need for word lists based on direct tests of learner knowledge to
  inform L2 pedagogy. The Knowledge-based Vocabulary Lists (KVL) are
  introduced, and a description of the theoretical and practical basis for
  their development is given, highlighting pedagogical and assessment
  situations in which it is beneficial to know whether learners are likely
  to be able produce and correctly spell the words they know"-- Provided
  by publisher.
Identifiers: LCCN 2023023608 (print) | LCCN 2023023609 (ebook) | ISBN
  9781800504134 (hardback) | ISBN 9781800504141 (paperback) | ISBN
  9781800504158 (ePDF) | ISBN 9781800504547 (ePub)
Subjects: LCSH: Second language acquisition. | Vocabulary--Study and
  teaching. | English language--Study and teaching--Foreign speakers.
Classification: LCC P118.2 .S364 2024 (print) | LCC P118.2 (ebook) | DDC
  401/.4--dc23/eng/20231019
LC record available at https://lccn.loc.gov/2023023608
LC ebook record available at https://lccn.loc.gov/2023023609

Typeset by S.J.I. Services, New Delhi, India

CONTENTS

LIST OF FIGURES

Credits

Figure 1.1: Reproduced by permission of Cambridge University Press from *Vocabulary in Language Teaching* by N. Schmitt and D. Schmitt, © Cambridge University Press 2020.

LIST OF TABLES

Credits

Table 1.1   Reproduced by permission of UTP Journals from How large a vocabulary is needed for reading and listening? by P. Nation, *Canadian Modern Language Review*, 63(1), © UTP Journals 2006.

Table 2.3   British National Corpus (BNC) data reproduced by permission of the BNC Consortium (2007). The British National Corpus, XML Edition, 2007. Oxford Text Archive. http://hdl.handle.net/20.500.12024/2554

ACKNOWLEDGEMENTS

A research project of this size and scope inevitably requires help and cooperation from a large number of people. We are extremely grateful for the assistance provided by the following collaborators. We have endeavoured to include everyone who contributed to the project, but offer apologies to anyone we have inadvertently omitted.

- For access to his crowdsourced L1 test results and SUBTlex lists: Marc Brysbaert.
- For providing frequency-based lists of lemmas based on the COCA corpus: Mark Davies.
- For providing test results from his Japanese university students: Aaron Gibson.
- For providing feedback on the development of the KVL, at conferences and privately: Batia Laufer.
- For helping develop the initial Spanish pilot version of the KVL test, and the item-writing protocols: Beatriz González Fernández, and Marijana Macis.
- For helping develop the initial Chinese pilot version of the KVL test, the item-writing protocols, and the Chinese test items: Xu Xiaofan.
- For support in encouraging respondents to participate in the pilot and/or main stage data collection: Michelle Alejandra Batarse Saieh, Mireya Aguilera Munizaga, Mark Bowthorpe, Paula Díaz, Marion Durbahn, Claudia Harsch, Friederike Jaene, Phobe Lin, Rosa Manchon, Imma Mirelpex, Carme Muñoz, Ana Pellicer-Sánchez, Rachel Serrano, Alexandra Vraciu, Andrea Revesz, Marlene Schwartz, Judith Sebastiani, Wen-ta (Thomas) Tseng, and Xuelian Xu.
- For helping with the direct publicity for the *Vocabulary Challenge*: Vicky Ainsworth, Viviana Caicedo, and Ruth Groth.
- For translating/checking/revising test items into Spanish, German, or Chinese: Mia Aghajari, Viviana Caicedo, Arianna Carrizo Ruiz, Kathrin Eberharter, Beatriz González Fernández,

Uwe Grabher, Ruth Groth, Stefanie Hollenstein, Yuanfang Hua, Xiaojun Lu, Bernadette Maguire, Sean McDonald, Xiao Sa, Ana Pellicer-Sánchez, Danni Shi, Ulrike Trodler, Jin Yan, Andi Wang, and Judy Wang.

ABOUT THE AUTHORS

Norbert Schmitt is Emeritus Professor of Applied Linguistics at the University of Nottingham, specialising in second language vocabulary issues. He directed the project from a lexical perspective, and carried out the main data analysis.

Karen Dunn is a senior researcher at the British Council specialising in measurement and evaluation in language testing; she contributed to early decisions about data collection and carried out data analysis, specifically the Rasch-based analysis of the test results. Karen also acted as the general manager of the project, as the communications liaison between the members of the research team, and as the coordinator of the various parallel strands of research.

Barry O'Sullivan is Head of Assessment Research and Development at the British Council. He headed the measurement aspects of the project, as well as securing funding for the project overall.

Laurence Anthony is Professor in the Faculty of Science and Engineering at Waseda University in Japan, specialising in information technology for language research and pedagogy. He consulted on vocabulary issues in the study, built and maintained the web-based platform for crowd-sourced data collection, and managed the resulting dataset.

Benjamin Kremmel is Head of the Language Testing Research Group Innsbruck at the University of Innsbruck. He contributed to the lexical aspects of the research, particularly the vocabulary measurement issues.

CHAPTER 1

THE NEED FOR KNOWLEDGE-BASED VOCABULARY LISTS (KVL)

Vocabulary is the key type of knowledge necessary for any language use because if the words used to express concepts are not known, all syntactic and discourse knowledge is of little use. This is true for both first languages (L1) and second languages (L2). But while first language vocabulary is mainly learned incidentally from the massive exposure to language which children receive, much of second language vocabulary is typically learned in instructed environments. This means that second language pedagogy must have a way of prioritising which words to teach from among the multitude available. The focus of this monograph is on English vocabulary knowledge, a language which is estimated to have 10 million different individual words (Brysbaert et al., 2016a).

For English in particular, word lists have been used to inform this prioritisation of teaching for the last century. These lists have largely been based on word frequency, i.e., how often a certain word appears in typical (usually L1) discourse. While the word lists have proven useful, frequency has its limitations when predicting which words might be known by L2 learners. Therefore, there is a need to complement this information with word lists based on what language learners actually *know*.

This book describes the development of the ***Knowledge-based Vocabulary Lists*** (KVL) among English language learners from selected language backgrounds. It reports the rationale and creation of the KVL, presents the lists, and discusses their intended uses.

This chapter provides background information on word lists, and outlines the rationale and need for the KVL.

1.1 What vocabulary to focus on? A brief history of word lists

The question *What vocabulary to focus on?* may seem unnecessary but in fact the vocabulary of any language can be broken down into several quite distinct types. Schmitt & Schmitt (2020) discuss commonly used categories and the roles they play in discourse. Perhaps the most constrained category might be called *survival vocabulary*, which consists of the most essential words and phrases that allow someone to achieve the most basic needs of life. It is largely functional in nature, e.g., enquiring whether a hotel has an available room. Nation & Crabbe (1991) developed one survival list of about 120 words and phrases, which includes the following items.

Hello	Delicious	I want ___
No	Entrance/exit	Excuse me [to get attention]
How much [cost]	Please speak slowly	Where is ___

It was developed by asking people who had spent a month overseas what useful vocabulary they had needed/learned. This was compared to items listed in guidebooks and criteria such as frequency and learnability. The list can be found in 23 languages on Paul Nation's website (www.wgtn. ac.nz/lals/resources/paul-nations-resources/vocabulary-lists).

While surviving on a short overseas trip is a start, many people wish to do more using their second language, such as study or work professionally. This has led to lists of specialised vocabulary which have mainly revolved around notions of academic vocabulary and technical vocabulary. *Academic vocabulary* is defined as the sub-technical vocabulary that commonly occurs in academic discourse (cf. Paquot, 2010). There is no intrinsic property that makes any particular word or phrase 'academic' – rather, academic vocabulary is usually defined statistically by its relatively higher frequency in academic texts compared to general texts. The best-known academic word lists are the *Academic Word List* (AWL) (Coxhead, 2000), the *Academic Vocabulary List* (AVL) (Gardner & Davies, 2014), and the *Academic Formulas List* (AFL) (Simpson-Vlach & Ellis, 2010). Examples of academic vocabulary from these lists include the following items.

AWL	AVL	AFL
acquire	describe	it is important to
investigate	literature	on the basis of
scope	section	such as the
widespread	study	to some extent

Technical vocabulary is the specialised vocabulary used to represent the specific concepts necessary in a particular field. For example, in the field of law, an *appellant* is a person who appeals the decision of a court.

Technical words can name things (*trachea, chromosome*), classify concepts (*rhodophyta, omnivore*), describe processes (*hybridization, photosynthesis*), or describe states (*androgynous, nocturnal*). They can also be everyday words with technical meanings, e.g., *file* (an electronic document) and *cap* (as in blasting cap, used to set off explosives) (Fang & Schleppegrell, 2008). Applied linguistics also has technical vocabulary, some of which will be used in this book (e.g., *corpus, lemma, validity*).

Lists of specialised vocabulary are useful but the most influential word lists have been those that cover what might be called *general vocabulary*. When frequency-based criteria have been used, this has also been referred to as *high-frequency vocabulary*, and some scholars have conceptualised it as *core vocabulary*. Regardless of the terminology, this general vocabulary is essential, because it forms the foundation upon which all language use is based. Attempts to identify what constitutes general vocabulary have a long history. In 1864, Thomas Prendergast, objecting to the archaic word lists used in the Grammar-Translation method, compiled a list of the most common English words by relying solely on his intuitions (which proved to be surprisingly accurate) (Zimmerman, 1997).

Empirically determined corpus-based accounts of general English came to the fore in the first half of the 20th century when the *Vocabulary Control Movement* focused on efforts to systematise the selection of vocabulary. It used corpus evidence and systematic criteria, particularly frequency, to select the most useful words for language learning. Several researchers worked in this area during the period, and their efforts merged in what came to be referred to as the *Carnegie Report* (Palmer et al., 1936). The report recommended developing a list of vocabulary which would be useful in the production of simple reading materials. The list was finally published by Michael West as the *General Service List of English words* (GSL) in 1953. The GSL was highly influential, informing materials development and syllabus design for decades. However, it inevitably became dated (with words like *plough* and *shilling*), having been based on corpus evidence from the first half of the 1900s. There have been several attempts to update the GSL; the latest and best-known iteration is the *New General Service List* (new-GSL) (Brezina & Gablasova, 2015).

It is interesting to look at how general vocabulary was defined in these lists. The roughly 2,000 headwords in the original GSL (West, 1953) were selected based on a range of criteria (see below), with frequency being primary. The 2,494-lemma new-GSL (Brezina & Gablasova, 2015) was compiled by drawing on word lists based on four diverse corpora, and then selecting the top words from those lists based on frequency and distribution criteria. Thus, for both the GSL and the new-GSL, frequency was the driving force in word selection. In fact, the notions of general vocabulary and frequency are inexorably linked. This makes it worth looking at the role of frequency in word list compilation in greater detail.

1.2 Frequency in word lists: Strengths and limitations

It is understandable why frequency is so important in the compilation of general English word lists. In simple terms, a relatively small number of the most frequent words in a language make up the vast majority of discourse. This phenomenon is captured in Zipf's law (see Sorrell, 2012), which shows that a relatively small number of words are extremely frequent, but then frequency drops off dramatically, with most words being relatively rare. This becomes obvious when we look at *coverage*, i.e., the number of words necessary to provide certain percentages of textual coverage (sometimes called *lexical coverage*). Nation (2006) provides a good demonstration of this for both written and spoken discourse. Table 1.1 summarises a number of his coverage analyses, using the counting unit of *word family*. A word family consists of the base form of a word (e.g., *access*), its inflections (e.g., *accessed, accessing, accesses*), and derivations (e.g., *accessibility, accessible, accessibly*). The table shows that the 1,000 most frequent word families make up around 80% of discourse, but beyond this, the coverage drops precipitously.

Word families	Approximate written coverage (%)	Approximate spoken coverage (%)
1st 1,000	78–81	81–84
2nd 1,000	8–9	5–6
3rd 1,000	3–5	2–3
4th–5th 1,000	3	1.5–3
6th–9th 1,000	2	0.75–1
10th–14th 1,000	<1	0.5
Proper nouns	2–4	1–1.5
14,000+	1–3	1

Table 1.1: Vocabulary size and text coverage across nine written and spoken corpora (Nation, 2006, p. 79)

The Zipfian nature of vocabulary is good news for L2 learners, because a relatively constrained set of words does the majority of work in English. This set of high-frequency, high-value words makes an obvious, and relatively manageable, goal for learning. Nation (2013) notes that all teaching/learning has costs, in terms of time, effort, and attention. Using a cost/benefit approach, he argues that teachers should prioritise words that have a high benefit for learners, regardless of the cost (essentially high-frequency vocabulary), because this vocabulary is useful in all contexts, and so should be learned by everyone. Conversely, low-frequency vocabulary is probably not worth focusing upon (unless it is specific to a particular topic relevant to the learner), and so little or no instruction time should be spent on it. If learners are interested in these words, they can learn them independently through vocabulary learning strategies.

Nation's general approach to high/low-frequency vocabulary surely makes sense but does not take into account the full nature of frequency. His definition of high-frequency words was the traditional 2,000 most frequent items. This figure partly came from the GSL, which includes about this many headwords, and research by Schonell et al. (1956) which showed that 2,000 word families covered around 99% of the spoken language they studied. All vocabulary beyond the 2,000 level (often abbreviated as **2K** level), was counted as low-frequency vocabulary, with the exception of academic vocabulary. However, Schmitt & Schmitt (2014) argue that the 2K cut-point is too low, and that a 3,000 cut-point (3K) is more pedagogically sound.

Schmitt & Schmitt (2014) go on to argue that the high-frequency/low-frequency dichotomy is too crude, and that an intermediate *mid-frequency* level is also required. The main reasons for this come from research into coverage. Van Zeeland & Schmitt (2013) found that 95% coverage enabled around 80% comprehension of information in spoken passages drawn from the Internet. Approximately 3,000 word families are necessary to achieve 95% coverage in this conversational discourse. Nation (2006) looked at a wider range of speech styles (i.e., formal, semi-formal, and informal speech) in the Wellington Corpus of Spoken English, and also calculated that it took 3,000 word families to give 95% coverage. Thus, Schmitt & Schmitt's (2014) 3K cut-point should allow considerable listening comprehension in English. However, for a more complete comprehension of spoken discourse that a 98% coverage would enable, it would take 6,000–7,000 families (plus proper nouns).

Laufer & Ravenhorst-Kalovski (2010) found higher requirements for reading, largely because written text is generally denser and more lexically diverse than spoken discourse. They carried out one of the most extensive analyses of lexical requirements for reading and identified two thresholds. The first was the ability to understand authentic English texts adequately with some support (e.g., teachers or resources like dictionaries). They called this the *minimal* threshold, that required 95% coverage, while the *optimal* threshold for independent reading required 98% coverage (see also Laufer, 1989). Schmitt et al. (2011) found that 95% coverage enabled comprehension of about 60% of the information in a written text. In terms of coverage, 95% equates to a vocabulary size requirement of 4,000–5,000 word families, while 98% requires 8,000–9,000 families. Thus, in order to read non-simplified texts, even with help, learners will need to know far more than 3,000 high-frequency words; they will need to know vocabulary at least at the 4–5K level, and vocabulary at the 8–9K level in order to read independently. Therefore, Schmitt & Schmitt set their mid-frequency range at between 4,000 and 9,000 word families. According to this scheme, 1–3K would be considered high-frequency vocabulary, 4–9K mid-frequency vocabulary, and vocabulary beyond the 9K level would be considered low-frequency (see Figure 1.1).

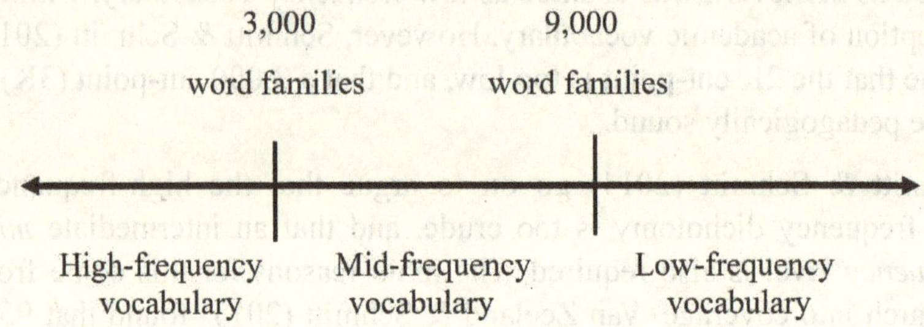

Figure 1.1: High-, mid-, and low-frequency vocabulary (Schmitt & Schmitt, 2020, p. 81)

This distinction is a very useful way to categorise words in terms of pedagogy and more nuanced than the high/low dichotomy. High-frequency vocabulary is so essential that it needs a strong focus, both in explicit instruction and self-study. Mid-frequency vocabulary is important for more advanced language use, and should also be learned. But there are so many words in this category that explicit instruction alone will not be feasible, which means large amounts of exposure (reading and listening) leading to incidental learning will also be necessary. Low-frequency vocabulary is relatively less useful, and should not be emphasised unless specifically needed.

There is also evidence that people learning English as a second or foreign language (hereafter ESL) acquire more vocabulary in higher frequency bands than lower frequency bands. This typically manifests itself as a 'stair-step' pattern in vocabulary test results, where each successive frequency band has lower scores than the previous band. This is well illustrated in the validation evidence for the *Vocabulary Levels Test* (Schmitt et al., 2001). Figure 1.2 shows the mean scores for the 2K, 3K, 5K, and 10K frequency bands for 801 ESL learners of various proficiencies and L1s who took part in the study. The stair-step phenomenon is quite robust for groups of words and groups of learners. But it is important to note that there are typically large variations among individual learners in the vocabulary they know. Frequency is not nearly as predictive of learner knowledge for individual learners, or individual words.

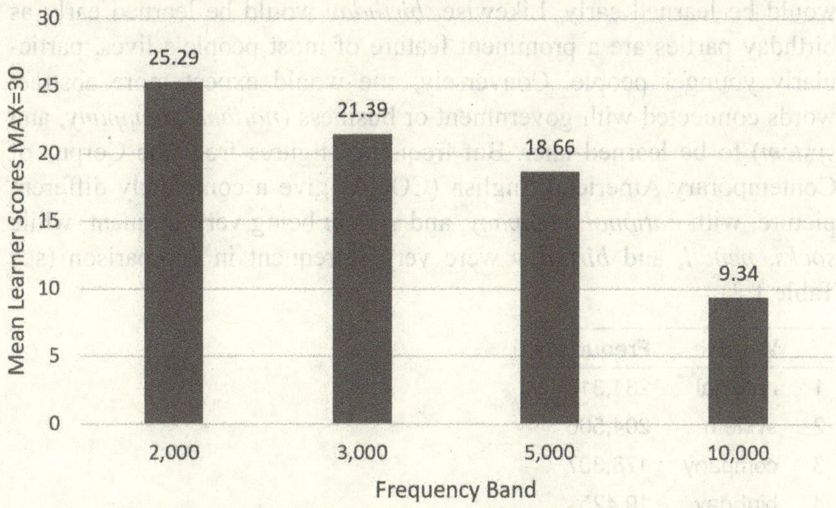

Figure 1.2: Mean vocabulary scores at the 2K, 3K, 5K, and 10K frequency bands

Up to this point, the discussion has shown the importance of frequency in language learning and use – there is no surprise it has been used as the major factor in selecting which words to teach, to place on word lists, and to use in vocabulary tests. In essence, the rationale has been: Teach the most useful words in a language, and the most frequent words are the most useful. Thus, frequency lists have been used to grade the 'difficulty' of vocabulary for around a century, and they seem to work, at least in an approximate manner.

However, inevitably it is not so straightforward and there are limits as to how well frequency can predict which words will be learned and known. This can be shown by the following short activity. First rank the words in the order that you think L1 or L2 learners might learn them, i.e., 1 = first learned, 6 = last learned.

    ____ birthday
    ____ company
    ____ national
    ____ pencil
    ____ system
    ____ socks

If you are like most people who have done this exercise, your intuition is that everyday objects (*socks*) and classroom-based materials (*pencil*) would be learned early. Likewise, *birthday* would be learned early as birthday parties are a prominent feature of most people's lives, particularly younger people. Conversely, one would expect more abstract words connected with government or business (*national, company*, and *system*) to be learned later. But frequency figures from the Corpus of Contemporary American English (COCA) give a completely different picture, with *national, company*, and *system* being very frequent, while *socks, pencil*, and *birthday* were very infrequent in comparison (see Table 1.2).

	Word	Frequency
1	national	231,318
2	system	204,500
3	company	178,307
4	birthday	19,425
5	socks	6,660
6	pencil	6,277

Table 1.2: Frequencies from the 520-million-word COCA (4 October 2019)

Of course, we chose the above words to make a point, and clearly L2 words are learned with some relationship to frequency, e.g., words we would expect to be learned early like *man* (370,606) and *good* (510,181) are very frequent, while words expected to be learned later are infrequent in comparison: *inhabitant* (321), *analogy* (4,026). But the illustration above shows that using frequency to predict knowledge of L2 vocabulary is imperfect and may have many mismatches. The extent of the mismatches was previously unknown as there were few large-scale, empirically-based listings of the rank order in which L2 students learn words with which to compare frequency. The *Knowledge-based Vocabulary Lists* (KVL) allow this comparison, and show many cases where frequency does not predict learner knowledge very well – see Chapter 7 for the results.

There are numerous possible reasons for frequency–knowledge mismatches. First, corpus-based frequencies are massively affected by the composition of the particular corpora from which they are derived. For example, the frequency ranking of words in spoken discourse will be different from that in written discourse. However, while many general corpora have both spoken and written components – e.g., COCA, British National Corpus (BNC) – most are biased towards written discourse, because historically this has been much easier to collect. Without the availability of highly accurate transcription software, building a corpus of truly spontaneous, everyday speech still requires an expensive and time-consuming process of collecting speech samples, manually transcribing the data, and linking that data to metadata about the speakers. (To avoid this process, most spoken corpora have been built by using transcripts of spoken radio and television programs, which introduces another problem – see below.) Overall, the 100-million-word BNC has only about 10 million words of spoken discourse, while the 520-million-word COCA contains around 118 million spoken words, at the time of writing. This design choice emphasises words that are more common in written texts.

Corpora can also be skewed by other elements of their composition. For example, language in novels and newspapers tends to be more colloquial than language in academic texts and technical manuals. So, if a corpus is weighted towards representation of a particular genre of written language, the relative frequencies of colloquial vs formal vocabulary will be affected if the corpus is processed as a single monolithic object, which is often the case.

Second, learning is driven by the input to which learners are exposed. In a perfect world, a corpus would accurately reflect the complete range of language styles, genres, and contexts that a learner is exposed to. This would likely lead to corpus frequencies that closely predict L2 vocabulary knowledge. But in practice, this is far from the reality, and researchers have to resort to using the corpora available to them, despite the limitations. For example, most large general corpora (with their written bias) do not represent the input young L1 children receive, as they typically do not read newspapers and magazines, and most of their input is oral. Using the spoken component of a large general corpus would perhaps be better, but even here, the spoken components are usually made up of transcripts of talk-show radio and television, and do not reflect the simplified and child-directed caretaker talk that children hear.

It is also important to remember that the language knowledge of L2 learners will greatly differ from that of their L1 counterparts, due to their learning context and their different stages of literacy and age development. As an example, although input from the digital world is increasing, for many L2 child and adult learners, input still largely comes from their textbooks. In this regard, there are many corpora of textbook language, which can more closely reflect the language input that learners receive. Even so, these corpora only reflect a partial view as they are unlikely to include the additional language input that learners get through teacher interaction as the textbooks are being used.

Again, in an ideal world, L2 learner textbooks themselves would reflect the language distributions of the real world. This could be done (imperfectly) by following corpus evidence, but the majority of textbooks do not do this. They are largely written to include diverse 'jaunty' and interesting topics and whatever vocabulary goes with them, with little regard for a principled approach to vocabulary selection (Schmitt, 2019). This means that L2 learners using different textbooks may be exposed to widely varying vocabulary – it is no wonder that the words they learn do not always match well with frequency figures.

This all explains that, while frequency can give a crude indication of learner knowledge of vocabulary, it can be misleading in many cases. We could look at other criteria used in word list development to supplement and sharpen the limited predictive power of frequency. In particular, the GSL used a number of diverse criteria, as shown below (Howatt, 2004, p. 289).

1.   word frequency
2.   structural value (all structural words included)
3.   universality (words likely to cause offence locally excluded)
4.   subject range (no specialist items)
5.   definition words (for dictionary-making, etc.)

6. word-building capacity
7. style (colloquial or slang words excluded)

However, looking at these criteria, they all either *describe* vocabulary, or try to quantify its *usefulness*. 'Word frequency' simply indicates how common individual words are, and so has been used as the main marker of usefulness. Likewise, 'structural vocabulary' (words like *the*, *by*, and *there*, now better known as *function words* or *grammatical words*) is useful because it is extremely frequent and appears in all discourse regardless of topic. These function words are needed for constructing sentences for topics ranging from food to carpentry to astrophysics. 'Word-building capacity' is also a measure of usefulness, as words that can be used as a base for many other words (e.g., *nation* → *national, international, nationalize, nationally*, etc.) are worth knowing. 'Definition words' are obviously useful for using dictionaries and understanding the definitions. 'Universality' and 'style' are exclusion criteria, removing words which may prove offensive or are considered too colloquial. Similarly, 'subject range' basically excludes technical vocabulary. Thus, we see that all these criteria describe the characteristics of words themselves, not the likelihood of the words being known. In fact, frequency, although imperfect, is the best traditional indicator of this.

But there are times when practitioners would benefit from information about the likelihood of their learners knowing particular words. For example, if learners know certain words (*human, hour, book*), are they also likely to know others (*hero, change, fruit*)? If they know some members of a lexical set (*apple, orange*), are they also likely to know other members of the set (*banana, pear, peach*)? If we want to measure learners' vocabulary size, which words should we put on the test that learners have a reasonable chance of knowing? In these cases, frequency has limited usefulness, e.g., *pear* is one-tenth as frequent as *orange*, even though pears might be a much more common fruit in some learners' homes.

This suggests the need for a completely new criterion relating directly to learner knowledge, i.e., empirically-based evidence about what learners *actually* know, compared to what frequency *predicts* they know. The only way to gather this evidence is to <u>test</u> learners for their knowledge of a wide range of words. It would then be possible to determine which words are better known by learners (and thus typically learned earlier) and which are lesser known (typically learned later). The *Knowledge-based Vocabulary Lists* (KVL) are the result of such work, providing lists of words, ranked according to the probability of learners knowing each one. Subsequently, the KVL can be used for numerous purposes:

- to provide teachers, syllabus designers, and textbook writers with information on the words that are less likely to be known by students from a given L1 background and thus require careful treatment
- to provide test developers with information on how vocabulary development occurs, with implications for vocabulary testing (i.e., some high-frequency words are less well-known than other words of a similar frequency and so the difficulty of test items will likely reflect the knowledge rankings more closely than the frequency rankings)
- to serve as a resource in any pedagogic application where knowledge of the typical acquisition order of vocabulary would be beneficial (e.g., teachers may choose to spend more classroom time focusing on key words for a given topic that have been shown to be less likely to be known by learners)
- to be used in tandem with frequency information, to give a fuller understanding of learner knowledge (i.e., frequency-based lists have value in providing useful *prescriptive* information on words that learners are likely to need to know for a particular purpose, whereas knowledge-based lists provide useful *descriptive* information about the words they are likely to know)

These purposes will be taken up again in Chapter 10, which describes how the KVL should (and should not) be used. The next chapter explains the development of the KVL, starting with how we created the list of candidate lemmas that would be used in our vocabulary test.

CHAPTER 2

CREATING A LIST OF LEMMAS TO TEST

Creating the KVL was a lengthy process that involved multiple stages, as follows:

1. conceptualising the list(s) and making decisions about scope
2. developing a list of target items which we would test with our L2 respondents
3. creating a feasible test format to measure the thousands of target words
4. making the test available online and generating the surrounding publicity
5. collecting data and monitoring progress of responses
6. analysing response data to create the three *Knowledge-based Vocabulary Lists* (KVL)

In practice, the stages occurred concurrently, with decisions about each affecting the others. However, to make the description in this book clearer, each stage is presented sequentially. This chapter covers the first two stages: describing issues involved in conceptualising the KVL; and creating a list of target words to measure.

2.1　Deciding on the counting unit

Chapter 1 outlined a number of pedagogical uses for a word list to indicate the relative probabilities of learners knowing particular words. Our goal was to produce such a list, and so all decisions in developing it were based on pedagogical utility. This began with the initial conceptualisation of the list, and what it might ultimately look like. Two issues in particular would shape the final form of the list: the counting unit the list would employ; and the length of the list, i.e., how many items it would contain.

Up to this point, we have spoken of *words*; however, this is not precise enough for research. The problem is that, in English, meanings are related to word forms in complex ways (Schmitt & Schmitt, 2020). For instance, consider the following items: *die; expire; pass away; bite the dust; kick the bucket;* and *give up the ghost*. These six examples are synonymous with the meaning 'to die'. However, they are made up of one to four words. *Die* and *expire* are single words, *pass away* could be described as a phrasal verb, and the last three are idioms. Thus, there is not necessarily a one-to-one correspondence between a meaning and a single word. Often, meanings are represented by multiple words.

There are also issues with the various grammatical and morphological permutations of vocabulary. This relates to how we 'package' words together and revolves around the degree to which learners can recognise morphologically-related words. For example, can learners recognise that *survival* is the noun form of the verb *survive*? In a detailed discussion of the issue, Nation (2016) refers to the affixation hierarchy developed by Bauer & Nation (1993), which lists different degrees of packaging words. Level 2, the first level beyond the word itself, includes straightforward inflectional suffixes. The taxonomy moves through Level 3 and Level 4 with regular and frequently applied affixes, to Level 5 with less frequent but still regular affixes and Level 6 which expands to include irregular affixes, to the top level, Level 7, which encompasses a huge range of associated words (Bauer & Nation, 1993, pp. 258–262). For native speakers, Nation (2016) suggests that word knowledge extends to Level 6 on the hierarchy. Most scholars would refer to the items at Level 6 as *word families* (stem + inflections + derivatives, i.e., *nation, nations, national, nationalize, nationally, international*, etc.). Nation argues that word families make sense for native speakers, as they are likely to have a reasonable grasp of morphology, and will recognise the members of a family as related. This is supported by Brysbaert et al. (2016a) who estimate that the average 20-year-old English native speaker knows about four members per word family. For beginning L2 learners, Nation suggests that Level 2, typically labelled as *lemma* (stem + inflections only: i.e., *country, countries*), is more appropriate because these learners often have limited morphological knowledge. This is supported by McLean (2018), who shows that learners seem relatively able to produce the Level 2 inflected forms, presumably because they are based on rules which generally operate in a regular and consistent manner, e.g., the progressive form of a verb involves *-ing*. However, at higher levels of proficiency, the question of which unit of counting to use becomes more complicated. In terms of *productive* ability, there is convincing evidence that learners do not reliably know all of the various word family members (i.e., Level 6), and so they will not necessarily be able to write or speak the appropriate derivative forms when required (Schmitt & Zimmerman,

2002; Ward & Chuenjundaeng, 2009). For *receptive* knowledge, there is also evidence that learners might have problems in recognising the members of a word family. González-Fernández & Schmitt (2019) tested 144 Spanish speakers of English on their knowledge of four word classes (noun, verb, adjective, adverb) for 20 target words. Table 2.1 shows the mean percentages of four derivatives correctly recognised on the multiple-option test. As the results show, the majority of derivative forms were not recognised by most learners (although it must be noted that the words were presented in isolation rather than in context).

Correctly identified	% of participants
0	12.0
1	24.9
2	28.1
3	20.0
4	15.0

Table 2.1: Mean percentages of four derivatives correctly recognised on the multiple-option test

Nation (2016, p. 35) explains that learners 'differ greatly' in their morphological awareness. This observation is tied to the learners' characteristics, including their L1, age, exposure to the L2, and a host of other factors. This means it is difficult to set a level beyond lemmas (Level 2) that would be suitable for a broad range of learners. Thus, until we have research specifying a level of awareness that can be assumed for most learners, the safest approach is to use the relatively conservative counting unit of lemmas (Level 2), as Nation suggests (see also Kremmel, 2016).

In addition to the issue of morphology, there is another rather mundane reason for using lemmas as the counting unit rather than a unit such as 'word family'. End users, like teachers (and also some researchers), may not understand the concept of word family and simply interpret the figures as 'individual words'. This could lead to a misleading sense of the vocabulary knowledge required. For example, needing 3,000 'lexical items' to watch television and movies (see Webb & Rodgers, 2009a, 2009b) may seem like a challenging, but not impossible, task. The reality is that 3,000 word families translates into over 19,000 individual words (types), which is a much more demanding proposition.

For these reasons, we opted to use lemmas as our counting unit in the KVL project. The list is meant for pedagogical purposes for ESL learners, and we felt a lemma was the unit best matched to the morphological knowledge that most learners involved with the list would be likely to know.

It is interesting to note some recent discussion about another counting unit, the *flemma*. A flemma is similar to a lemma, but combines all of the varying word classes. For example, whereas *crack* the verb (break) and *crack* the noun (narcotic) are two different lemmas because they belong to different word classes, they merge into a single flemma. There is some initial evidence that flemmas may be a suitable unit for some L2 teaching and learning purposes (e.g., Brown et al., 2020; McLean, 2018), but this research arrived after our decision to use lemmas for our study.

The issue of multi-word lexical units was more difficult. We were aware of the importance of formulaic sequences (Schmitt, 2010), but incorporating them into our study would have proven very problematic. First, formulaic sequences (also referred to as multi-word units) come in all shapes and sizes, for example, idioms, collocations, lexical bundles, phrasal verbs, phrasal expressions, and variable expressions/concgrams. Each of these categories has its own characteristics (Schmitt & Schmitt, 2020). With this variety, it is not surprising that there is little agreement on what comprises a formulaic sequence. With no clear definition, it would have been impossible to search for formulaic sequences or test them in our study.

A second problem is that most computer software is still based on word forms. For example, if you type *expire* into a concordancing program, it will search for only exact orthographic examples. It is not yet possible to search for the meaning 'to die'. This type of meaning-based search must still be carried out manually, although this may change in the future.

Thus, based on definitional ambiguity and the limited software available at the time of the project, the decision was taken to focus on single lemmas only, and (regrettably) to disregard formulaic language.

2.2   The number of lemmas to include on the KVL

Given the intended pedagogic purposes of the list, its length needed to correspond broadly to the number of lemmas necessary for learners to function in English. However, specifying this number is quite difficult. As we have seen, Zipf's law indicates that a relatively limited number of very high-frequency words account for the majority of the running words that occur in a text (see Figure 1.1). This has led to the use of frequency bands (e.g., 1K, 2K, 3K, etc.) to probabilistically describe the words that learners are likely to need to utilise English. We used this frequency-band-based approach to vocabulary size requirements to inform our decision on the eventual size of the KVL.

The KVL will be denominated in lemmas; however, almost all of the research on vocabulary size to date has been based on the word family unit, largely because of Paul Nation's influence. He produced a number of influential tools for measuring and researching vocabulary, all using word families: the Vocabulary Levels Test (Nation, 1990); the vocabulary analysis program, Range (www.wgtn.ac.nz/lals/resources/paul-nations-resources/vocabulary-analysis-programs); and several lists of vocabulary (e.g., the BNC–COCA list) (www.wgtn.ac.nz/lals/resources/paul-nations-resources/vocabulary-lists). Despite word families and lemmas being different counting units, research has shown that, on average, word families translate into lemmas in a ratio of roughly 1 to 3–4 (i.e., 1 word family→3–4 lemmas) (Brysbaert et al., 2016a; Nation, 2016). This means that word family counts can still provide useful guidance in terms of lemma requirements.

To determine how much vocabulary is required to function in a second language, two things are necessary. The first is the percentage of words in a written text/listening passage (i.e., *coverage*) which a person needs to know in order to understand it. The second is the number of words necessary to reach this percentage. Laufer & Ravenhorst-Kalovski (2010) found that 95% coverage was minimally adequate for understanding written texts, and calculated that this required 4,000–5,000 word families (including proper nouns). For more independent reading comprehension, they found that 98% coverage was necessary, requiring 8,000–9,000 word families. Van Zeeland & Schmitt (2013) looked at conversational spoken narratives and found that 95% coverage was adequate, requiring around 2,000–3,000 word families, while Nation (2006) found that it took 6,000–7,000 families (plus proper nouns) to reach a higher 98% coverage (see Chapter 1). Research into watching television and movies showed that it took knowledge of the most frequent 3,000 word families to reach 95% lexical coverage and about 6,000–7,000 families to reach 98% coverage, although there was considerable variation among the individual programs and movies in terms of the amount of vocabulary required (Rodgers & Webb, 2011; Webb & Rodgers 2009a, 2009b) (see the discussion earlier in this chapter).

In summary, there is no one vocabulary size which is adequate in all cases. The required amount varies depending on the type of discourse (oral or written), and the comprehension needs of the reader or listener (beginning to access authentic texts with help, or independent usage). While independent listening and reading can take 6,000–9,000 word families, learners who are striving to move on to authentic materials can do with less than this, especially if they are involved in a pedagogical environment where help is available. In these cases, around 3,000 families gets them to the 'minimal' 95% coverage in listening and watching television and movies, and around 4,000–5,000 families does the same for reading.

On balance, around 5,000 word families seems to be a reasonable minimum requirement for learners to operate in the 'pedagogic zone' when using English, including reading. The higher end of this zone is somewhere around 8,000–9,000 word families, where learners are becoming more independent and able to engage with a wider range of listening and reading. If we take 5,000 word families as a minimal pedagogic requirement, that would convert into around 15,000–20,000 lemmas based on the conversion ratio of 1 to 3–4 (Brysbaert et al., 2016a; Nation, 2016). After considering the advantages of investigating larger numbers of lemmas with the feasibility constraints of collecting extremely large amounts of data and maintaining a rigorous testing approach, we decided a reasonable compromise was 5,000 lemmas. While this is far short of 15,000–20,000 lemmas, several factors convinced us that a logistically feasible 5,000 lemma list would still prove useful.

First, research shows that lemmas do not all have equal pedagogic value. As an example, take the word family for *avoid*. The frequencies for the COCA are given in Table 2.2 which shows that, although the word family for *avoid* is made up of seven members, the lemma accounts for over 95% of the occurrences in the COCA. The three derivatives *avoidance*, *avoidable*, and *avoider* hardly occur in comparison. Thus, the lemma is virtually performing as the whole word family in terms of coverage provided. Moreover, *avoid* is not an isolated case. Laufer & Cobb (2019) analysed a range for text types and found that basewords and inflections (i.e., lemmas) accounted for over 94% text coverage on average. We also find high coverage figures for lemmas even if we consider only the most frequent ones. Brown (2018) found that basewords and inflections of the 5,000 most frequent words constituted 86.6% of the BNC corpus. The word family members in the lemma carry the vast majority of load for the complete family. Thus, opting for 5,000 lemmas for the KVL provides most of the coverage value of 5,000 word families, and should make the KVL viable pedagogically.

Word	COCA frequency	% of word family
avoid	73,465	68.8
avoided	12,910	12.1
avoiding	12,463	11.7
avoids	3,186	3.0
Total for the lemma *avoid*	102,024	95.5
avoidance	3,969	3.7
avoidable	775	0.7
avoider	38	<0.1
Total for word family *avoid*	106,806	100

Table 2.2: COCA frequencies for the members of the word family 'avoid' (January 2021)

The figure of 5,000 was also chosen because, for the most part, English language learners have rather limited vocabulary sizes. Laufer (2000, p. 48), for example, reports that most learners have sizes of less than 2,000–3,000 families. However, as learners often do not know many or most of the derivative members of a family (McLean, 2018; Schmitt & Zimmerman, 2002; Ward & Chuenjundaeng, 2009), in reality their true knowledge may well be closer to 2,000–3,000 lemmas. Thus, a 5,000-lemma list would be informative for the majority of ESL learners worldwide, while still being feasible to develop.

Additionally, as words become less frequent, they tend to be more context- and domain-specific (Gardner, 2013). There is no one frequency point where 'general vocabulary' ends, but certainly by the 5,000 level, words become noticeably more connected with specific topics and domains. The most pedagogically useful vocabulary to include in the KVL will therefore be higher-frequency vocabulary that is used across a wide variety of contexts.

A related issue is that people are exposed to different vocabulary depending on their circumstances and interests, meaning that lower-frequency vocabulary will be more context-dependent. For example, a medical student learning in an English-medium medical environment will be exposed to quite different language to an agricultural student learning about crop prices and the weather. Thus, as vocabulary becomes less frequent, the knowledge of any given word by any given learner becomes more and more idiosyncratic. We wanted the KVL to show the kind of vocabulary knowledge that is generalisable to most learners, but after the 5K level, it is likely that such knowledge would be more difficult to identify due to this idiosyncratic learning behaviour. These reasons supported our decision to settle for 5,000 lemmas.

2.3   Choosing the reference corpora to use

To establish a list of lemmas likely to be among the 5,000 best-known, it was necessary to consult one or more corpora as a starting point. The best corpus to use in any situation depends on the purpose of your research or pedagogy (Pinchbeck & Schmitt, 2018). For example, for English for Specific Purposes, it can make sense to use a corpus of specialised vocabulary, e.g., a medical corpus to inform materials designed to help medical students (Wang, Liang, & Ge, 2008) or an engineering corpus if the goal is to understand language used in engineering textbooks (Ward, 1999). Since the intended purpose of the KVL was to inform the pedagogy and assessment of general English, a corpus which represents English across a wide variety of contexts and functions was most suitable. Also, based on the pedagogical decision to use the lemma as counting unit, it would be best to use a lemmatised corpus, i.e., a corpus that disambiguates words at the lemma level.

This narrowed the field with the major contenders being the suite of corpora developed/adapted by Mark Davies (2008–), and available on his website (www.english-corpora.org). The english-corpora.org possibilities revolved around five major corpora and their sub-corpora: the *Corpus of Contemporary American English* (*COCA*), the *Global Web-based English* (*GloWbE*), the *Wikipedia Corpus* (*Wikipedia*), and the *Corpus of American Soap Operas* (*Soap Operas*), as well as the *British National Corpus* (*BNC*), which Mark Davies was given permission by the BNC Consortium (2007) to make available through his site. Three sources not from english-corpora.org were also considered. Two were based on subtitle corpora: the *Subtitle Corpus* from American films and television series (*SUBTlex–US*) (www.ugent.be/pp/experimentele-psychologie/en/research/documents/subtlexus) and the corresponding *Subtitle Corpus* from British films and television series (*SUBTlex–UK*) (http://crr.ugent.be/archives/1423). The third source was the *Pearson GSE* ranking of words (*GSE*) (www.pearsonelt.com/about/gse/teacher-toolkit.html). This is not a corpus, but a ranking of word difficulty based on a combination of frequency and teacher judgements. The details of the corpora are listed in Table 2.3. GSE is based on words extracted from three corpora: Longman Corpus Network, ukWaC (a British Web Corpus from the .uk domain), and the COCA Spoken.

Corpus	Size	Language/dialect	Time period
COCA	560 million	American	1990–2017
COCA Spoken	117 million	American	1990–2017
COCA Fiction	112 million	American	1990–2017
COCA Magazine	117 million	American	1990–2017
COCA Newspaper	113 million	American	1990–2017
COCA Academic	111 million	American	1990–2017
BNC	96 million	British	1980s–1993
BNC Spoken	10 million	British	1980s–1993
BNC Fiction	16 million	British	1980s–1993
BNC Magazine	7 million	British	1980s–1993
BNC Newspaper	10 million	British	1980s–1993
BNC Non-academic	16 million	British	1980s–1993
BNC Academic	15 million	British	1980s–1993
BNC Misc.	21 million	British	1980s–1993
GloWbE	1.9 billion	20 countries / web	2012–2013
Wikipedia	1.9 billion	English	2014
Soap Operas	100 million	American	2001–2012
SUBTlex–US	51 million	American	1900–2007
SUBTlex–UK	201 million	BBC broadcasts	2010–2012

Note: The British National Corpus (BNC) is made available through permission given by the BNC Consortium (2007).

Table 2.3: Details of candidate corpora for the KVL project

Given that the purpose of the KVL was to indicate the relative probability of learners knowing lemmas, in order to choose from among these corpora and sub-corpora, one approach was to see how well the frequency rankings from each corpus matched up with the acquisition order based on actual test results. Corpora whose frequency figures correlated strongly with test results from learners would presumably be better suited to the purpose of reflecting learner knowledge than those corpora whose frequency figures did not match so well.

List frequency ranking ⟷ Test results ranking

The frequency information from each of the corpora was easily available but finding test results proved more difficult. Since every vocabulary-size test measures different words, there were few common words between tests which could be used for this exercise. This narrowed the possibilities to three main sources of data, including common target words.

The first test scores were supplied by Marc Brysbaert from Ghent University, Belgium. With colleagues Stevens, Mandera, and Keuleera (2016a), he administered a crowdsource-based test of English vocabulary knowledge. His team collected 1,000 responses per target lemma through crowdsourcing, with all respondents being US and UK native speakers. The test asked respondents to indicate whether they knew the word or not. It was a self-report Yes/No checklist with no demonstration of knowledge (although nonwords were included to control for overestimation) and 11,600 lemmas were reported known by 95% or more of the respondents. The next set of test results came from work by Benjamin Kremmel, who developed a new computer-based vocabulary test (Kremmel, 2017), which he administered to Austrian learners to test their knowledge of 400 English words. The test format was multiple-choice, with 40–100 examinees per lemma. The last main source of test results was from a study published by Shiotsu (2011) who administered his test to 116 first- and second-year Japanese university students. The students self-reported whether they knew the 2,532 target headwords in a Yes/No checklist format.

A comparison between the rank orders of knowledge from each of the three studies indicated there were very few lemmas with the same rank order across all three. While some lemmas were generally better known and some less known, there were few lemmas with consistent rankings. This is perhaps not surprising given that test-takers were from different countries and included both L1 and L2 speakers. One issue was that Shiotsu's data concentrated on words suitable for his less-advanced Japanese students, and so was only useful for the highest-frequency, best-known lemmas. Therefore, we focused on the Brysbaert and Kremmel figures. Ultimately, we found only 28 lemmas where the order matched in the Brysbaert and Kremmel data, with the Shiotsu data generally corresponding, but with some discrepancies (see Table 2.4). Note that the negative and positive logits indicate better-known and lesser-known lemmas respectively. For example, *body* was the best-known word for the Austrian ESL learners (logit = −4.61) and *beetle* was the least-known (logit = 4.40).

Lemma	Brysbaert et al. (proportion known)[a]	Kremmel (logits)	Shiotsu (logits)
body	0.9976	−4.61	−5.70
read	0.9967	−4.37	−5.70
girl	0.9955	−4.03	−5.69
force	0.9947	−3.53	−1.26
kitchen	0.9939	−3.35	−5.70
bird	0.9929	−3.14	−5.70
bus	0.9928	−2.57	−5.68
opening	0.9924	−2.25	
relative	0.9920	−2.03	
enjoy	0.9912	−1.98	−5.70
recovery	0.9905	−1.38	
coast	0.9895	−0.99	−0.11
populate	0.9887	−0.54	
divide	0.9881	−0.26	−0.24
observer	0.9859	−0.07	
storage	0.9856	0.18	
fragment	0.9852	0.70	
sadly	0.9849	0.92	
crowded	0.9842	1.02	
cube	0.9834	1.27	
milky	0.9826	1.60	
stabilize	0.9802	1.85	
accommodate	0.9775	2.39	3.80
poetry	0.9753	2.49	
fold	0.9750	3.19	1.70
liquor	0.9688	3.61	
devastation	0.9612	3.90	
beetle	0.9548	4.40	

a. Figures in this column are shown at four decimal places as the differences were very small.

Table 2.4: Knowledge rankings from the Brysbaert et al. (2016a), Kremmel (2017), and Shiotsu (2011) data

The aim of this exercise was to identify a set of lemmas that were empirically shown to be known in a reliable order so we could judge which corpus produced frequency orders that best matched with this demonstrated knowledge ranking. Although only a small sample of lemmas met this requirement, these 28 ranked target lemmas were used as a basis for comparison with frequency figures from the various corpora and sub-corpora. The results of the Spearman's rank correlations for this (admittedly small) number of lemmas are shown in Table 2.5.

COCA	−0.77
COCA Spoken	−0.71
COCA Fiction	−0.69
COCA Magazine	−0.72
COCA Newspaper	−0.74
COCA Academic	−0.63
BNC	−0.78
BNC Spoken	−0.69
BNC Fiction	−0.67
BNC Magazine	−0.73
BNC Newspaper	−0.77
BNC Non-academic	−0.64
BNC Academic	−0.59
BNC Misc	−0.77
GloWbE	−0.68
Wikipedia	−0.59
Soap Operas	−0.52
SUBTlex–US	−0.57
SUBTlex–UK	−0.74

Note that the correlations are negative because the better-known lemmas had low numbers (e.g., 1, 2, 3), while high-frequency figures from the corpora had high numbers.

Table 2.5: Spearman correlations of corpus frequency with 28 ranked target lemmas

The correlations from the corpora – discussed here as positive values to indicate the absolute strength of the correlations – ranged from 0.52 (Soap Operas) to 0.78 (complete BNC). The two best-known and most-widely-used corpora (COCA and BNC) had the strongest correlation figures and produced very similar results (0.77 and 0.78 respectively).

The correlations for the complete COCA and BNC were also higher than for each of their various sub-corpora, although the differences are often not great. We also confirm the increasingly common observation that corpus size is not everything; the massive 1.9-billion-word GloWbE and Wikipedia corpora had lower correlations (0.68 and 0.59 respectively).

The subtitle SUBTlex–US and SUBTlex–UK corpora have been gaining attention recently (e.g., Bao & Xu, 2022; Pinchbeck et al., 2022; Smolík & Filip, 2022) as research shows that data from these corpora corresponds more closely than other corpora with participant behaviour in psycholinguistic experiments, such as lexical decision times (Brysbaert et al., 2016b). This is presumably because the SUBTlex frequencies better describe the vocabulary which many people know. The SUBTlex corpora are made up of subtitles from popular US and UK movies and television shows, and so probably better represent the everyday language that English speakers (both native and non-native) use on a regular basis. The SUBTlex–US correlated surprisingly less strongly (0.57) than the SUBTlex–UK (0.74), but the SUBTlex–UK performed nearly as well as the COCA and BNC complete corpora.

Although not part of our corpus selection methodology, for interest's sake, we also looked at the ranking of the Pearson GSE scale for vocabulary. It had the highest correlation (0.80), slightly higher than the COCA and BNC complete, indicating that the combination of frequency data and teachers' ratings of difficulty was slightly better at predicting knowledge of the 28 target lemmas than frequency alone, as with the COCA and BNC.

The ultimate decision was taken to use the COCA as one source for the target lemma list. Although the COCA and the BNC had similar correlations, the COCA has several advantages which made it preferable for the KVL research.

- It was designed from the start to be lemma-based, which fits with our selected counting unit.
- It is large, containing around half a billion words at the time of this research. This is about five times the size of the 100 million-word BNC. (Note that in early 2020, the COCA was expanded to one billion words.)
- It is a monitor corpus that represents language from 1990 to the present day, with new language data added each year. This contrasts with the BNC, which is a snapshot, static corpus.

- It is balanced, containing roughly the same amount of five registers: spoken, fiction, popular magazines, newspapers, and academic journals.
- Although it should be considered primarily a written corpus, it still contains a substantial element of unscripted spoken English taken from TV dialogues. Davies (2021) makes a case that this type of spoken communication is similar to informal conversation.
- The corpus was free to access online at the time of the study.

2.4   Compiling the list of candidate lemmas to test

The KVL was to be compiled by testing large numbers of ESL learners on their knowledge of English target words. The intended result was a ranked-ordered list of the best-known 5,000 lemmas in English. Without starting from a position of knowing exactly which were the best-known lemmas, testing more than 5,000 words was essential. The goal was set to select the best-known 5,000 lemmas from a pool of 7,000–8,000 lemmas. As well as frequency, it was important to draw upon other criteria for inclusion in the long list. For this, two sources of input were used.

The first source was a measure of knowledge. We have seen that frequency figures from the SUBTlex–UK performed well in our corpus selection exercise. This and the SUBTlex–US list were used as the basis for the tests which Brysbaert et al. (2016a) used in their study. Therefore, we felt sanctioned to use the SUBTlex-derived list of the best-known 11,600 lemmas from the study by Brysbaert and colleagues. From it, we extracted the best-known 6,000 lemmas. Although their study used a self-report Yes/No test format and their L1 respondents probably had varying impressions about what 'knowing' a word meant when answering the test, it was one of the only sources of large-scale empirically-based evidence of the knowledge of a large number of English words available at the time of the project. Note that this list was based on L1 respondents. For the purposes of the KVL project, a knowledge list based on L2 respondents would have been preferable. Unfortunately, an L2-based list did not become available until 2020 (Brysbaert et al., 2020). This L2-based list is compared to the KVL in Chapter 9.

The second source of input was frequency. As discussed earlier, this is not always accurate for individual words or for individual users, nonetheless a long history of research has shown that most people, most of the time, tend to know higher-frequency words in general better than lower-frequency words, at least until about the 5,000 frequency level. The highest-frequency words (above the 5,000 frequency level) are also the most stable and remain in language over time, because they describe the things, ideas, and acts which people need to express across a range of contexts (see Schmitt, 2010 for more discussion of these points). Indeed, Gardner's Core Vocabulary (2013) is essentially the combined first 4,000 items from the BNC and COCA. Thus, generalised information on frequency provides an essential input.

Based on our corpus comparison described above, COCA provided the frequency information. This is combined with a measure of dispersion through the corpus, a metric indicating to what extent a lemma occurs in a wide range of texts rather than just in a specific topic or genre. Davies (2017; see also Davies & Gardner, 2013) uses a simple formula that takes both frequency and dispersion into account (frequency x dispersion), and the lemma lists can be ranked according to this combined score. We extracted the top 6,000 lemmas from Davies' list of the highest-scoring 60,000 lemmas in the COCA in rank order. The final input, to ensure we were not missing any very commonly-used words, were the head-words from Nation's BNC-COCA 1K–5K word lists (see www.wgtn. ac.nz/lals/resources/paul-nations-resources/vocabulary-lists for this and other word lists).

The two 6,000 lists (plus Nation's BNC-COCA additions) had a large amount of overlap, but with considerable differences as well. This result matches that of Dang & Webb (2016), who also found many discrepancies between four of the most commonly used word lists in the field. For our study, the TextLexCompare function on the *Lextutor* website (www.lextutor.ca) was employed to collate the lists and remove redundant lemmas. This compilation ended up with 8,454 unique lemmas. However, a number of lemmas on the list were unsuitable or did not match our research focus and so the list needed to be cleaned. The first deletions were function words because our focus was content words, and also function words are difficult to measure in vocabulary tests. For this, we referred to Gardner's (2013, p. 165) Core A list of 461 function words (including grammatical words and numerical words: *eight, eighth, eighty*). However, many function words on Gardner's list have content meanings. For example, the word *all* is coded as both a preposition (*at all*), and an adverb, meaning 'everything'. Due to practical constraints, it was impossible to do an in-depth corpus analysis of each function word, so we used the COCA codings, and looked to delete lemmas that were coded as *i* (preposition), *d* (determiner), *a* (article), *p* (pronoun), *m* (number), and *c* (conjunction). However, prepositions (*i*) with clear definable relations (*beneath* = under something, *in* = inside something) were kept. For lemmas coded as *r* (adverb), we kept items that seemed definable in terms of a meaning and deleted those that we could not easily classify. Some other classes also had lemmas deleted for the same reasons (e.g., the verb *be*). This procedure was admittedly somewhat subjective, but preferable to keeping or deleting all function words regardless of their meaningfulness.

Further to this, redundant items were identified and removed. The COCA part-of-speech labelling system had several categories which seemed to overlap somewhat in terms of definability, especially the adverb category. For example, *ahead* is listed separately as an adverb and as a preposition, which seemed quite difficult to distinguish clearly in a translation/definition. We therefore deleted the adverb entry because the preposition entry was intuitively more familiar to people. Similarly, the colour *blue* was listed as an adjective (*blue sky*) and as a noun (*dresses in blue*). Essentially the meaning is the same, so we deleted the less frequent noun entry.

The list included numerous other items which required a decision on whether to retain. As far as possible, we followed the principles below, but some arbitrary decision-making was inevitable.

- Items with different British and American spellings were conflated into single items. The eventual final target lemma spreadsheet showed both British and American spellings, but under a single spreadsheet row entry. This allowed us to give respondents the choice of using either American or British spellings on the test. (See below for more details.)
- Compounds were deleted (e.g., *African American*) plus all hyphenated words (e.g., *full-time* and *long-term*), as the meaning can usually be gained from understanding the individual words (*full-time = full + time*), and also these items would be difficult for our test format (see below).
- Basic words like *do* and *can*, which cannot easily be defined, were removed.
- Exclamations like *ha, huh, mm, hmm, oh, uh, yeah* were not included.

- Swear words like *bastard*, *bitch*, *fuck*, *fucking* and *shit* were removed since the purpose of the KVL is pedagogical and these would not be part of teaching materials.
- When possible, compound words with a space were joined to form a single word: *health care* → *healthcare*.
- Abbreviations like *i.e.*, *e.g.*, *vs*, and *re* were removed. However, *AM* and *PM* were retained as representing individual items with a meaning connected with time.
- Cardinal directions (*north south, east, west*) and their adjectives (*northern, southern, eastern, western*) were retained, but not sub-compass points (e.g., *northwest, southeast*).
- For numbers, the most basic numbers were included (*one, two ... ten, twelve, hundred, thousand, million*), but nothing more complex.
- Prefixed lemmas were generally not included. For example, *un-* is transparent, and if a learner knows *acceptable*, then they are likely to know *unacceptable* as well. Also, almost any word can be negated with *un-*, which would have quickly doubled the list length. In these cases, the prefixed lemmas were not included. On the other hand, some very frequent and well-known words with the prefixes were kept, e.g., *incorrect, informal, unpopular,* and *unusual*. This decision process was somewhat subjective, but preferable to keeping or deleting all function prefixed lemmas.
- Plurals were not included as they are inflectional suffixes. The singular and plural forms of a word are always part of the same lemma. Similarly, comparatives and superlatives (e.g., *bigger, biggest*) were not included because they are part of the same lemma.
- Further deletions included:
  o contractions of not: *n't*
  o proper names: such as *Atlantic* (as in ocean)
  o measure terms: *mile, gram, kilogram*
  o month or day names: *January, Sunday*
  o holidays: *Christmas, Easter, Halloween*
  o money units: *dollar, cent*
  o very colloquial lemmas: *dude, papa, mummy*
  o technical vocabulary (which is obviously difficult and/or specific): *electromagnetic, electrotherapy, multicellular*

    o words which do not make much sense alone, but are used in compound words, e.g., *keeping* which is mainly used in words like *beekeeping* and *peacekeeping*. Similarly, *shaped*, which is mainly used in compounds like *pear-shaped*. Other examples of words like these included *kept* (*well-kept, best kept*) and *lived* (*short-lived, long-lived*).

After this cleaning, the original 8,454 unique lemmas were reduced to 7,762 lemmas. Considering that these included the best-known 6,000 lemmas from a major crowdsource study (Brysbaert et al., 2016a), the most frequent 6,000 lemmas from a major corpus (COCA), and the most frequent 5,000 headwords from one of the most influential pedagogical word lists (Nation's BNC-COCA list), we felt confident that we had captured nearly all of the lemmas best-known by L2 English learners. There may have been a small number of well-known lemmas missed from the list, but the number is likely to be very small and should not affect the pedagogical value of the KVL.

2.5 British and American spelling variants

The team was always aware of the differences between British and American spellings. However, during the development of the translation test format (see Chapter 3), it became apparent that both spelling variants would need to be available to the test respondents, because the test would measure the ability to recall and spell the target words (i.e., form-recall level of mastery). This meant that both spellings needed to be included in the target word list so the website could be programmed to show either spelling variant, depending on the preference of the particular respondent.

To identify and describe the British and American spellings, several sources were drawn upon. First, the information available on the *English Oxford Living Dictionaries* website (https://en.oxforddictionaries.com/spelling/british-and-spelling), which outlines the main differences between American English (AmE) and British English (BrE):

- words ending in -re: *centre/center, litre/liter*
- words ending in -our: *colour/color, humour/humor*
- words ending in *-ize* or *-ise*, with verbs in British English that can be spelled with either *-ize* or *-ise* but are always spelled with *-ize* in American English: *apologize* **or** *apologise/apologize, organize* **or** *organise/organize*
- words ending in -yse: *analyse/analyze, paralyse/paralyze*

- words ending in a vowel plus l: in British spelling, verbs ending in a vowel plus 'l' double the 'l' when adding endings that begin with a vowel, while in American English, the 'l' is not doubled: *travelled/traveled, traveller/traveler, fuelled/fueled, fuelling/fueling*
- words spelled with double vowels: British English words spelled with the double vowels '*ae*' or '*oe*' are just spelled with an '*e*' in American English: *leukaemia/leukemia, manoeuvre/maneuver, paediatric/pediatric*
- some nouns that end with *-ence* in British English are spelled *-ense* in American English: *defence/defense, licence/license, offence/offense*
- some nouns that end with *-ogue* in British English end with either *-og* or *-ogue* in American English: *analogue/analog* **or** *analogue, catalogue/catalog* **or** *catalogue, dialogue/dialog* **or** *dialogue*

The site also has a list of 1,739 words which have both BrE and AmE spellings. This is illustrated with the five entries below.

BrE	AmE
authorising	authorizing
axe	ax
backpedalled	backpedaled
bannister	banister
baptise	baptize

Second, the lead researcher (Schmitt) drew on his intuitions based on his experience with both AmE (native speaker) and BrE (living in the UK for over two decades as scholar, author, and editor). Third, Schmitt consulted the *Cambridge Online Dictionary* (http://dictionary.cambridge.org/dictionary/english/) to confirm any questionable items. Fourth, to verify his additions, and to add any BrE spellings he may have missed, Dunn (a native speaker of BrE and an experienced researcher and scholar) checked the list. She confirmed the British spellings he had identified.

Furthermore, during the test item-writing process (see Chapter 5), the item writers sometimes queried the various corpora on the english-corpora.org site to determine whether an alternative British spelling might be possible that was not on the list. An example of this was *disk*, where the British spelling *disc* was queried. In many cases an alternative spelling was common, and the variant was added. In some cases, it was not: *jail/gaol*. In the BNC, *jail* occurred 1,207 times, and *gaol* 255 times. So, although *gaol* does exist as an alternative in BrE, the spelling *jail* is the norm, and so *gaol* was not included as the British variant. Ultimately, **145** lemmas were identified on the list with different British and American spellings. The alternative British vs American spellings were to have significant implications when it came to testing the lemmas, as the next chapter will show.

CHAPTER 3

DEVELOPING THE VOCABULARY TEST

This chapter describes the process by which different approaches to the vocabulary test format were evaluated, the decisions that were made, and, moving forward, the considerations involved in setting up the protocols for item writing, and other arising issues.

3.1 Deciding on an item format

Vocabulary tests can take different forms depending on their purpose (Schmitt et al., 2019). The KVL were envisaged to have broad pedagogic value for teachers, syllabus designers, textbook writers, and test developers (see Chapter 1). The varying requirements of these specialist groups cannot be limited to narrow vocabulary competences. For example, they are not limited to either receptive or productive knowledge. Likewise, they will include both spoken and written modes. The purposes envisaged for the KVL span both *teaching* vocabulary and *testing* it. However, these intended purposes did not suggest any obvious testing format which would support every requirement. Nevertheless, the aim was to test at a level of mastery which could be interpreted as having a robust knowledge of the target lemmas, entailing the ability to employ them to some reasonable degree. Following the compilation of the target item list therefore, the next key step was to select/devise an item format that would provide valid and reliable information relating to the intended purposes, and, at the same time, allow the testing of a large number of lemmas (7,762).

Various item formats were reviewed to determine the format which would match the greatest number of our intended purposes.

Interviews are interactive and give the best chance to probe examinees about their lexical knowledge. However, they are extremely time-intensive. Although they might be useful in the piloting and validation stage, they would be impractical as a main testing approach.

Multiple-choice item types are well known and have the advantage of being easily adapted to a computerised format. They also give some demonstration of knowledge. However, examinees usually try to answer unknown items using test-taking strategies, typically being able to correctly guess around 25% of unknown answers on a four-option item (Gyllstad et al., 2015). This makes it difficult to know whether an item is answered correctly because it is known, or because of a successful guess. Another major disadvantage is that item writing is time-consuming, and the items need to be piloted before use. With nearly 8,000 items to write and pilot, it was not possible to consider multiple-choice item formats any further.

Yes/No (checklist) self-report formats have the major advantage of being quick to take, which allows for the inclusion of a relatively high number of items on a test. They are also easy to automatically score. Because of these advantages, this format has been popular for vocabulary size studies, particularly larger-scale ones, such as Brysbaert et al. (2016a). However, there are some substantial disadvantages. First, there is no demonstration of knowledge, and so it is impossible to know how well the target words are actually known, or even if they are known at all. To address this issue, nonwords are typically added to the list of target words. Because respondents cannot know these nonwords, if they check them as 'known', they are clearly overstating their knowledge. A number of adjustment formulas have been applied to adjust the vocabulary size estimates based on the number of nonwords checked. However, there is no consensus on which adjustment formula works best, and Pellicer-Sánchez & Schmitt (2012) found that different formulas worked best for different populations with different levels of proficiency. Also, the addition of nonwords substantially cuts down on the number of target items which can be tested, eroding much of the speed advantage of the Yes/No format. Since the KVL are intended to be based on learner knowledge of words, we wanted a test format that gives more convincing evidence of this knowledge.

A **dual sentence format** initially looked very interesting. It was suggested by Marc Brysbaert (personal correspondence) as it had worked well in a Dutch study of around 150 words, although it proved to be a lot of work to develop. The format uses a target word in two sentences, one that makes sense and one that does not, plus an option indicating no knowledge of the target word. Two examples of this format follow, with the first one testing the real word *lambada*, and the second one the nonword *smaggle*.

Lambada
1. They enjoyed drinking a **lambada** and went home late.
2. They enjoyed dancing the **lambada** and went home late.
3. I've never heard of the word **lambada**.

Smaggle
1. I like to **smaggle** at the beach.
2. I like to **smaggle** at home.
3. I've never heard of the word **smaggle**.

However, for the purpose of the KVL project, several problems were identified. One is the multiple-choice nature of the format, where the researcher cannot be sure that the participant has not simply guessed one of the two sentences. Brysbaert had addressed this by adding nonwords (*smaggle*) into his tests and adjusting the scores downwards according to the number of nonwords answered by options 1 or 2. However, this would entail adding a substantial number of nonwords to our tests, when we already had a very large number of lemmas to test. It also did not exclude the possibility of guessing. The suggestion was made to add a second distractor sentence. This would certainly have helped, but it would make the items much more time-consuming to write. Feedback from our KVL presentation at the 2017 American Association for Applied Linguistics (AAAL) conference in Portland led to the conclusion that the format was not viable in terms of item development time, the likelihood and impact of guessing, and in terms of score interpretation.

Translation formats have a time-honoured history in vocabulary assessment and can test either *recognition* or *recall* knowledge. Recognition formats however employ multiple-choice or matching responses, and these were eliminated from consideration for the same reasons as multiple-choice formats in general. Recall formats meanwhile require examinees to produce either the word form or meaning given a prompt. Most vocabulary size tests (including the one envisioned for this KVL study) measure the link between word form and its meaning.

There are two different directionalities of recall in this type of test item. If the L2 form is given, the examinee must recall and produce its meaning, demonstrating this with an L1 translation. This level of knowledge would be termed *meaning recall* and corresponds to the receptive skills of reading and listening, e.g., a learner sees a word form on a page and must recall its meaning (Schmitt, 2010). Conversely, if the L1 meaning is given, the examinee must produce the L2 word form (*form recall*). This corresponds to the productive skills of writing and speaking, where the learner has a thought in his head, and then must recall the L2 word form to represent that thought. An example is given below for an L1 Spanish learner of L2 English.

Type of format	Prompt given on test	Learner produces
Meaning recall	home	casa
Form recall	casa	home

One advantage of translation tests is that they allow the testing of a wide variety of L2 words, as the corresponding L1 translations should always be comprehended by the test-taker. This is particularly important for high-frequency L2 words, which are difficult to define with even higher-frequency L2 definitions. An additional advantage is that a translation test requires a relatively advanced form-recall level of mastery which was our preferred option.

Nevertheless, translation formats have considerable disadvantages for large-scale testing. If a meaning-recall level of mastery is desired, then the target lemma is given in the L2, and either an L1 translation is required, or an L1/L2 definition:

> 1. *home* ________________

This format would be very easy to write (simply placing the L2 lemmas on the test) but scoring would be extremely difficult, as the participants could provide a wide range of translations or definition formulations which could all demonstrate acceptable knowledge. This would necessitate either manual scoring which would be infeasible, or wide piloting to build an 'acceptable answer' list for each individual item, which would also strain practicality.

In the case of a form-recall level of mastery, the scoring is not necessarily any more straightforward:

> 2. *casa* ________________

With a 'lenient spelling' criterion, we would have to decide on, or pilot, a list of spellings which showed reasonable knowledge of the lemma in question, even if the exact spelling were not achieved. For example, the acceptable answers for the following item (*jealousy*) might be set as *jealousy, gealousy, jelousy, jealosy,* etc. This scoring procedure has the advantage of giving credit for partial knowledge but is disadvantaged by a lack in clarity as to where to draw the line on incorrect spellings, as each lemma will be different.

With an 'exact spelling' criterion, on the other hand, scoring is simplified, as there would be only a single correct answer (although potentially two with both AmE and BrE spellings accepted). An advantage is that the scores would be clear to interpret: either participants are able to produce the exact spellings or they are not. If they are, presumably, they would be able to use the lemmas in their writing, and perhaps in their speaking (although we would not be testing oral language). Form-recall knowledge has consistently been shown to be more difficult and later-acquired than meaning-recall knowledge (Laufer & Goldstein, 2004; Laufer et al., 2004), so if the form-recall items are correctly answered, we can also assume that the participants would be able to comprehend the lemma if seen in its written form (e.g., while reading). However, a disadvantage is that the participants may know a lemma well enough to understand it while reading, but may be unable to produce the correct spelling, and so such a test may miss considerable amounts of lexical knowledge.

Another disadvantage of translation formats is that they are language-specific. In the KVL project we hoped to test three separate languages: German (English is a Germanic language), Spanish (a cognate Romance language), and Chinese (an unrelated language). Translation formats would require the test to be produced in three different versions for these three languages. Although this idea was initially rejected by the project team, insightful feedback from Batia Laufer at the 2017 AAAL conference encouraged us not to discount translation as a test format.

Ultimately, all item format possibilities have limitations and inherent scope for error, and there is no ideal solution, especially when testing a large number of lemmas. Nevertheless, for the purposes of the KVL, the team saw the advantages of the form-recall translation format, especially because it tested lemmas at a relatively advanced stage of the knowledge continuum. Furthermore, Dunn's experience with translation tests suggested that they generally have good psychometric qualities (Dunn, 2014). A disadvantage was the additional costs of translating nearly 8,000 lemmas into three different languages (especially if example sentences were to be included alongside the L2 word form). A major advantage, on the other hand, would be the ability to interpret correctly answered lemmas as being relatively well-known. Also, using an 'exact spelling' criterion would allow us to score the test without manual scrutiny of each lemma.

Having considered all options, we concluded that the form-recall translation format with exact scoring was the most valid and viable for our purpose.

3.2   Designing the final item format

Once the form-recall (exact spelling) criterion was selected, it was possible to begin developing the item format in more detail. Reviews of the CATSS test (Laufer et al., 2004) and the technical requirements necessary to place the test online indicated that a practical way of writing the exact scoring format was to use individual blanks for each letter of the correct spellings. For example, for Spanish-speaking respondents, *casa – home*:

> casa h __ __ __

Giving the first letter and the exact number of letters required would constrain the respondents into supplying the desired target lemma rather than an alternative synonym (e.g., not something like *house* or *dwelling*). It also made it easier to program the web application, as each blank had only one correct input. Importantly, if a respondent does not know a lemma, this format is almost impossible to guess.

To help disambiguate the targeted English lemma, and to fully indicate the meaning of the lemma we were aiming to elicit, an example L1 sentence was included along with the L1 translation. For example, for the target lemma *house,* the Spanish item would be the following:

> casa Vivo en una **casa** grande que tiene tres dormitorios.
> h __ __ __ __
>
> [English]
> house I live in a large **house** that has three bedrooms.
> h __ __ __ __

The exact spelling criterion had an additional complication: the variation in length between some AmE vs BrE spellings. In some cases, there would only be variation in the spelling:

> advis<u>e</u>r and advis<u>o</u>r
> reali<u>s</u>e and reali<u>z</u>e
> defen<u>c</u>e and defen<u>s</u>e

But, in other cases, the number of blanks would change:

> col<u>ou</u>r vs col<u>o</u>r
> dialo<u>gue</u> vs dialog

We needed to accept both spelling and length variations as our test respondents may have been taught either AmE or BrE, or a combination of both. To allow for this, the web application was designed to ask respondents at the outset of the quiz to indicate their language of preference (AmE or BrE). Then, the application would display the correct number of blanks for each target lemma according to this initial selection and score the words accordingly. (See Chapter 6 for more detail on how this was done.)

It was hoped this would allow respondents to show their knowledge of the spelling of the target lemmas. However, we knew it was only a partial solution. With the worldwide reach of the Internet and ever-increasing use of World Englishes (e.g., Singaporean English, Indian English; see the journal *World Englishes*), learners are exposed to a variety of Englishes. They may be taught in more than one variety, and are likely to be exposed to versions of both AmE and BrE. Therefore, expecting learners to consistently answer the test with only AmE or BrE was optimistic. In cases where the number of letters differ between the two Englishes, if respondents knew the alternative spelling which was different from the version of English they initially chose, they often would not be able to answer the test item. So, even though they knew a perfectly acceptable spelling, the respondent would not be able to gain credit for their knowledge. We knew the AmE/BrE spellings were problematic for our test format, but it was impossible to know in advance the scope of the problem. We resolved to move forward with this item format, and to place the lemmas with AmE and BrE spellings onto the test, but then decide later, based on the subsequent analyses, whether we could generate reliable rankings with the limitations of the test format in mind.

The finalised item format therefore consisted of two parts: a **prompt** and a **response**. Each prompt further consisted of two parts: a **translation** and an **example sentence**. These components are illustrated in Table 3.1. The correct response is known as the **target lemma**. This terminology will be used in the rest of the book to describe the various parts of an item when necessary.

	Prompt		Response
Item	Translation: casa	Example sentence: Vivo en una **casa** grande que tiene tres dormitorios.	h _ _ _ _

Table 3.1: The components of a KVL test item

3.3   Developing the item-writing process

The time-consuming element of writing translation-based form recall test items lies in developing the prompt, especially the example sentences. We developed the item-writing process in two initial languages: Spanish and Chinese. To do this, the 28 lemmas from the corpus selection study above were used, plus two low-frequency lemmas we added to make sure there were some quite difficult lemmas included (*escalation, serenity*). The 30 lemmas in this development phase are listed below:

body	read	girl	force	kitchen	bird
bus	opening	relative	enjoy	recovery	coast
populate	divide	observer	storage	fragment	sadly
crowded	cube	milky	stabilize	accommodate	poetry
fold	liquor	devastation	beetle	escalation	serenity

3.3.1 Item-writing protocol

The item writers needed guidance on several issues. A particular concern for the Spanish items was the use of cognates in the prompt. If a Spanish cognate was given, then the prompt often had a very similar word form to the English target, or even the exact same form: e.g., English *bus* = Spanish *autobús*. To create prompts without making the answers too transparent based on cognate similarity (cognate prompts ended up having a strong influence on learner performance, see Chapter 8), we decided on the following guidelines for writing test items.

1. If there is a one-word equivalent translation that expresses the meaning perfectly on its own, this is the preferred option (e.g., *cuerpo* = body). If there are two words that express the same meaning, and one is a cognate, use the non-cognate word (e.g., *alojar* instead of *acomodar* = accommodate).

2. If there is only one word that expresses the particular meaning, and this word is a cognate, it is better to use a definition (e.g., coast = *orilla del mar, de un río, de un lago*, etc., *y tierra que está cerca de ella*). Also, if that definition would lead to another word that starts with the same letter and is very similar in meaning but is not the word form we want to retrieve (e.g., *destruction* for *devastation*), then specify that the response should not be that word ('NOT destruction').

3. If two words are needed to capture the specific meaning (i.e., one word only would be misleading or not informative enough), then use both words (e.g., *chica, niña* = girl).

4. If more information than two words is needed to capture the specific meaning and retrieve the right word form, then use a definition. There might be cases where the definition has to be extended to make the word form clear, e.g., *polar*: relating to the very cold regions in the north or south parts of the world. The earth rotates around the axes located in these regions.

3.3.2 Polysemy

There are many cases where a lemma has multiple meanings in a given word class, each of which necessitated a decision as to which should be included on the test. Without a concrete way of knowing which meaning senses were the most likely to be known, we used frequency as a guide under the assumption that this meaning sense would be the most useful for the majority of learners. Based on this, we decided on the expedient of using learner dictionaries (e.g., by Cambridge University Press, Oxford University Press, Longman, Macmillan) to get the most frequent meaning for each lemma (in its own word class), because these dictionaries list senses in their frequency order. In most cases, the various dictionaries agreed on the primary meaning sense. However, in cases where the dictionaries disagreed, the lead researcher (Schmitt) made a final decision after carefully checking the frequency data on the different meaning senses.

3.4   Developing the test instructions

After considering the results of an initial pen-and-paper pilot of the test (see the following section), these instructions and examples were developed for the full pilot:

You will see a Spanish (Chinese) translation or definition and need to write the correct English word that expresses this meaning. In order to help you, the first letter of each word is provided. You need to write one letter on each of the blanks. In the example below, there are 5 blanks, so you must fill in 5 letters only. If you do not know the English word, just move on to the next word on the test.

Example:

ventana	w _ _ _ _ _

Answer:

ventana	w i n d o w

Note that in the pilot studies, the respondents were instructed to answer each item, to make sure they engaged with each item. If they did not know a lemma, they were instructed to write an equivalent of 'I don't know', typically *no se* for Spanish. This was done to ensure we would have very little missing data.

3.5   Initial pilot (pen and paper)

We piloted the paper-based 30-item test with Spanish-L1 and Chinese-L1 ESL learners. The pilots generally showed that the item format worked well.

3.5.1 *Spanish results*

The Spanish version of the 30-item test was developed and administered to 40 participants in May 2017. Seven respondents were from Spain (professionals or students), one was from Mexico (Spanish instructor living in the US), and the remainder (32) were university students in Santiago, Chile. The participants rated their English proficiency as follows: 3 elementary, 28 intermediate, and 9 advanced. Their gender was 24 women, 16 men, and 1 no response. Key findings from the Spanish pilot are outlined below.

1. If the respondents knew the lemma, they typically were able to answer the item. We see this from the high-frequency words, where nearly all respondents answered correctly, e.g., *body* 39/40, *girl* 40/40, *bird* 39/40, *enjoy* 40/40. There were 1,200 cases (40 participants x 30 items). Overall, the respondents answered 62% of the items correctly (745/1,200). As might be expected, the format seemed clearest to participants for very easy, high-frequency words, with an obvious translation.

2. Sometimes, the respondents seemed to know the word, but did not have mastery of the spelling, making errors like: *bird*→berd, *read*→reed, *coast*→coust, *divide*→devide. However, this was not a major problem, as it occurred 20 times in 1,200 responses (1.6%).

3. The respondents sometimes seemed to know the basic word but produced the wrong word class: *opening*→opened, openness; *recovery*→recovered, recover; *storage*→storement; *stabilize*→stability; *poetry*→poetic. This occurred only 20 times in 1,200 cases (1.6%). Also, 10 of the cases occurred for the lemma *stabilize* alone, which in retrospect is not surprising because the

number of blanks for *stabilize* and *stability* are the same (8). This situation was kept in mind when writing items. This pattern of derivative confusion is to be expected; research has shown that learners typically do not know all word family members, and our lemma-based form-recall test format measures this aspect of word knowledge. The fact that the wrong derivatives were produced was interpreted as indicating that respondents did not know the lemma in question. However, we must accept that there could be other explanations (for a discussion of this point, see Iwaizumi & Webb, 2021). For example, the results might indicate that in some cases the lemma itself is too big a unit of counting. It could also be the case that the respondents used test-taking strategies and wrote the most frequent word form based on the number of letters and meaning provided in the item prompt, but this strategy did not always work. Importantly, this finding highlighted the need for item writers to clearly distinguish which lemma is targeted in a prompt (i.e., which part of speech), and the need to indicate to participants that they should consider word class when answering the test.

4. Occasionally, respondents answered with a Spanish (L1) word, or Spanish-influenced spelling: *cube*→cubo, *population*→problation, *storage*→estorage, *liquor*→licour. This occurred 9 times in 1,200 cases (<1%).

5. In order to indicate they did not know a lemma, respondents typically wrote *no se* (I don't know) or something similar. This occurred 335 times (28%). The high occurrence of this response, and the amount of time it took participants to write it, suggested that we needed an 'I don't know' option in order save time on the eventual, much longer tests.

6. In a very few cases (5: 0.004%), the participants provided no response at all. This shows that almost all respondents engaged with the test and were able to follow the test instructions.

7. Generally, giving the initial letter of the lemma and the number of spaces seemed to constrain the respondent answers to the desired target item. However, there were cases where the respondents simply ignored the number of spaces and wrote longer or shorter answers. In the final version of the test, the maximum number of keystrokes was 'locked'.

The Spanish pilot test results are summarised in Table 3.2. Overall, it seemed that the test worked well, as the respondents either knew the word and answered correctly, or made no response, or wrote *no se* in 1,085 cases out of 1,200 (90%). If we add the cases where a completely wrong word was produced (probably just being a guess), the total becomes 1,139 cases out of 1,200 (94.9%). Although in the remaining 5% of cases the respondents may have had some knowledge of the word which fell short of full form-recall, this percentage seems acceptably small. It is probably much less than the amount of error we would have to accept with other test formats (e.g., guessing in multiple-choice formats). Also, the difference between scores based on an exact spelling criterion (used here) and a lenient spelling criterion would only involve these 5% of cases, and not even all of these. The advantage of moving to a lenient criterion (i.e., picking up this relatively small percentage of partial knowledge) was not sufficient to justify the substantial problems involved in manual scoring and eventual analysis.

Correct	No response	Wrote 'No se' (I don't know)	Probably known, but misspelled	Wrong derivative form	L1 influence	Completely wrong word	Other
745	5	335	20	20	9	54	12
62%	<1%	28%	1.6%	1.6%	<1%	<1%	1%

Table 3.2: Spanish pilot results (N = 40, K = 30, Responses = 1,200)

3.5.2 Chinese results

The Chinese version of the 30-item test was also developed and administered in May 2017 to 40 Chinese participants (professionals or students). Overall, the Chinese respondents were of higher English proficiency than the Spanish respondents. In most aspects, the results mirror the Spanish results. Key findings from the Chinese pilot are noted below.

1. If the respondents knew the lemma, they typically were able to answer the item. We could see this from the high-frequency words, where nearly all respondents answered correctly, e.g., *body* 40/40, *girl* 40/40, *bird* 40/40, *enjoy* 40/40. As with the Spanish results, there were 1,200 cases (40 participants x 30 items). Overall, the respondents answered 76% of the items correctly (907/1,200) (in comparison, the Spanish respondents answered 62% or 745/1,200 of the items correctly). As might be expected, the format seemed clearest to participants for very easy, high-frequency words, with an obvious translation.

2. Sometimes, the respondents seemed to know the word, but did not have mastery of the spelling, making errors like: *recovery*→recowery; *divide*→devide; *stabilize*→stabalize, stabilize, stabelize; *accommodate*→acommodate, accomodate; *beetle*→beatle. This was particularly noticeable for *stabilize* (11 cases) and *divide* (8 cases) (problems with unstressed vowels), *accommodate* (7 cases, double letters), and *beetle* (18 cases, the influence of rock-and-roll with the spelling 'Beatle'), and would be the kind of words English-L1 speakers might also have trouble with. For example, the *English Oxford Living Dictionary* lists *accommodate* as one of the most misspelled words in English   (https://en.oxforddictionaries.com/spelling/common-misspellings). Overall, misspellings occurred 51 times in 1,200 cases (4.2%), but 44 of these cases occurred from just the four words cited above. The misspelling problem was certainly not widespread across items, and around 4% should probably not be considered problematic for the test format.

3. As with the Spanish respondents, the Chinese respondents some-times seemed to know the basic word but produced the wrong word class. Ten of the cases occurred for the lemma *recovery*, where the respondents ignored the number of blanks and wrote the shorter *recover*. Ten cases also occurred for *populate*, where the respondents often wrote *population*, which was too long for the blanks. There were also problems with *accommodate*→ac-commodation (8). Overall, inappropriate derivative forms occurred 61 times in 1,200 cases (5%), but 28 out of the 61 cases occurred with just the three words mentioned above. The deriv-ative issue is certainly not pervasive across all items, and around 5% should probably not be considered problematic for the test format.

4. With only a single exception, the Chinese participants did not use a Chinese (L1) word in an attempt to answer the item.

5. To indicate they did not know a lemma, respondents typically wrote in Chinese 'I don't know' (忘了, 不知), or attempted just a letter or two, or wrote 'xx'. This occurred 61 times (5.1%).

6. In only a few cases (16, 1.3%), the participants made no response at all. This shows that almost all respondents engaged with the test and were able to follow the test instructions.

7. In some cases, there was a consistent wrong response. This was the case for *relative*. The item writer chose its adjective meaning

and explained it as 'related' in the prompt. However, many respondents replied with the answers *relevant* and *relating*. In the main test, its noun meaning (family member) was used, which is more frequent. In cases that a non-target lemma could be foreseen as a common response, it was clearly necessary to indicate to respondents to avoid this answer, e.g., 'The answer is not *relevant*'.

Correct	No response	Indicated 'I don't know'	Probably known, but misspelled	Wrong derivative form	L1 answer	Completely wrong word
907	16	61	51	61	1	107
76%	1.3%	5.1%	4.2%	5%	~0%	8.9%

Note: Owing to difficulty in categorisation, 4 responses were doubled coded.

Table 3.3: Chinese pilot results (N = 40, K = 30, Responses = 1,200)

The Chinese pilot test results are summarised in Table 3.3. The findings are in general similar to Table 3.2, but the Chinese respondents were more proficient overall, and answered an average of 76% of the items correctly compared to 62% by Spanish participants. The Chinese respondents also gave somewhat more misspellings, incorrect derivatives, and wrong words than the Spanish, but the higher English proficiency of the Chinese L1 speakers probably explains this. If they did not know the correct word form, their relatively higher proficiency gave them the chance to try with a different derivative form (usually a higher-frequency one), even if it was incorrect. It also seems to have made them more inclined to try words for which their spelling was still shaky.

Overall, the test seemed to work well. The misspellings + wrong derivatives added up to around 9% of the total responses, and the derivative problems could be reduced substantially with enhanced instruction rubrics. This percentage seemed acceptable. As discussed above, any other test format was likely to have problems greater than those we found in this pilot for the form-recall translation format (exact spelling).

3.5.3 Timing

The Chinese pilot also tracked the time taken to complete the 30 items. The fastest time was 103 seconds (1 minute 43 seconds), the slowest was 2,986 seconds (49 minutes 46 seconds). However, this slow time was very much an outlier; the next slowest were 1,742, 1,036, and 1,026 seconds. The descriptive statistics (excluding the respondents with times of 2,986 and 1,742 seconds) are shown in Table 3.4.

	Seconds	Minutes	Seconds per item
Mean	599.03	9.98	19.97
Median	546.50	9.11	18.22
SD	246.68	4.11	
Minimum	103	1.72	3.43
Maximum	1036	17.27	34.53

Table 3.4: Timing for the Chinese pilot participants (30 items)

The mean time to take the test was just under 10 minutes. As there were 30 items on the test, the mean time per item was 19.97 seconds, rounded to 20 seconds. The median time per item was 18.22 seconds. Respondents were thus able to answer approximately three items per minute.

Overall, the piloting showed that the test format was viable and that we were justified to proceed with it.

CHAPTER 4

PILOTING THE ONLINE TEST

The development of the online vocabulary test, the *Vocabulary Challenge*, included practical and functional aspects, such as ensuring the test worked well across all digital platforms, considerations of how to motivate learners to take part, and ways to encourage participants' prolonged engagement with the questions.

4.1 Aims of the pilot online test

The paper-and-pencil pilot indicated that the test format worked well, so the next step was to pilot it online, as this is how the eventual study would be administered. We aimed to explore three issues with this pilot. The first key issue was the number of items we could put on each test. With 7,762 lemmas to measure, it would be advantageous for each respondent to answer as many items as possible. However, there is obviously a point where respondents will lose interest and refuse to go further. The first question was how much time respondents would be willing to put into the test; the Chinese time results suggested a rate of about three items per minute. A second issue concerned the clarity of the test, especially whether the background material necessary to set up the test for the respondents was clear. This included practical issues, such as whether the instructions and example items were comprehensible and unambiguous. The third issue was whether the test format would work well on a web-based platform. It seemed fine in the pen-and-paper format, but an online environment could change the dynamics and affect the format adversely.

To address these three issues, an online pilot test was developed. We originally thought of making one 40-item test, one 60-item test, one 80-item test, and one 100-item test, to see how participants would respond to each length. However, a more 'game-based' approach in which participants were offered 262 items of which they could answer as many items as they liked allowed us to gain an idea of learners' endurance in taking the test. Using this approach, the web application would randomly sample items from a 262-item bank one at a time, for as long as the participants wished to proceed. At the end of the test, participants were given their scores and the information about which lemmas were answered correctly and incorrectly.

This format was piloted with Spanish respondents. Drawing upon the lessons learnt from the paper-based pilot, the test items were developed by two Spanish-English bilinguals, cross-checking each other's work. Spanish language instructions were developed and translated, also drawing on feedback from the first small pilot. The online pilot was carried out from mid-December 2017 until mid-February 2018 with 108 Spanish respondents from Catalonia.

4.2   Pilot test results

4.2.1 Number of items on the test

The percentage of Spanish participants who completed various numbers of items is given in Table 4.1. From this, we can see that over two-thirds of the participants completed 10 or fewer items. Only about a quarter did at least 30 items when left to their own devices. Based on these results, we felt the safest approach was to formulate the test in sets of items, with feedback after each set. The first decision to make was how many items to include in each set, therefore. Larger sets (e.g., 20 or 30 items) would lead to more data gathered. On the other hand, too large a set might put off respondents, with some likely to quit before reaching the end of the set. Also, we felt it was more motivating to get feedback relatively soon, rather than after a large number of items.

Another issue was technical. Because feedback was to be given after each set, the more items per set, the more information that would have to be shown on the feedback page. On small devices like smartphones, anything over 10 answers would require scrolling, which in design terms is undesirable. Balancing these issues, we ultimately plumbed for sets of 10 items. This way, respondents would get their interim scores quickly, and hopefully this would encourage them to take on another set of 10 items. We hoped that most respondents would go on to do two or three sets of words, giving us a total of 20–30 lemmas per test administration. It also indicated the need to think about other motivational techniques to keep the respondents involved with the test.

Items answered	0–10	at least 20	at least 30	at least 40	at least 50	at least 60	at least 70	at least 80	at least 90	at least 100
Number of participants	77	39	26	18	16	11	9	7	6	5
Percentage of participants	71	36	24	17	15	10	8	6	6	5

Table 4.1: Number of items attempted by Spanish participants on the online pilot test (N = 108)

4.2.2 Clarity of test

We asked for respondent impressions about the clarity of the test format with the following question.

> *Were there any items on the test for which the Spanish translations and sentences were confusing?*
> a) *none (that I remember)*
> b) *a few*
> c) *more than 5 words*

The results showed that 27 respondents answered 'none', 52 answered 'a few', and 1 respondent answered 'more than 5 words' (not all participants answered the question). Looking at the actual test item responses, most respondents were able to answer a considerable number of items. This suggests that the majority of the 'a few' responses were because the respondents did not know the target word in question rather than that the item prompts themselves were confusing. Unfortunately, due to the anonymous nature of the pilot study, and the fact that it was delivered online, it was impossible to follow up with interviews to confirm this.

There was also an open-answer perception question, where no respondent commented on any problems with the instructions or example items. Given that the participants were able to proceed successfully with the test (see the section below), we concluded that the background information was satisfactory.

4.2.3 How well did the participants do on the online pilot test?

Looking at the item responses, a number of patterns appeared. First, there were a number of spelling errors, where the target word was evidently known, but not the correct spelling – *revelutionary, Japanisse, countain* (contain), *deleite* (delete). (Note that although the web application had a character limit, a bug in the program allowed some respondents to type in more letters than they should have, e.g., those with iPhones that did not correctly limit the number of blanks.) It might seem harsh to penalise these students for slight spelling errors, but it is instructive to look at other words that were spelled correctly. Here are some examples.

> Respondent 1: revelutionary, but also philosophical, financially, astronaut, discriminate
>
> Respondent 2: Japanisse, but also revolutionary, collaboration, philosophical
>
> Respondent 3: countain, but also usually, professor, undefined
>
> Respondent 4: deleite, but also legislator, projection, memorable

Clearly, these respondents knew how to spell at a high level in English, and so the misspellings must be seen as simply not fully knowing the target lemma in question, rather than as symptomatic of a wider weakness in spelling proficiency.

Second, unsurprisingly, a common spelling problem was double consonants, which also plagues English-L1 speakers. Some examples include: *regrett, tecnollogical, accepptancy, cammel*. However, this again shows that the target words are not mastered to the level of form-recall, which is the standard of knowledge we are using as a criterion.

Third, the test sometimes exposed a lack of derivational knowledge. Stems were correctly produced, but with the wrong affix, as in the following examples.

arrogance:	arrogancy
missionary:	missionnaire
disturbing:	disturbiate
widespread:	widespreaded
desirable:	desireful

Productive knowledge of derivations is one of the most difficult types of word knowledge to master (González-Fernández & Schmitt, 2019), so it is unsurprising that the test answers sometimes demonstrated such weakness in derivational knowledge.

Fourth, in a very few cases, respondents made up words as responses.

skyline:	sunline
moonshine:	madebrand

Since this was uncommon, it should not be seen as a problem for the test itself, but rather as a strategy used by respondents to answer items where they did not know the correct answer.

Fifth, in the majority of cases, the respondents either answered the items correctly, or left them blank (note that an 'I don't know' option was not possible in the free formats – *Survey Monkey/Google Forms* – used in the pilot). They sometimes attempted the item with made-up responses that were clearly incorrect, as in the above examples. Sometimes, however, they attempted the item with responses that were far from the correct answer, as in the following examples.

polished:	pulitated
absorb:	absrove
unchanging:	unmobable
struggle:	shdjdnc
tremble:	troumble
hacking:	hackerie

Overall, the test seemed to work well, in that if the respondents knew the target lemma and its spelling, they were able to answer the item correctly. In cases where the responses were incorrect, they tended to be clearly wrong, and not even close to the correct spelling of the target lemmas.

4.2.4 *Other issues*

A number of other issues arose from the pilot.

Two respondents repeated the first letter of the target word, even though it was already given. This made the spelling incorrect, as the number of blanks would not then fit.

g g a r b a g
p p u z l e

A number did this with the odd word, not in all their answers. We considered adding an instruction line to avoid this redundancy, but decided against this in the end, in the interest of concise instructions (see below).

A more common issue was respondents capitalising the first letter of the answer (15/108 respondents), e.g., *casa* h O u s e. This often seemed to be caused by their input device (e.g., iPhone) or browser (e.g., Firefox) automatically capitalising the first letter of the input. However, this did not cause any problems for the automatic scoring, as the web application was programmed to disregard capitalisation. The problem was also addressed by redesigning the web application to only allow lower case letters to be typed as input.

There was also an issue with the sampling procedure. The test would present 10 lemmas per set. These 10 lemmas needed to be sampled from the 7,679-lemma list (a few lemmas were deleted from the 7,762 list – see Chapter 5 for details). We could sample randomly, which would generally select a variety of lemmas, from easier to more difficult. However, there was a danger that this approach could lead to individual respondents receiving only difficult items in their first batch which might dissuade them from continuing. To address this possibility, the team consensus was that a stratified sampling would be better. We thus divided the 7,679 lemmas into 10 'bins' based on frequency. One lemma would be automatically selected from the most frequent bin for the first item presented, from the second bin for the second item, etc. This ensured that the items would appear in an easier-to-more-difficult order, broadly speaking.

We needed to streamline the front-end of the test to get respondents into the test much more quickly. Our solution was to move two example test items from the instruction pages into an EXAMPLES tab in the upper left-hand side of the screen. This allowed respondents to check them if they felt the need, but most respondents were able to go straight into the test. Next to the EXAMPLES tab, we placed the FAQ tab with all of the background information. It was thus available, but not obtrusive.

These changes left the introduction page of the website with the minimum amount of information necessary for introductory, motivational, and legal reasons. It included a brief introduction and buttons to select the language of the test (Spanish, German, Chinese). We then included a brief description of the donation the project would make to UNICEF for motivational reasons (see the following section). Finally, the opening page contained a legal notice that the respondents' answers would remain anonymous, and that we would use the data for research purposes only.

We also revised our biodata collection approach, which had originally included eight questions. This was shortened to four items.

1. What is your age in years?
2. How many years have you studied English?
3. How many hours a week do you use English? (This may include reading, speaking, watching television or using social networks, the Internet, or videogames.)

4. Would you like to take the Vocabulary Challenge in American English or British English?

This last question was essential, as the web application needed to know which list of spellings (American English vs British English) it would present (the test would eventually be known as the *Vocabulary Challenge*). We felt many respondents would not consciously know which national variety to check, so we presented a short list of alternative spellings. Note that none of these words appeared on the actual test, so that no priming could potentially occur (see Figure 4.1).

Some words are spelled differently in American English and British English. Please look at the examples below to see which spellings you are most comfortable using.

American English	British English
Agonize	Agonise
Liter	Litre
Savor	Savour
Analog	Analogue

Figure 4.1: Reproduction of the AmE vs BrE instructions on the online test

4.2.5 *Motivational issues*

Given that just over one-third of pilot participants completed at least 20 items, we needed to find ways to encourage more prolonged engagement. First, we agreed to provide enhanced feedback on the respondents' answers. After each set of 10 items, a page would appear showing the number of correct answers. Additionally, each lemma would be indicated as being answered correctly or not. Finally, the correct answers would be shown for incorrect answers.

We consulted a motivational expert on how to make the test more appealing. She indicated that the 'look' of the webpage was important and helped design an attractive website with British Council branding. It was felt that having this branding would lend credibility and gravitas to the test, and perhaps induce the respondents to take it seriously and stay with it longer. A series of screenshots that give an idea of the look and feel of the website are shown in Appendix 3.

The test was given the user-friendly name, *Vocabulary Challenge*, echoing the game-like feel and potentially encouraging respondents to challenge themselves beyond the first set of 10 items. It also fit well with the 'challenge between friends' aspect made possible by social media. We attempted to harness the potential exponential spreading of news about the test by including a Twitter button on the final page of the test, encouraging respondents to Tweet their scores to their friends and challenge them to do better (see Figure A3.7). This design choice introduced a very small but real possibility that respondents might resort to dictionaries to improve the scores that they shared on social media. However, a review of the Twitter feed revealed that only 23 respondents posted their scores during the run of the test and even here, only 2 respondents posted perfect scores, so we felt that this was not a major concern.

The last idea of how to encourage more participation came from the *Free Rice* website (http://freerice.com/#/english-vocabulary). This is a vocabulary quiz website which donates 10 grains of rice to the United Nations World Food Program for every correct answer given. We decided to support UNICEF with the KVL project. For every 10 words a respondent correctly answered on the *Vocabulary Challenge*, the British Council donated 1 pence (£0.01) to UNICEF, up until a maximum of £2,000 (which was donated to UNICEF in July 2021). This money was targeted to supporting innovative education programs across the world that give the most vulnerable children the chance to learn.

We hoped that these improvements would encourage respondents to engage more fully with the *Vocabulary Challenge* while also indirectly supporting a worthy charity.

CHAPTER 5

WRITING AND REVISING THE TEST ITEMS, DEVELOPING THE ONLINE TEST, AND MAIN DATA COLLECTION

The process of item writing and approval involved translation of the selected lemmas into Spanish, Chinese, and German, along with associated prompts in each language. These were embedded into the *Vocabulary Challenge* website backend database, which included a mechanism for allocating items to participants and collecting response data. Promotional channels were employed to ensure good reach across the relevant regions.

5.1   Writing the items in Chinese, German, and Spanish

Item writers for the three languages were recruited to the project. The principal Chinese item writer was a fluent bilingual who had completed a PhD in language studies. For German, the work was split across multiple bilingual writers, who were experts in applied linguistics and language testing. The principal Spanish item writer was a fluent bilingual, a language consultant and teacher with many years of experience gained at the British Council. In all cases, the writing process was supervised through consultations with project members. In particular, the principal Chinese item writer, who was first recruited, worked closely with the lead researcher (Schmitt) and through regular meetings generated best practices that were later communicated to other item writers on the project.

The team of bilingual item writers were provided with the following information.

- Rank: the frequency rank for the lemma, based on the COCA 60K database information
- Lemma: the target item
- Word class: part of speech for the lemma (many lemma forms have multiple word class, e.g., *access* = noun, *access* = verb)
- Spelling: British/US

- Dispersion: how widely the lemma is distributed across the COCA
- Total frequency: frequency in the COCA
- Score: Davies & Gardner's (2013) simple formula for combining frequency and dispersion (frequency x dispersion)

To carry out their task, the item writers were interested in the 'Lemma', which indicated the target word, and 'Word class', which helped to limit the translations to the desired part of speech. The British spellings would be used by the web application to offer either British or American spellings, according to the respondents' preferences. Other information had been used mainly in the process of building the candidate word list (i.e., Rank, Dispersion, Score, and Total frequency; see Chapter 2).

The item writers were required to provide the following pieces of information.

- Translation: the translation prompt for the lemma
- Example sentence: the contextualised sentence prompt for the lemma
- Highlight: this informed the web application which word(s) in the sentence to highlight in bold; usually the highlighted word(s) was the same as the translation prompt
- Comments: any specific information about the lemma which might be useful in a post-hoc manual analysis

If there was anything particularly unusual or noteworthy about the lemma and its translation/sentence, this was recorded in the 'Comments' column for future reference, in case any issues with the lemma turned up during the analysis.

The writing of the Chinese items informed the initial process for the item writers for the other two languages. Once a workable item-writing procedure had been established in liaison with this item writer, Schmitt wrote up instructions to send to all item writers (largely based on results of the earlier piloting) to ensure comparability across the three languages. The instructions are reproduced in Appendix 1.

Although these instructions clarified the procedure for most item writers, some additional discussion about cognates was necessary with the German item writers, especially regarding how to write a meaningful sentence for cognates. Some of the English lemmas had no German substitute. Words like *pizza, pipeline, quantum,* and *zebra* have the exact same spelling in German, and any kind of circumlocution would probably make the item much harder than it needed to be. Similarly, some lemmas had very similar, but not exact, spellings: *pistol/pistole, pump/ pumpe, psychologist/psychologe,* and *psychological/psychologisch,* and the same would apply to these. Taking *pizza* as an example, a German translator tried the following example sentence.

> *In vielen italienischen Restaurants kann man diese Speise bestellen. Es handelt sich dabei um dünn ausgerollten und mit Tomaten, Käse und anderen Zutaten würzig belegten Hefeteig.*

> *[English equivalent] In many Italian restaurants you can order this dish. It is a thinly rolled out yeasty dough covered with tomato, cheese and other savoury ingredients.*

Exact or very similar cognates like this were a conundrum. We obviously did not want to give away the spelling of the answers if possible, but the circumlocution in the pizza sentence could be too confusing and might make the learner think that the answer is not *pizza.* Thus, we tried to balance these two aspects by using exact translation spellings when necessary, but using the definition approach when it made sense to do so.

Some English/German lemma pairs meanwhile had considerable overlap in spelling, but were not identical: *professionalism/professionalität, politician/politiker, plantation/plantage,* and *programming/programmierung.* The decision was taken that pairs like these were different enough in spelling to elude guessing on the part of participants who did not know the word. Item writers were therefore advised to use these translations without seeking further discussion. Ultimately, we trusted the item writers to use their expert judgement of how to handle each individual lemma, realising that for some words the best option would be to use the exact/close cognate. (We eventually had to rewrite some items which avoided cognate prompts, see a later section of this chapter.)

Once the items were written, they went through a review and revision process by qualified bilinguals. The spreadsheets with the completed Spanish, Chinese, and German items were then checked to ensure that they worked with the web application. Once this was confirmed, we assumed the item-writing stage of the project was completed.

As a retrospective note, however, the amount of freedom that the item writers were given to choose the example sentences to best exemplify the target lemmas, and to formulate informative, unambiguous, and inoffensive example sentences, perhaps led to some avoidable issues further down the line in the project. While it was inevitable in 7,679 items that a few misleading example sentences might sneak into the *Vocabulary Challenge*, the number of questionable items identified by stakeholders (subsequent item writers, British Council local offices, participants) as problematic was larger than expected. Chapter 7 includes an analysis of problematic test items based on the example sentences.

5.2   British Council item vetting

The final step before entering the main data collection phase of the study (i.e., launching the *Vocabulary Challenge* website online) was a review by the British Council to confirm we met their standards for research and online presentation. This was important because the British Council was funding the research project, and the test carried its branding.

This review looked at several aspects of the research.

- Were any of the lemmas potentially controversial, offensive, or culturally sensitive, and with which the British Council would not wish to be associated?
- Were there any translations or example sentences that might prove controversial, offensive, or culturally sensitive, and with which the British Council would not wish to be associated?
- Did our website design meet the British Council brand criteria?

To vet our lemma list, we engaged the help of bilinguals who would be sensitive to any cultural issues and could check for any potential issues with the lemmas. We asked them to delete any offending item entries from their spreadsheets by deleting the entire row including all information about that particular item. They also kept a list of the deleted items, so the other two L1 spreadsheets could have those items deleted as well. This resulted in 28 items being deleted, most of which related to sex, but some referred to violence, drugs, and derogatory words. The list of deletions is given in Appendix 2. After this cleaning, the total number of lemmas which would appear in the *Vocabulary Challenge* was **7,679**.

These reviewers also checked the prompts. They looked for any that might cause unease or offence, but we also asked them to review the quality of the items, and whether they would lead the respondents to the intended target lemmas. They were instructed to change any offensive or weak translation/example sentence they encountered. The Spanish and Chinese checkers found relatively few problems (only 2.7% or 205/7,679 of the Spanish items needed revision; the Chinese checker made even fewer changes). The German checkers changed almost 1,000 items, with most of the discrepancies relating to cognate items and the best way to render cognates with informative translations and sentences, without giving away the L2 spelling unnecessarily. The checkers also proofed the example items and instructions. A final check for harmonisation and completeness across spreadsheets was conducted by Schmitt, before uploading the items to the online *Vocabulary Challenge* platform.

The website was designed to be attractive to the test respondents. Three stakeholders in the British Council checked the test and website design to comply with the organisation's digital branding requirements, and to ascertain whether the site functioned as expected in China.

It was anticipated that the *Vocabulary Challenge* would be accessed on devices with varying screen sizes, e.g., desktop computers, smart phones, iPads and other notebook devices. A responsive layout design ensured the test would be legible and look attractive across each display (e.g., the sidebars were set to automatically disappear on narrow displays and the menu bar would reduce in size). Similarly, the website was designed to work identically across different web browsers.

Finally, a 'stress test' was performed before launching to ensure the website could handle multiple respondents simultaneously.

5.3   The Vocabulary Challenge website

The *Vocabulary Challenge* website provisionally went live on 20 June 2018 to collect some 'real-world' data for our final validity check. As we wished to collect data from a wide range of ESL proficiencies in the three target languages, we decided to present the website instructions and background information in the respondents' respective L1s, so that L2 language proficiency would not hamper taking the test. Wording in English was agreed upon, and translated into Spanish, German, and Chinese. This was converted to website page templates for display based on each respondent's language choice.

The web page format can be seen in the selection of screenshots in Appendix 3. An excerpt of the information on the home page is provided in Figure 5.1.

Have you ever wondered how many English words you know? Maybe you are a student, you are learning English in your free time, or you use English as part of your job? If so, you can try the British Council's Vocabulary Challenge to check your English word knowledge!

We are looking for Spanish, German and Chinese native speakers to take the Vocabulary Challenge and be a part of this international project.

Supporting UNICEF

By taking the Vocabulary Challenge, you are not only testing your knowledge and perhaps learning some new English words, you are also supporting UNICEF. For every word you attempt in the Vocabulary Challenge the British Council will donate to UNICEF on your behalf. [...]

Why are we collecting this information?

Some words are more likely to be known by English learners than other words. The Vocabulary Challenge project aims to find out which of 7,000 of the most common English words Spanish, German or Chinese learners of the English language know.

All information collected through the Vocabulary Challenge is anonymous and will be used for research purposes only.

Figure 5.1: Excerpt of background information on the Vocabulary Challenge home page

Examples of the question format were given, as well as a list of FAQs and answers; an excerpt is provided below, with the full list in Appendix 3.

- Who can take the Vocabulary Challenge?
- How can I participate?
- Where should I take the Vocabulary Challenge?
- How long is the Vocabulary Challenge?
- What type of feedback can I expect?
- Why are you asking for background information before I take the Vocabulary Challenge?
- How am I supporting UNICEF by taking the Vocabulary Challenge and will it cost me any money?
- What if I experience a technical problem when taking the Vocabulary Challenge?

Once the language was chosen, the site took the respondent to a bio-data page. It then showed some words with American and British English spellings and asked the respondent if they preferred to take the *Vocabulary Challenge* in American English or British English. The next page contained the instructions, also in the L1 selected. We tried to make these short so that the respondent could quickly launch the challenge itself. The English translation of the instructions is shown in Figure 5.2.

> **Your challenge is to complete the words in English! You will see a word in Spanish and a sentence with this word underlined. You must enter the word in English of the underlined word.**
>
> We will show you 10 words to try initially and give you your first score when you complete the section. After that you can try more words and try to improve your score! We will give you your final score when you finish.
>
> Once you have tried a word, or if you do not know it, click NEXT.
>
> Remember, the more correct answers you get, the more money you will help raise for the world organization, UNICEF!
>
> Now you are ready to start the VOCABULARY CHALLENGE.
> Good luck!

Figure 5.2: Instructions to test respondents (English translation)

The items were all presented in the same format. Figure 5.3 shows the presentation of the item for the lemma *apart* from the Spanish language version.

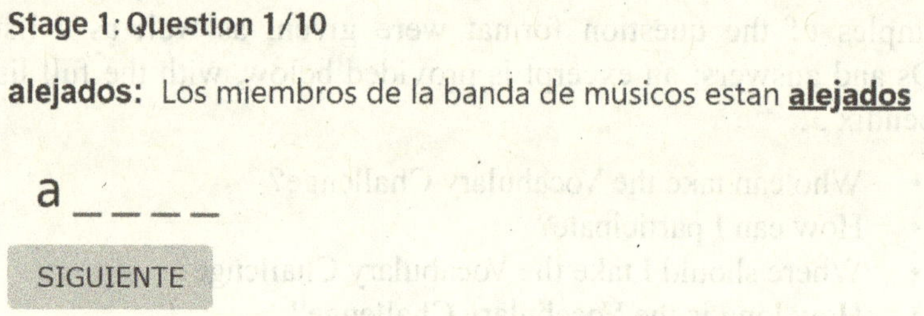

Stage 1: Question 1/10

alejados: Los miembros de la banda de músicos estan **alejados**

a _ _ _ _

SIGUIENTE

Figure 5.3: Item presentation for the lemma 'apart' (Spanish)

After every 10 items, a feedback page appeared, providing the total score, feedback on correct and incorrect answers, and offering the decision to continue the test or terminate. Figure 5.4 is an example feedback page after 10 items have been attempted, i.e., feedback on Stage 1 (items 1–10), with the English translation provided in the box below.

> Congratulations, now you have reached 10 words. Your current score is 5/10! Keep trying more words, and remember, for each correct answer you are helping the British Council raise money for UNICEF. Here are your scores from Stage 1: . . .

Bien hecho, has alcanzado 10 palabras. Tú puntaje actual es 5/10. Continúa intentándolo con más palabras, y recuerda, ¡por cada respuesta correcta estás ayudando al British Council a recaudar dinero para UNICEF!

Aquí están tus puntajes de la etapa 1:

```
1: ✗ asdfs (apart)
2: ✗ csdf (connection)
3: ✗ developed (discovered)
4: ✓ golf
5: ✗ iilsdfsdf (institutional)
6: ✓ matrix
7: ✗ polic (pound)
8: ✓ rolling
9: ✓ stroll
10: ✓ undetermined
```

CONTINUAR   TERMINAR

Figure 5.4: *Example of results presentation (Spanish)*

Clicking the Continue button took the respondent on to the next stage of 10 items. Clicking the Finish button took them to the closing page, where they received their final total score and an encouragement to share their score on Twitter. The page also encouraged them to come back and try the *Vocabulary Challenge* again, as shown in Figure 5.5.

Congratulations, you have finished the VOCABULARY CHALLENGE!

Your final score is 4/20.

Share your score on social networks and challenge your friends!

"I just completed the VOCABULARY CHALLENGE, my score was 4/20."

[Twitter button]

Each time you take the Vocabulary Challenge, you will be given new words to try. So you can take the challenge as many times as you want!

Thank you for being part of the VOCABULARY CHALLENGE!

Figure 5.5: *Closing page of the Vocabulary Challenge (English translation)*

5.4   Initial results and further revisions

Analysis of the initial findings was carried out to ensure that both the test and website were functioning well. Inevitably with such a large number of test items, a number of issues appeared. It became apparent that some of the German and Spanish items with close cognates were confusing participants because the cognate translations were avoided (see Appendix 1: Instructions to the item writers). That is, respondents may have known the English word (e.g., *telepathy*), but would enter an incorrect answer because the typical close cognate translation (e.g., *telepatía*) was not used in the prompt. Because of such discrepancies, all prompts were reviewed again in all three languages, and any problematic items were rewritten.

Second, some items (e.g., *conceive*) were surprisingly not known by anyone after 20 or so responses were gathered. We conducted an item analysis of poorly answered items to determine whether the items were faulty, or whether they simply represented difficult lemmas. Defective items were rewritten. Third, we received qualitative feedback that a small number of items had straightforward errors and needed to be corrected. For example, we found that 'flood' was erroneous, having the prompts for 'food' *essen*. All of the revisions were incorporated into the *Vocabulary Challenge* website.

A huge wave of respondents accessed the *Vocabulary Challenge* site in its early days, resulting in some items gaining a large number of responses (e.g., 99) while others had few responses (e.g., 6). Therefore, the programming was adapted to ensure that the lemmas would be allocated to participants in a more balanced manner.

Following promotional pushes by the British Council on Facebook, we received feedback from some German respondents who were not happy with some of the German items. Negative comments indicated that some participants had slightly misunderstood the aim of the *Vocabulary Challenge*, expecting in all cases to be providing a direct translation equivalent. Based on this, we reviewed a sample of the German items which had no correct responses, to see if the difficulty resided in the words themselves, of if any of the items were misleading. It was established that, while some items would benefit from further revision, some respondents were overly translation-focused in their criticisms. For example, for these respondents, the prompt for the target word *seaside* was seen to relate to *coast* and nothing else, based on the German translation cognate *küste*. While the meaning of *coast* is correct, it did not fit into the item format, i.e., *s _ _ _ _ _ _* (seaside). To ensure respondents understood that the test was based on meaning, and not simply strict translation equivalents, we revised our instructions to include a specific example, as shown in Figure 5.6 (with the English translation of the relevant portion provided in the box).

Your task is to fill the appropriate English words in the given gaps! For each task, you will see a German word and an example sentence where that word is used. The word is always underlined. You then have to write the word in English in the gaps.

The Vocabulary Challenge is designed to test the breadth of your vocabulary. Therefore, it tests more than just the most common words. For example:

stale: The beer tastes **stale**.

s _ _ _ _

The most obvious translation for **stale** would be **flat**, but this word starts with an "s". So, what other words do you know that mean the same thing?

s t a l e

Deine Aufgabe ist es, die passenden englischen Wörter in die jeweils vorgegebenen Lücken zu füllen! Bei jeder Aufgabe siehst ein deutsches Wort und einen Beispielsatz, wo dieses Wort verwendet wird. Dabei ist das Wort immer unterstrichen. Du musst dann das gesuchte Wort auf Englisch in die Lücken schreiben.

Die Vocabulary Challenge ist so entworfen, dass sie die Bandbreite deines Wortschatzes prüfen will. Daher testet sie mehr als nur die geläufigsten Wörter. Zum Beispiel:

abgestanden: Das Bier schmeckt **abgestanden**.

s _ _ _ _

Die naheliegendste Übersetzung für **abgestanden** wäre **flat**, aber dieses Wort beginnt mit einem "s". Also, welche anderen Wörter kennst du, die dasselbe bedeuten?

s t a l e

Am Anfang werden dir 10 Aufgaben gestellt und du erhältst nach diesen ersten Fragen einen Punktestand. Danach kannst du dann noch mehr Wörter versuchen, um deinen Punktestand zu steigern. Deinen endgültigen Punktestand erhältst du, wenn du die Challenge beendest.

Klicke auf WEITER, wenn du deine Antwort abgeben willst oder das Wort nicht kennst.

Vergiss nicht, je mehr richtige Antworten du gibst, desto mehr Geld geht an UNICEF!

Du kannst jetzt die VOCABULARY CHALLENGE starten.

Viel Glück!

WEITER

Figure 5.6: Elaboration on instructions to broaden participant responses beyond direct translation equivalents

Once we were satisfied that the test items and the site were working well, the *Vocabulary Challenge* website was ready to officially launch for the final data collection. Obviously, for items that had been revised, we needed to start from scratch with the new items. But for unchanged items, there was no reason to discard the data already gathered. We felt it justifiable to keep it and add it to the forthcoming data, as: the items were identical to how they appeared in the main data collection stage; the type of crowdsourced participant was the same; and the online elicitation platform would be identical. We also needed to collect very large amounts of data (i.e., ~150 responses for 7,679 lemmas) so there was no good reason not to employ this valuable data in the final study.

5.5   Promotion and data collection

Promotion of the *Vocabulary Challenge* involved activation of both professional and British Council networks, in addition to paid campaigns over social media platforms. A marketing kit was produced to share with the marketing contacts involved in promotion. It included both static and animated digital assets developed to appeal to potential participants and pique their interest. Because the *Vocabulary Challenge* was aimed at participants from such a wide range of demographics, we took a broad-based approach to promotion.

British Council contacts utilised internal and external British Council social media links in relevant countries. Additional contacts (mainly teachers and university staff) in Spanish-, Chinese-, and German-speaking countries were asked to promote the test among their students.

For promotion amongst Spanish learners, we had many colleagues encouraging the use of the *Vocabulary Challenge* in their Spanish school, university, and language school contexts. As well as Spain, we benefited from the large number of Latin American countries with Spanish as their L1, from which we could draw respondents. These included colleagues in British Council centres in Argentina, Chile, Colombia, Mexico, Peru, and Venezuela. The major share of the participation was driven by two paid campaigns on Google and Facebook which reached people in Spanish-speaking countries across the globe.

A similar approach was taken with the Chinese version of the test. Colleagues who helped promote data collection included university colleagues, plus colleagues in British Council China. We paid for promotions to encourage uptake on the Chinese platform *WeChat* but this was not as successful as with the Spanish respondent population.

In seeking German participants, we received good support from colleagues working at German and Austrian universities, as well as British Council colleagues from Austria, Germany, and Switzerland.

We are immensely grateful for the support and input of colleagues and volunteers across the globe for promoting the *Vocabulary Challenge* during the data collection phase. Please see the Acknowledgements at the front of this monograph for details.

5.6   Final item response numbers

Our goal was to collect a minimum of 150 responses per lemma for each language version of the *Vocabulary Challenge*. The most successful promotional effort was achieved across the Spanish-speaking world. We achieved the 150-responses-per-lemma target for our Spanish respondents within 19 months of the *Vocabulary Challenge* being live online. For various reasons, the numbers were not as easily achieved in the Chinese context, and the Chinese data collection lagged behind that of the Spanish. The German uptake saw additional problems. This was partly because of the prompt revisions that were required for the German items following the initial launch (see discussion above), which meant that the German test was late in becoming fully operational. As a result, the German data collection was affected by the COVID-19 slowdown and associated budget cuts.

In fact, the pandemic slowed the number of daily respondents drastically. At this point, with no reliable way of knowing when the effects of the pandemic would end, we decided to close Chinese data collection just shy of the target, with 90% of the lemmas having 140 responses or more, and eight lemmas having fewer than 135 responses. The German participant numbers were lower than this. The final German dataset saw a minimum of 120 responses per lemma, with two exceptions at 117 responses. Overall, there were around 11,000–12,000 fewer participants for German than for Spanish or Chinese. A more detailed breakdown of the final respondent tallies is reported in the next chapter.

CHAPTER 6

ANALYSIS AND RANKING OF LEMMAS

Chapter 5 described how we collected data from a very large sample of Spanish-, Chinese-, and German-speaking participants. Although the resultant dataset was vast, the collection procedure was designed so that there would be relatively little cross-over in terms of response data by item and by test-taker. This is because each of the approximately 20,000–30,000 participants across each of the three different language versions of the *Vocabulary Challenge* was randomly allocated a selection from the 7,679 items from the relevant language list (stratified across the 10 difficulty bins as described earlier). This meant that as respondents progressed through the test, Participant A might be randomly allocated a particular lemma (e.g., *burn*) in their first round of 10 items, while it might come up for Participant B in their 50th round. While some participants completed as few as 10 items, and a very small percentage of respondents across all three languages (around 350) answered more than 1,000 items, the median number of responses per session across the three language groups ranged from 25 to 33.

6.1　Descriptive statistics for the KVL data

Between 940,000 and 1.2 million valid responses were collected per language, giving a total of over 3.3 million individual item responses for the project overall. The data came from 30,000-plus testing sessions for the Spanish- and Chinese-speaking groups, and over 20,000 for the German-speakers (Table 6.1). The majority of respondents were 24 years of age or over, although the Chinese group also had a sizable number of 17- to 23-year-olds. The majority also reported to have studied English as a second language for 10 years or more. The responses to 'Hours of using English per week' were more evenly distributed, although many respondents indicated either 1–2 hours per week, or 5 hours or more. The Spanish and German speakers favoured British English, while the Chinese speakers chose American English more often (Table 6.2).

Facility values (the number of times an item was answered correctly over the total number of times the item was presented) were calculated to give an immediate indication of the difficulty of the items. With a mixed population taking the test, this straightforward Classical Test Theory approach is broadly informative. However, to generate the estimates to rank the word knowledge order, we used an Item Response Theory (IRT) approach which provides a more sophisticated indication of item difficulty as it also accounts for the ability of each respondent in the calculation. We built a single parameter (1pl) IRT model within a General Linear Mixed Model (GLMM) framework, as this methodology could accommodate the sparsity of the dataset without causing estimation problems. Please see Appendix 4 for the full technical explanation of GLMM. Both facility values and the IRT GLMM values are summarised in Table 6.3.

One of the limitations of the form-recall test format used in the *Vocabulary Challenge* was capturing knowledge of lemmas with alternative BrE and AmE spellings (e.g., *disc/disk, aluminium/aluminum*) (see Chapter 3). These lemmas were included in the test, in hopes that limitations would not be unsurmountable. Unfortunately, close analysis of the responses to these items indicated multiple problems, and, ultimately, reliable knowledge rankings for these lemmas could not be generated. Therefore, lemmas with alternative BrE and AmE spellings were not included in subsequent analyses and not included in the KVL. The excluded BrE/AmE lemmas are listed in *Supplementary List A: Lemmas with alternative British vs. American spellings that are not included in the KVL* at the end of the online User Manual (www.britishcouncil.org/exam/aptis/aptis-expertise/knowledge-based-vocabulary-lists-kvl). Following these exclusions, the total number of lemmas included in the analyses was **7,532**.

	Spanish	Chinese	German
Total number of valid responses recorded and used in the GLMM model	1,265,443	1,104,962	942,150
Number of testing sessions engaged in by respondents[a]	31,315	32,726	20,681

a. Participants could log into more than one testing session, so the total number of individual participants is less than this.

Table 6.1: Summary of response numbers for the KVL data

Question	Response	Spanish (% participants)	Chinese (% participants)	German (% participants)
Age	10 years or younger	468 (1.49%)	795 (2.43%)	263 (1.27%)
	11–16 years	1,999 (6.38%)	2,054 (6.28%)	2,531 (12.24%)
	17–23 years	2,493 (7.96%)	13,237 (40.45%)	3,590 (17.36%)
	24 years or older	26,355 (84.16%)	16,640 (50.85%)	14,297 (69.13%)
Years studied English	3 years or fewer	4,998 (15.96%)	2,467 (7.54%)	1,286 (6.22%)
	4–6 years	5,228 (16.69%)	3,479 (10.63%)	4,240 (20.50%)
	7–9 years	4,691 (14.98%)	6,112 (18.68%)	6,606 (31.94%)
	10 years or more	16,398 (52.36%)	20,668 (63.15%)	8,549 (41.34%)
Hours per week using English[a]	None	3,511 (11.21%)	3,687 (11.27%)	1,296 (6.27%)
	1–2 hours	8,167 (26.08%)	11,982 (36.61%)	6,445 (31.16%)
	3–4 hours	5,858 (18.71%)	6,063 (18.53%)	4,456 (21.55%)
	5 hours or more	13,779 (44.00%)	10,994 (33.59%)	8,484 (41.02%)
Language variety selected	US	8,125 (25.95%)	19,277 (58.90%)	6,669 (32.25%)
	UK	23,190 (74.05%)	13,449 (41.10%)	14,012 (67.75%)

a. This included reading, speaking, watching television, using social media, the Internet, and video games.

Table 6.2: Description of KVL participants by language group

Metric	Statistic	Spanish	Chinese	German
Lemmas tested	Total	7,679	7,679	7,679
Lemmas included in the analyses	Total	7,532	7,532	7,532
Responses per lemma	Minimum	154	137	120
	Maximum	216	228	222
	Median	167	146	125
	Mean	168.01	146.88	125.11
	s.d.	6.54	6.27	4.91
Lemma facility values	Minimum	.00	.00	.00
	Maximum	1.00	1.00	1.00
	Mean	0.59	0.62	0.69
	s.d.	0.27	0.24	0.24
GLMM intercept values[a]	Minimum	−5.90	−5.93	−6.50
	Maximum	5.14	4.84	4.32
	Mean	−0.02	−0.02	−0.05
	s.d.	1.87	1.67	1.78

a. These can be considered as broadly equivalent to 'difficulty' estimates from a 1pl (Rasch) model with the signage reversed.

Table 6.3: Summary of KVL responses and difficulty (easiness) estimates

6.2 Relative knowledge of the target lemmas by the three language groups

Each language group was tested on the final KVL target list of 7,679 lemmas. Ultimately, we were able to collect a minimum of 153 responses per lemma from the Spanish respondents, 130 from the Chinese respondents, and (with the exception of two lemmas) 120 from the German respondents. Overall, the target lemmas as a group were known by around one-half to two-thirds of the respondents, with the mean facility value for the Spanish respondents being 0.59, the Chinese respondents 0.62, and the German respondents 0.69. This means that, for example, when all of the lemmas were averaged together, about 59% of the Spanish respondents answered correctly. While the facility values do not take into account the ability levels of the test-takers, with such large and broadly targeted participant groups for each language background, some degree of random equivalence can be assumed. These statistics were used to give an insight into the comparative knowledge levels of the learners before the more complex statistical analyses were run, which do account for participant ability based on all their responses.

The first thing to note is that the various lemmas varied widely in their difficulty. A few were very difficult and answered correctly by no respondent (Spanish: *unchallenged, received*; German: *indictment, orthodox*; Chinese: *arresting, unchecked*). Conversely, some lemmas were extremely well-known and answered correctly by all respondents (Spanish: *city, dance, jet, zoo*; Chinese: *car, cat, dream, just*). The German group produced by far the most lemmas known by all respondents, 23 in total: *better, blog, bomb, burger, cat, dance, day, drive, eat, elite, English, fit, hungry, ice, idol, jeans, kiss, Korean, not, orange, sun, west, wind*. Interestingly, there is no overlap between the language groups in terms of completely unknown lemmas, only two lemmas (*cat, dance*) were completely known by at least two language groups, and there was no lemma completely known by all three language groups. The facility values for the lemmas, broken into 10 bands (unrelated to the 10 difficulty bands used during the collection process), are shown in Table 6.4 and illustrated in Figures 6.1 to 6.3.

For all three language groups, there was a greater percentage of lemmas in higher facility value bands than lower ones. In general, there were relatively few lemmas which had very low facility values, i.e., 0.00–0.09 and 0.10–0.19. Conversely, there was a relatively large percentage of lemmas that had very high facility values, i.e., 0.80–0.89 and 0.90–1.00. Perhaps this is not surprising, as the purpose of the KVL project was to identify the *best-known* 5,000 lemmas, and so the 7,679 lemmas to be tested were selected based on high frequency and Brysbaert et al.'s (2016a) previous knowledge results, and were always likely to be relatively well-known. The table and figures also confirm that the German respondents were the strongest in terms of vocabulary knowledge, with an exceptionally high percentage of lemmas (26.1%) with the highest facility value (0.90–1.00).

Facility value	Number of lemmas in facility value band (%) Max = 7,532		
	Spanish	German	Chinese
0.90–1.00	1,165 (14.4)	1,964 (26.1)	996 (13.2)
0.80–0.89	1,030 (13.6)	1,267 (16.8)	1,146 (15.2)
0.70–0.79	872 (11.4)	1,014 (13.5)	1,069 (14.2)
0.60–0.69	862 (11.5)	823 (10.9)	1,030 (13.7)
0.50–0.59	793 (11.0)	728 (9.7)	909 (12.1)
0.40–0.49	741 (9.6)	603 (8.0)	773 (10.3)
0.30–0.39	675 (9.2)	494 (6.6)	717 (9.6)
0.20–0.29	598 (8.1)	381 (5.1)	504 (6.7)
0.10–0.19	530 (7.3)	200 (2.7)	281 (3.7)
0.00–0.09	266 (3.5)	58 (0.8)	107 (1.4)

Table 6.4: Facility values of the target lemmas

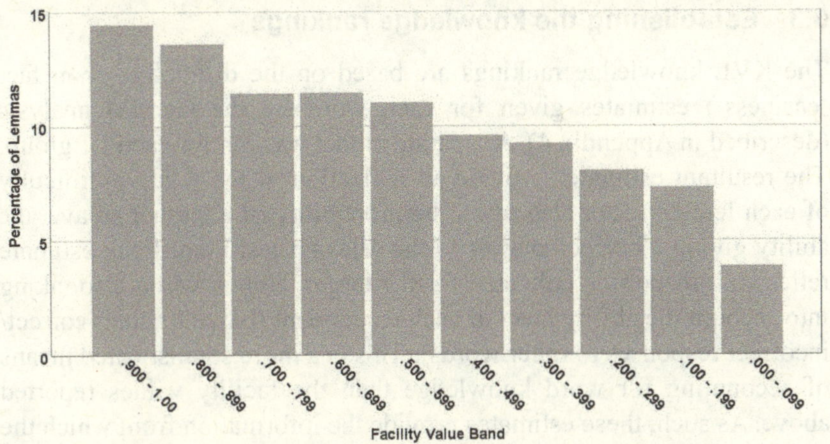

Figure 6.1: Facility values for Spanish respondents

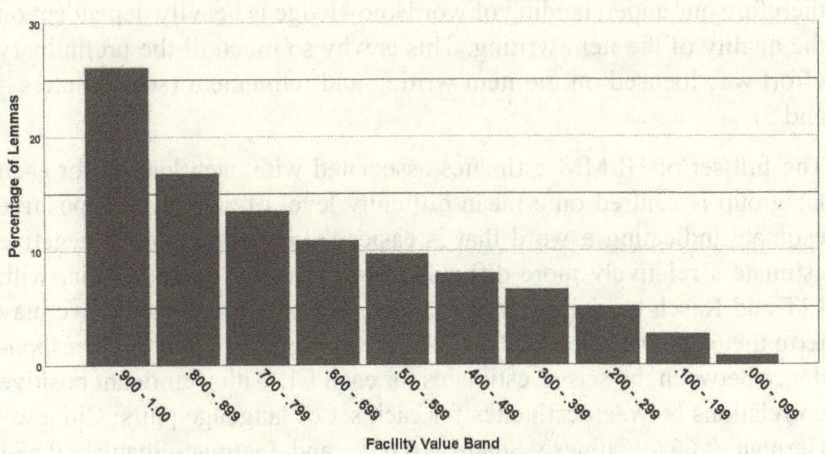

Figure 6.2: Facility values for German respondents

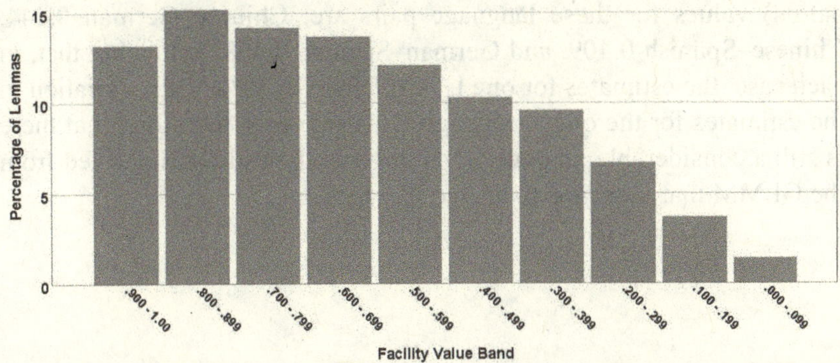

Figure 6.3: Facility values for Chinese respondents

6.3   Establishing the knowledge rankings

The KVL knowledge rankings are based on the difficulty (or in fact 'easiness') estimates given for each word by the GLMM analysis (described in Appendix 4). A separate model was run for each L1 group. The resultant estimates provide an indication of the relative difficulty of each lemma tested, based on the probability of a learner of average ability giving a correct answer to the relevant test item. Each estimate reflects all responses collected for the target lemma, while also taking into account the ability level of each respondent (based on their correct/ incorrect responses to other words). This is a more sophisticated means of accounting for word knowledge than the facility values reported above. As such, these estimates provide the information from which the KVL rank order lists were constructed. It is important to note that the statistical model is directly linked to responses given to the test items, therefore our understanding of word knowledge is heavily dependent on the quality of the item writing. This is why so much of the preliminary effort was focused on the item writing and refinement (see Chapters 4 and 5).

The full set of GLMM estimates associated with each lemma for each L1 group is centred on a mean difficulty level of zero, with a positive estimate indicating a word that is easier than average, and a negative estimate a relatively more difficult word (note: for those familiar with IRT and Rasch modelling, this is a *reversal* of signage, hence we may term them 'easiness' estimates). There was a good degree of correspondence between the sets of estimates for each L1, with significant positive correlations between estimates for each set of language pairs: Chinese– German 0.667, Chinese–Spanish 0.639, and German–Spanish 0.684 (Pearson correlations; all $p<0.01$). The relationship is illustrated by the scatterplots in Figures 6.4, 6.5, and 6.6. The r^2 (coefficient of determination) values for these language pairs are: Chinese–German 0.444, Chinese–Spanish 0.409, and German–Spanish 0.468, indicating that, in each case, the estimates for one L1 explain over 40% of the variation in the estimates for the other language. This suggests, therefore, that there is still a considerable amount of variation in the estimates derived from the GLMM that is *unique* to each of the lists.

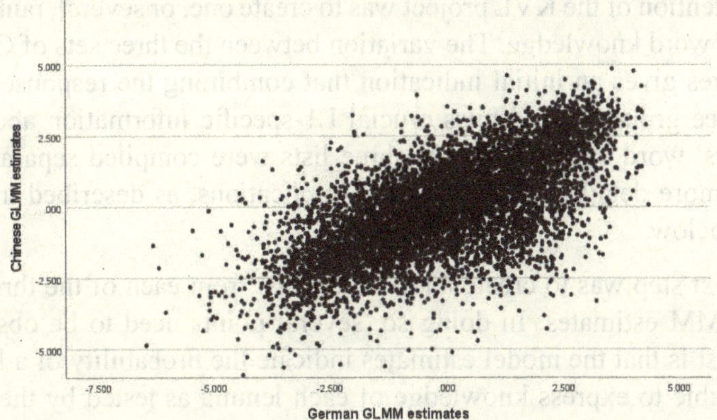

Figure 6.4: Scatterplot of Chinese and German GLMM estimates

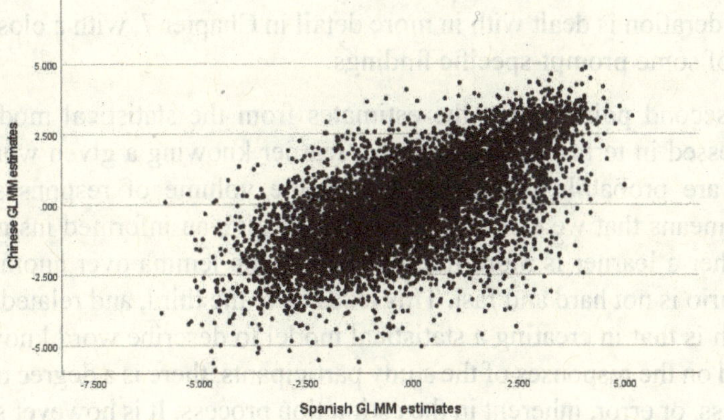

Figure 6.5: Scatterplot of Chinese and Spanish GLMM estimates

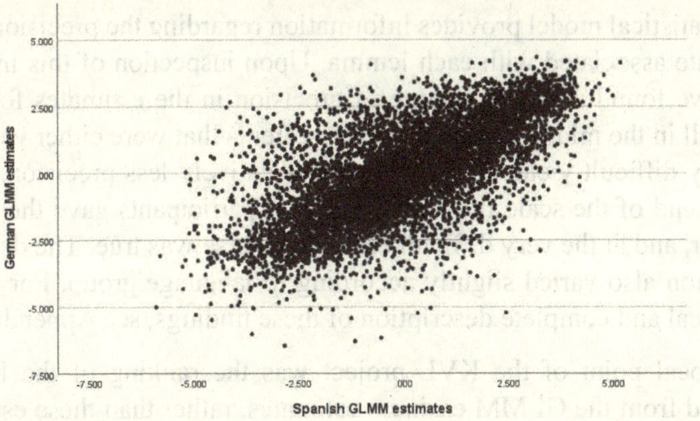

Figure 6.6: Scatterplot of German and Spanish GLMM estimates

The intention of the KVL project was to create one, or several, rank order lists of word knowledge. The variation between the three sets of GLMM estimates gives an initial indication that combining the responses from the three groups would miss crucial L1-specific information about the learners' word knowledge. The three lists were compiled separately to allow more detailed scrutiny of the implications, as described in more detail below.

The next step was to create a rank order list from each of the three sets of GLMM estimates. In doing so, several points need to be observed. The first is that the model estimates indicate the probability of a learner being able to express knowledge of each lemma as tested by the given prompt. This means that the estimate for each lemma is inherently tied with the design of the prompt; some of the differences between the lists will therefore reflect discrepancies in the item prompts across L1s. This consideration is dealt with in more detail in Chapter 7, with a close scrutiny of some prompt-specific findings.

The second point is that the estimates from the statistical models are expressed in terms of the odds of a learner knowing a given word, i.e., they are probability-based. Although the volume of responses gathered means that we can use the models to give an informed insight into whether a learner is more likely to know one lemma over another, this scenario is not hard and fast. This leads us to the third, and related, point, which is that in creating a statistical model to describe word knowledge based on the responses of the study participants, there is a degree of inexactness, or error, inherent in the estimation process. It is however statistically possible to describe the extent to which this inexactness affects our certainty, or confidence, in the estimates given.

The statistical model provides information regarding the precision of the estimate associated with each lemma. Upon inspection of this information, we found a greater degree of precision in the estimates for items that fall in the middle range of easiness. Items that were either very easy or very difficult yielded estimates with relatively less precision. At the easier end of the scale the majority of the participants gave the correct answer, and at the very difficult end, the reverse was true. The degree of precision also varied slightly according to language group. For a more technical and complete description of these findings, see Appendix 5.

The focal point of the KVL project was the ranking of the lemmas derived from the GLMM easiness estimates, rather than these estimates themselves. Inevitably, across the full sample of lemmas there were a large number of GLMM intercept estimates that fell very close to one another, and indeed a considerable number that shared values (to the nearest three decimal places). Looking in some detail at the three sets of estimates, it could be seen that the number of lemmas which shared a difficulty estimate with at least one other lemma from the list of 7,532 lemmas varied slightly between languages. The percentages were as follows: in the Chinese list, 68.8% lemmas shared an easiness estimate with at least one other lemma; in the German list, 66.9% shared an estimate; and in the Spanish list, 65.2%. In addition to these exact matches, the margin of error surrounding each of the estimates means that there is additional overlap in our degree of confidence that one lemma is more, or less, likely to be known than another lemma. Ultimately this means that in creating the rank order lists, there are words that have a higher or lower rank which are not significantly more or less easy than one another as estimated by the model.

In creating the ranked lists, it was therefore important for us to find out how distinct the easiness estimates for each lemma were from one another. This information allows us to understand the threshold at which we can be confident that one lemma is easier to know than another lemma for learners of each of the three language groups. To understand the practical impact of this (im)precision in the model, we ordered the lemmas based on their GLMM estimates, and then investigated how many lemmas fell into the bracket of uncertainty at regular points along the difficulty spectrum. Appendix 5 gives a detailed account of the process. In brief, the words were ranked according to their estimates, and a sample of 100 lemmas was taken from each list at 500-lemma intervals. The number of lemmas to fall between significantly different estimates was assessed in each 100-lemma sample. The findings are summarised in Table 6.5.

The interpretation of the results presented in this table indicate, for example, that for the Spanish respondents, we can be confident that lemmas ranked within the 200–299 band will be statistically accurate within ±44 places. That is, we are confident from the estimates given by the statistical model that Spanish learners of English are more likely to know *hat* (#250) than *online* (#295), and less likely to know *hat* than *dog* (#205). Conversely, we would not be confident that *hat* will be better known than *eye* (#270) or lesser known than *night* (#230). However, it must be acknowledged that the KVL rankings reflect a continuum, with no clear thresholds or divisions, so it makes sense to be cautious in how the precision of the rankings is interpreted. Overall, for Spanish and Chinese these findings show that if a lemma is ranked 100 places above another lemma in one of the KVL, we can have a strong degree of confidence that a learner has a greater probability of knowing that lemma over the other lemma. For the German learners this will also broadly hold, though we would not have the same degree of confidence.

Ranking band	Number of lemmas		
	Spanish	Chinese	German
200–299	44	55	78
700–799	53	56	102
1,200–1,299	61	60	96
1,700–1,799	53	80	108
2,200–2,299	68	71	99
2,700–2,799	54	95	108
3,200–3,299	51	94	89
3,700–3,799	69	76	85
4,200–4,299	54	79	97
4,700–4,799	44	72	68

Table 6.5: *Number of ranked lemmas between significantly different GLMM easiness estimates at 10 sampled points in the data*

6.4   Gradations in knowledge rankings

When developing the KVL, a key question was: in order to be pedagogically useful, how fine do the gradations in knowledge rankings need to be? To contextualise this question, it is useful to consider both the nature of English vocabulary overall and typical ESL acquisition patterns. Vocabulary follows Zipf's law, and the most frequent 8,000–9,000 word families will provide coverage of at least 98% of the running words in typical written texts and spoken discourse (Nation, 2006). As a consequence, a maximum of around 10,000 word families will ever typically be dealt with pedagogically (outside of a narrowly-focused English for Specific Purposes class). However, the typical ESL learner only knows somewhere in the range of 2,000–3,000 word families (Laufer, 2000), and most textbooks and instruction deal with only the first few thousand word families. This suggests that it would be highly desirable if the KVL had precision in reporting knowledge ranking within hundreds, and not thousands.

To illustrate this point, let us consider a typical classroom setting. It is unusual for more than 10 words to be taught per class session (and very often, fewer than this). Therefore, a gradation of 100 lemmas would be enough for 10 sessions. The 100 lemmas could be taught in any order during these 10 sessions, but there would still be a workable sequential structure where those 100 lemmas would be taught before the next 100 over the next 10 sessions. If the KVL only had precision in reporting a knowledge ranking within say 500 words, it would lead to the vocabulary being indicated for 50 sessions, which is a full academic year in many teaching contexts. This means that the KVL could offer no sequencing over the course, negating most of the value that the KVL could provide practitioners in terms of the logical sequencing of vocabulary instruction.

Similarly, graded readers are often graded into levels depending on how many different headwords occur in the reader. Often, the levels are differentiated by only a few hundred headwords (e.g., *Pearson English Readers – EasyStarts*: 200 headwords, *Level 1*: 300 headwords, *Level 2*: 600 headwords, *Level 3*: 1,200 headwords, *Level 4*: 1,700 headwords, *Level 5*: 2,300 headwords). A gradation of 500 lemmas or more would do little to help the writers of such graded readers to decide which words to include in particular levels. In testing, there is a parallel argument that finer gradations make sense for the most frequent/best known lemmas (Kremmel, 2016).

Pedagogical concerns such as these suggest that gradations of only a few hundred, and probably not more than 500, would make the KVL maximally useful. We have already seen above that within each list, the precision of the knowledge rankings gives us a good degree of confidence that if a lemma is ranked 100 lemmas above or below another lemma, then it is significantly better known, or less known, than the lemma with which it is being compared. This means that for each individual list, it is reasonable to make cut-points at intervals of fewer than 500 lemmas.

However, a major concern of the project was whether to produce a single KVL, i.e., one list to represent the ordering of word knowledge, or separate lists for each L1 background. The differentiation in difficulties assessed above only concerned the individual lists; first the decision needed to be made whether to combine the lists. To this end, analyses were conducted to assess the similarities and differences between lists. The rest of this chapter focuses on whether the rank orders to result from our difficulty estimates for each of the three L1 groups were similar enough to produce a single version of the KVL, or whether we needed three individual lists.

6.5   Comparisons between the rank orders from the three language groups

The rank order lists of words provide an indication of the probability of a learner from a given language background knowing one English language lemma over another lemma on the list. Since the use of the KVL refers to the rank order of word knowledge, it is of interest to compare these directly. While the correlations reported earlier show the correspondence between the three sets of GLMM estimates, this section examines the similarities and differences among the KVL rank orders for each language group.

When moving on to consider the rank order values attributed to each lemma, it is useful to bear in mind that the rankings are not independent of one another. If there is a group of words that are much better known for one group of learners than for another, and the obvious example is cognates, then the appearance of these words higher up in the ranked lists will displace other words that may not be dissimilar in terms of *absolute* difficulty for a learner from a non-cognate language background. We can illustrate this point with the word *republic*: the Spanish knowledge ranking is 157, a high score facilitated by the Spanish equivalent being a very similarly-spelled cognate (*república*). Because of this, it gains a place in the top 500 best known words for Spanish learners. The German equivalent is also a cognate (*republik*), but the German knowledge ranking is lower, at 1,177, although still within the top 2,000 known words. The non-cognate language Chinese unsurprisingly has the lowest ranking at 2,202. In terms of the implied order of learning, this and other cognate words will displace other non-cognate words in the Spanish and German lists, pushing them down to a lower ranking. Herein lies the usefulness of the lists – in teaching Chinese learners, the word *republic* may need fuller attention than for German and Spanish learners.

Kendall's tau (Kendall, 1955) provides an appropriate means of deriving a global comparison between rank order lists. This correlation coefficient compares the difference between one set of rank orders and another, based on the number of changes that are needed to transform one into the other (Abdi, 2007). To this end, Kendall's tau-b values were used to indicate the concordance between lists which incorporated the full 7,532 words, i.e., the extent to which the lemmas are ordered the same or differently across L1 rankings, with a correction for ties. The estimates were significant for all language pairs: Spanish–German 0.505, Spanish–Chinese 0.454, and German–Chinese 0.476 (all $p<0.001$). Rules of thumb for interpreting tau are not widely presented; however, values over 0.35 can be considered as strong associations (van den Berg, 2019). This overall measure does not however tell us anything about the nature of the differences, or similarities, between lists at different intervals in the rankings.

To gain a more detailed insight into the concordance between lists, we looked at the crossovers in the words appearing in each at different band levels. Since the full lists are to be set at 5,000 lemmas, a good place to start is to examine the overlap between the top-5000 lemmas for each L1 group. As noted above, the exact same set of lemmas will not appear across all lists, since language-specific reasons will cause variation in the rank order of difficulty. We found that there were more than 80% common words shared between the top 5,000 known lemmas for each pair of lists, with the highest crossover between the Spanish and German lists at 84.7% (see final row of Table 6.6). Since the full sample of lemmas with potential for inclusion in the lists was 7,532, the greatest distinction between any two lists of 5,000 drawn from this would have entailed a 49.4% crossover. Over 80% crossover for each pair of lists indicates a substantial increase on this, indicating a considerable degree of overlap between the words that made the top 5,000 for each L1 group.

Despite this overall crossover, it was of particular interest to examine how the rank ordering plays out within narrower ranges of words. Our second analysis into the commonality between the lists therefore involved taking a closer look at the percentage of lemmas that coexisted between the three language groups at various knowledge levels. We looked at 500-lemma bands, starting with 1–500 and finishing at 7,001–7,500. This finer-grained analysis of 500-lemma groups summarised in Table 6.6 indicates that there are considerable distinctions between rankings in each list. About half (~50%) of the very best-known lemmas (Band 1–500) are common between language comparisons, but at the next band (501–1,000) this drops to about one-quarter (~25%), and then for the vast majority of the bands (i.e., from 1,001–1,500 to 6,501–7,000) the range is typically 10%–20%.

At the least-known end of the continuum (7,001–7,500), the percentage overlap increases, but this is likely due to the ceiling effect, whereby a similar set of difficult words are clustered toward this end of the rankings. The overall pattern of crossovers is very similar between language groups, as is indicated by the visual presentation of this information in Figure 6.7.

Overall, the low level of commonality between ranked bands from 500 to 5,000 strongly suggests it would be difficult to create a single list which adequately describes the rank order of knowledge of all three language groups simultaneously. This means that the word lists are providing unique information about word knowledge for each of the L1 groups.

Knowledge band	Spanish ↔ German (%)	Spanish ↔ Chinese (%)	German ↔ Chinese (%)
1–500	48.6[b]	50.4	48.2
501–1,000	25.7	23.2	24.1
1,001–1,500	18.3	17.4	18.3
1,501–2,000	15.2	13.9	12.8
2,001–2,500	12.4	11.8	13.0
2,501–3,000	14.2	12.9	12.3
3,001–3,500	11.2	13.2	9.8
3,501–4,000	15.0	12.8	8.2
4,001–4,500	12.0	11.4	13.1
4,501–5,000	13.1	12.9	10.9
5,001–5,500	16.5	12.5	10.0
5,501–6,000	14.9	11.5	12.9
6,001–6,500	18.7	15.3	14.0
6,501–7,000	21.3	18.0	19.7
7,001–7,500	35.4	28.8	33.7
1–5,000	84.7[c]	82.4	83.3

a. Comparisons were made with the Text-Lex-Compare tool on the Lextutor website (www.lextutor.ca/cgi-bin/tl_compare/).

b. Percentage of lemmas that were common between the two languages at the specified knowledge band, e.g., 48.6% of the lemmas were shared between the 500 lemmas appearing in the Spanish 1–500 knowledge band and the 500 lemmas appearing in the German 1–500 knowledge band.

c. Percentage of lemmas that were common between the two languages at the combined 1–5,000 bands.

Table 6.6: *Percentage of common[a] lemmas within various knowledge ranking levels*

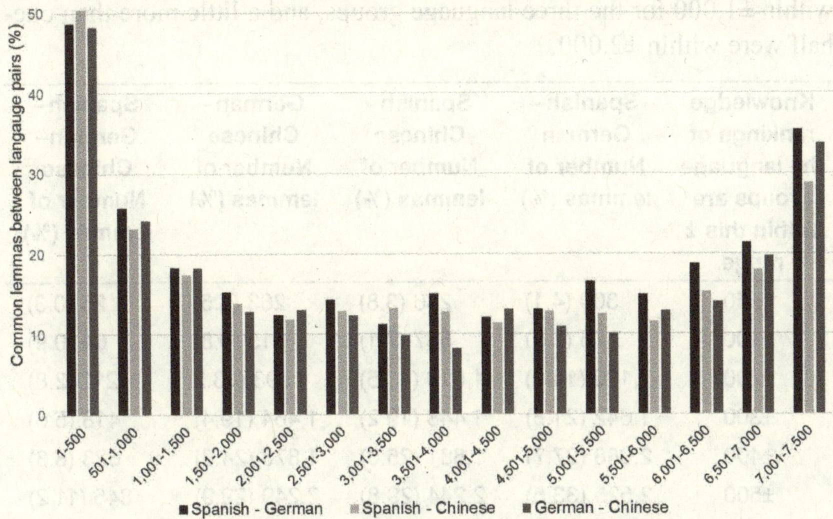

Figure 6.7: Plot showing percentage of common lemmas within various knowledge ranking levels

A further analysis examining the degree of correspondence in the knowledge rankings for the three language groups involved calculating the proximity of rankings across the different lists. This involved comparing the position of the same lemma between two and then all three lists to see how close they appeared in the rank ordering.

Table 6.7 reports the level of correspondence between language pairs beginning with what we would consider a very close correspondence (±50), and working towards only a very loose correspondence (±2,000). Again, we find rather modest levels of correspondence. The language pairs were within ±50 or ±100 for much less than 10% of the lemmas. They were within ±500 for about one-third of the lemmas, and within ±1,000 for about one-half of the lemmas. About 75% of the lemmas were within a very loose ±2,000 correspondence. The overall language pair analysis shows that the knowledge rankings for one language are not very near the knowledge rankings for another language.

The fifth column in this table is most important for the question of single vs multiple lists. It shows the number of lemmas in which *all three language groups* were within a plus/minus range. The figures here are unsurprisingly very much lower than for any language pair, and are very low overall. A bit over one-quarter of the lemmas were simultaneously within ±1,000 for the three language groups, and a little more than one-half were within ±2,000.

Knowledge rankings of the language groups are within this ± range	Spanish–German Number of lemmas (%)	Spanish–Chinese Number of lemmas (%)	German–Chinese Number of lemmas (%)	Spanish–German–Chinese Number of lemmas (%)
±50	309 (4.1)	286 (3.8)	263 (3.5)	26 (0.3)
±100	575 (7.6)	537 (7.1)	515 (6.8)	64 (0.9)
±200	1,126 (14.9)	1,016 (13.5)	993 (13.2	211 (2.8)
±300	1,642 (21.8)	1,448 (19.2)	1,464 (19.4)	418 (5.6)
±400	2,088 (27.7)	1,881 (25.0)	1,873 (24.9)	623 (8.3)
±500	2,525 (33.5)	2,244 (29.8)	2,249 (29.9)	845 (11.2)
±750	3,440 (45.7)	3,030 (40.2)	3,093 (41.1)	1,484 (19.7)
±1,000	4,150 (55.1)	3,703 (49.2)	3,827 (50.8)	2,130 (28.3)
±2,000	6,044 (80.2)	5,661 (75.2)	5,735 (76.1)	4,417 (58.6)

Table 6.7: Correspondence of lemmas known by Spanish, German, and Chinese speakers (complete dataset, Max = 7,532 lemmas)

The findings presented in this table bring our discussion back to considerations raised above, regarding the gradations in knowledge rankings. It is clear from the information about the crossover between combined lists that there is not enough congruence at the granular level to justify a single version of the KVL which is suitable for all three language groups. Therefore, our initial conclusion found that it is not feasible to produce a single Knowledge-based Vocabulary List. Further evidence supporting this conclusion will appear in Chapter 7.

6.6 Conclusion

Collecting the data for the KVL was a massive undertaking, with easily over three million data points collected from around 80,000 respondents across three language groups. Overall, mean facility values show that the average lemmas were known by around two-thirds of the respondents (with mean facility values of 0.59, 0.62, and 0.69 for Spanish, Chinese, and German respectively). Of course, the English language knowledge levels of participants varied widely. Therefore, to account for differing ability levels in the sample, the rank ordering of words for each L1 group was based on the more sophisticated analysis conducted within a GLMM framework. This resulted in internally comparable difficulty values for each lemma on each list, regardless of the range of participants presented with the relevant prompt. While these rank orders displayed a strong positive correlation with one another, for any individual lemma, the difficulty often varied considerably between the language groups, regularly affected by cognateness (see Chapter 8 for further discussion on this issue).

This led to the percentage of common lemmas within the different knowledge ranking bands to be quite low. In the 1–500 knowledge band, around 50% of the lemmas were common between language group pairs (Table 6.6), but other than this, the percentage of correspondence was typically in the mid-teens. Also, the percentage of lemmas which had knowledge ranks within ±500 for all three language groups was only 11%, and within ±1,000 only 28%. The lack of correspondence between languages means that it is not possible to create a single coalesced KVL which works for all languages simultaneously.

Therefore, in order to give knowledge information which best represents the three different language learner groups, we will present a customised KVL for each. This is in contrast to frequency lists, which effectively predict that every language group should get the same scores.

Our analyses so far show that knowledge and frequency are not the same thing, and the next chapter looks at the relationship between the two in much more detail.

CHAPTER 7

COMPARISON OF THE KVL WITH FREQUENCY LISTS

Frequency values from a corpus have been used for many decades to predict learner knowledge of vocabulary. The experience of both vocabulary researchers and practitioners shows that frequency lists do have predictive value, especially for groups of words (e.g., 1,000-word bands). However, the underlying rationale for creating the KVL was that corpus-based frequency lists of vocabulary (especially those based on corpora that represent the language of a different target population) are limited in that they give only a crude indication of the likelihood of any particular lemma being known by L2 learners from any given language background. Moreover, as mentioned in Chapter 1, the degree of correspondence between frequency and actual learner knowledge has heretofore been unknown, due to a lack of large-scale, empirically-based comparative data. With the KVL, this gap has been partially filled. Therefore, an important point of analysis of the KVL is to discern how well frequency matches with the empirically established KVL knowledge data.

7.1 The relationship between frequency ranking and knowledge ranking

As discussed in Chapter 2, word frequency information was drawn upon to select the most important lemmas for the data collection stage. Other words were also included in the sample, in particular from Brysbaert et al.'s (2016a) word knowledge list. This resulted in a sample of lemmas which spanned a broad range of frequency rankings, with the least frequent words included falling within the 50th thousand in the COCA corpus.

It is worth noting that the following discussion of KVL results utilises frequency and knowledge rankings, rather than raw figures. Therefore, the convention of 'higher' refers to better knowledge and higher frequency, which is indicated by lower rank figures. For example, for the

Spanish group, *city* has both a high knowledge ranking (#3) and a high frequency ranking (#290). Conversely, *positivity* has a low knowledge ranking (#7,521) and a low frequency ranking (#31,715). *Strategy* is a case with low knowledge ranking (#6,896), yet high frequency ranking (#845). The reader is advised to keep these distinctions in mind when reading the following results.

With respect to the statistics employed, correspondence comparisons are typically made using correlation statistics. The Kendall's tau correlation coefficient is the most appropriate statistic to measure the association between the two ranked sets of values, since it accounts for the ordered nature of the values (Kendall, 1955; see also Chapter 6). The ranked values derived from the sample of lemmas tested in the current study are bounded by the sample size, whereas the ranked values from a list like the COCA corpus span a much wider range. Kendall's tau compares the order of the ranks between the two lists, so these discrepancies in absolute numeric ranks will not affect the results. The first comparison is between the knowledge rank order of the lemmas included in the sample and the frequency rank order based on figures from the COCA corpus.

Kendall's tau correlation coefficients were as follows:

- 0.23 for the Spanish respondents
- 0.22 for the German respondents
- 0.40 for the Chinese respondents (all $p<0.001$)

Overall, these correlations indicate a very modest correspondence between the KVL rankings and the COCA frequency rankings, given that frequency has been the major way of grading difficulty of vocabulary for a century or so. This is based on the widespread understanding of word frequency as the main driver of lexical acquisition. However, it is important to note that this may not be equally true of receptive and productive mastery. Productive mastery requires a considerably greater amount of knowledge than receptive mastery (Schmitt, 2019). In reading, to comprehend a word, it might be enough to be able to recognise the spelling of a word and remember its meaning. All or most of the other word knowledge components are already in the text (e.g., its collocation and derivative form), and may or may not be utilised to aid comprehension. But when writing, one must know and produce all the various components independently without prompts. The same holds true for listening/speaking. The discussion so far involved all word knowledge components, but if we limit ourselves to just the form-meaning link (as in the *Vocabulary Challenge*), it is still much more difficult to know a word's spelling and morphology well enough to spell it correctly than to just recognise its form from a list of possibilities, as Laufer and colleagues showed in their validation of the CATSS test (Laufer & Goldstein; 2004; Laufer et al., 2004).

So, while a range of previous frequency-based testing research suggests that there is a useable link between frequency and receptive mastery (at least in terms of frequency bands), our results suggest that it is not so simple when it comes to a productive level of mastery. The low frequency–knowledge correlations for the Spanish and German language groups might be explained with reference to cognateness (see Chapter 8). But for the non-cognate Chinese speakers, other factors in addition to frequency must be driving their learning of productive English vocabulary to a large extent. Our study design does not inform us as to what these are, but we could speculate that the systematic factors might include, for example, which words are taught in the syllabus/classroom, which words are focused upon in examinations, and the personal preferences and interests of students. We also know that words have certain intrinsic qualities that can make them generally easier or more difficult to learn. For example, words that are shorter, morphologically transparent, phonotactically regular, concrete, more imageable, and register-neutral are generally easier to learn than those which are not (Dunn, 2014; Schmitt, 2010). For a further discussion of this topic, see Dang et al. (2022) as well as He & Godfroid (2019).

7.2   The degree of difference between frequency ranking and knowledge ranking

7.2.1 *Analysis of residuals*

A basic way to assess how closely the knowledge rankings and frequency rankings match is to simply subtract the knowledge rankings from the frequency rankings. To make the KVL and the frequency lists comparable, the lemmas that appear in each KVL are ordered according to frequency and ascribed a ranking (referred to herein as the 'sample frequency ranking'). This bounds the values between 1 and 7,532 in each list and provides a means of directly comparing the rank orders. A perfect correspondence would result in zero difference, while a similar correspondence would indicate a close relationship (e.g., Spanish data: *science, copper, softly, logistic*, are each ranked similarly in the KVL and sample frequency). Meanwhile a large difference indicates a serious lack of agreement between the two rankings (an example is *zoo* with a frequency ranking of 5,714, but Spanish KVL ranking of 4).

Plotting these differences shows the residuals of the data. Positive values indicate that the lemma was ranked higher in the KVL than the frequency list, suggesting that learners knew the lemmas better than frequency would have predicted (e.g., Spanish data: *German*, 7th best known lemma in the KVL, but with a sample frequency rank of 1,654). Negative values indicate that lemmas were not known as well as frequency would have predicted (e.g., *model*, 4,983rd best known lemma, but with a frequency rank of 391). Figures 7.1 to 7.3 show the 'frequency ranking minus knowledge ranking' results for the three languages.

The slight fading of density of dots at the top left and bottom right-hand sides of the scatterplots in Figures 7.1 to 7.3 indicates that the relationships tend to be tighter at the extreme ends of the scales (i.e., closer to the zero line), in particular for the Chinese learners, but still there is a lot of variation in the rankings across the board. At the centre of the plots, i.e., around the 4,000 level on the KVL ranking, it can be seen that approximately as many words are ranked higher in the sample frequency as lower, indicated by no patterning to the residuals. The downward slope of these residual plots reflects the bounded nature of the rankings, with the distinct edges on the plots indicating that many extreme differences exist between the two sets of rankings.

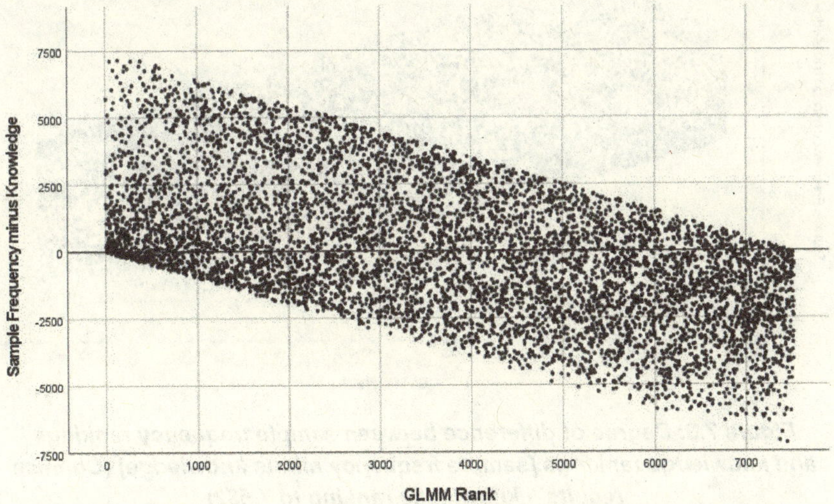

Figure 7.1: Degree of difference between sample frequency rankings and knowledge rankings [sample frequency minus knowledge] (Spanish results – knowledge ranking to 7,532)

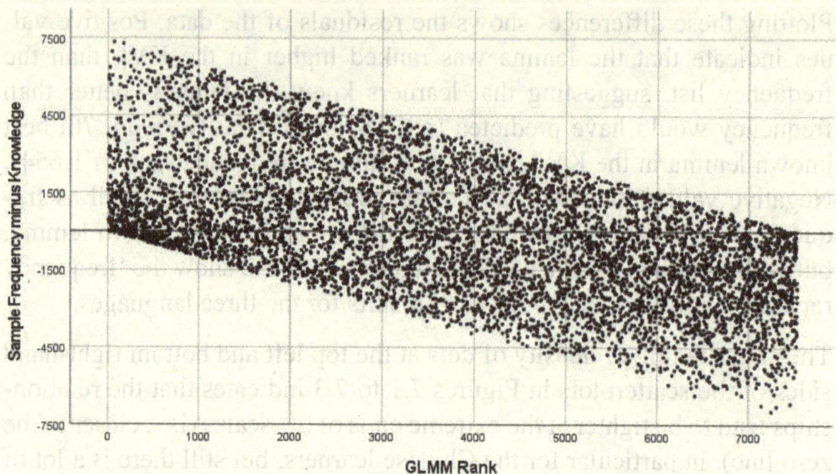

Figure 7.2: Degree of difference between sample frequency rankings and knowledge rankings [sample frequency minus knowledge] (German results – knowledge ranking to 7,532)

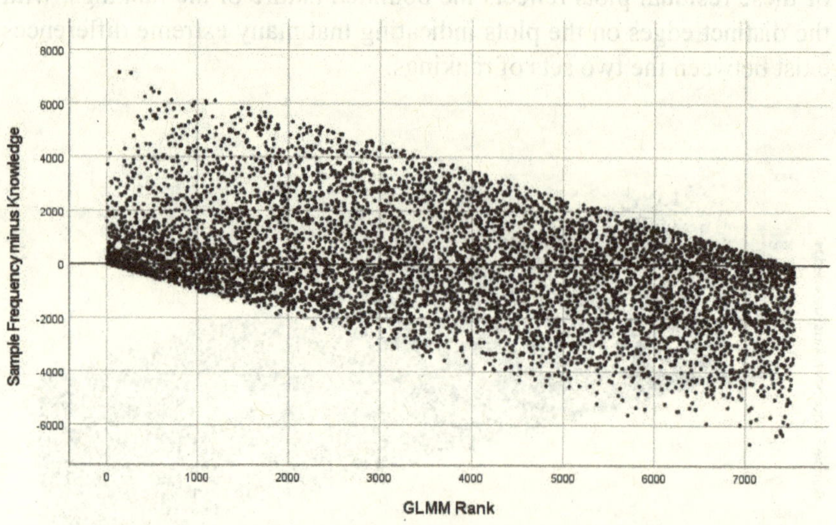

Figure 7.3: Degree of difference between sample frequency rankings and knowledge rankings [sample frequency minus knowledge] (Chinese results – knowledge ranking to 7,532)

7.2.2 Comparisons between KVL and frequency rankings

An important question is how great a difference between frequency and knowledge rankings might be acceptable without it posing difficulties for pedagogical purposes. In Chapter 6, we argued that it would be highly desirable for the degree of precision to be in the low hundreds, and probably not greater than 500. Similarly, if corpus-based frequency values were to be a good predictor of knowledge, the difference between frequency and knowledge should be denominated in the hundreds, and not the thousands. For instance, since a large number of learners never exceed an English vocabulary of around 2,000–3,000 word families (Laufer, 2005), frequency predictions that are 2,000 or more places off from actual knowledge rankings could be misleading and detrimental to effective pedagogy. Therefore, we carried out analyses to determine the percentage of lemmas at different degrees of difference. Please note: These analyses used the frequency rankings derived from corpus analysis, rather than the sample frequency rankings used in the residual analysis described earlier in this chapter.

We chose four levels of difference: 500, 1,000, 1,500, and 2,000. These are admittedly somewhat arbitrary, but they give a feel for the breadth of distinctions between frequency and knowledge rankings as established by the KVL. Tables 7.1 to 7.3 show these differences for fifteen 500-lemma knowledge bands (i.e., from 1–500 to 7,001–7,500).

Knowledge band	Number of cases within 500 ranks (%)	Number of cases within 1,000 ranks (%)	Number of cases within 1,500 ranks (%)	Number of cases within 2,000 ranks (%)
1–500	172 (34%)	235 (47%)	289 (58%)	332 (66%)
501–1,000	134 (27%)	217 (43%)	256 (51%)	293 (59%)
1,001–1,500	76 (15%)	184 (37%)	238 (48%)	278 (56%)
1,501–2,000	82 (16%)	151 (30%)	231 (46%)	267 (53%)
2,001–2,500	79 (16%)	160 (32%)	224 (45%)	285 (57%)
2,501–3,000	60 (12%)	150 (30%)	216 (43%)	280 (56%)
3,001–3,500	76 (15%)	134 (27%)	195 (39%)	264 (53%)
3,501–4,000	68 (14%)	146 (29%)	213 (43%)	274 (55%)
4,001–4,500	67 (13%)	120 (24%)	196 (39%)	258 (52%)
4,501–5,000	70 (14%)	151 (30%)	210 (42%)	255 (51%)
5,001–5,500	68 (14%)	124 (25%)	180 (36%)	220 (44%)
5,501–6,000	73 (15%)	119 (24%)	156 (31%)	215 (43%)
6,001–6,500	68 (14%)	96 (19%)	156 (31%)	204 (41%)
6,501–7,000	24 (5%)	74 (15%)	128 (26%)	168 (34%)
7,001–7,500	14 (3%)	29 (6%)	71 (14%)	134 (27%)

Table 7.1: *Number of cases where rank frequency is within X of rank knowledge (max 500 per band) (Spanish results)*

Knowledge band	Number of cases within 500 ranks (%)	Number of cases within 1,000 ranks (%)	Number of cases within 1,500 ranks (%)	Number of cases within 2,000 ranks (%)
1–500	161 (32%)	231 (46%)	285 (57%)	323 (65%)
501–1,000	125 (25%)	216 (43%)	251 (50%)	286 (57%)
1,001–1,500	112 (22%)	211 (42%)	267 (53%)	289 (58%)
1,501–2,000	86 (17%)	154 (31%)	235 (47%)	285 (57%)
2,001–2,500	51 (10%)	95 (19%)	187 (37%)	268 (54%)
2,501–3,000	65 (13%)	132 (26%)	192 (38%)	276 (54%)
3,001–3,500	67 (13%)	132 (26%)	197 (39%)	256 (51%)
3,501–4,000	71 (14%)	142 (28%)	212 (42%)	278 (56%)
4,001–4,500	60 (12%)	131 (26%)	196 (39%)	252 (50%)
4,501–5,000	63 (13%)	126 (25%)	173 (35%)	218 (44%)
5,001–5,500	81 (16%)	152 (30%)	201 (40%)	248 (50%)
5,501–6,000	69 (14%)	122 (24%)	171 (34%)	216 (43%)
6,001–6,500	42 (8%)	90 (18%)	145 (29%)	198 (40%)
6,501–7,000	15 (3%)	60 (12%)	113 (23%)	168 (34%)
7,001–7,500	18 (4%)	31 (6%)	83 (17%)	146 (29%)

Table 7.2: Number of cases where rank frequency is within X of rank knowledge (max 500 per band) (German results)

Knowledge band	Number of cases within 500 ranks (%)	Number of cases within 1,000 ranks (%)	Number of cases within 1,500 ranks (%)	Number of cases within 2,000 ranks (%)
1–500	237 (47%)	316 (63%)	373 (75%)	412 (82%)
501–1,000	178 (36%)	282 (56%)	328 (66%)	365 (73%)
1,001–1,500	139 (28%)	279 (56%)	329 (66%)	354 (71%)
1,501–2,000	105 (21%)	212 (42%)	294 (59%)	333 (67%)
2,001–2,500	100 (20%)	198 (40%)	286 (57%)	334 (67%)
2,501–3,000	90 (18%)	169 (34%)	250 (50%)	313 (63%)
3,001–3,500	91 (18%)	186 (37%)	254 (51%)	315 (63%)
3,501–4,000	90 (18%)	177 (35%)	242 (48%)	309 (62%)
4,001–4,500	72 (14%)	161 (32%)	238 (48%)	297 (59%)
4,501–5,000	64 (13%)	146 (29%)	214 (43%)	264 (53%)
5,001–5,500	96 (19%)	171 (34%)	220 (44%)	262 (52%)
5,501–6,000	72 (14%)	127 (25%)	176 (35%)	225 (45%)
6,001–6,500	34 (7%)	97 (19%)	152 (30%)	213 (43%)
6,501–7,000	17 (3%)	48 (10%)	108 (22%)	171 (34%)
7,001–7,500	15 (3%)	27 (5%)	77 (15%)	137 (27%)

Table 7.3: Number of cases where rank frequency is within X of rank knowledge (max 500 per band) (Chinese results)

The results from the tables are more easily understood with graphs. Figures 7.4 to 7.6 show the percentage of lemmas in which the frequency ranking is within ±500 of the knowledge ranking. The results are not close. In the best cases for the Spanish data, only 34% of the lemmas in the 1–500 knowledge band occurred within ±500, and only 27% in the 501–1,000 band. Beyond these bands, the figures are 16% or less. The German results are similar.

It could be expected that the Chinese frequency–knowledge figures would be more closely aligned than the Spanish or German ones. This is because there should be minimal effect of cognateness, and so frequency should be the main driver of knowledge. Therefore, we might anticipate a much stronger relationship between frequency and knowledge. There are indeed higher percentages of agreement at most knowledge ranking bands in the Chinese data, particularly at the highest knowledge rankings. At these highest bands, the percentages ranged from 47% (1–500 band) to 21% (1,501–2,000 band). While higher than for the other two languages, these are still underwhelming in absolute terms.

As the knowledge rankings decrease, the percentages of lemmas within ±500 also decrease for all language groups. Of course, as the comparative rank orders are affected by discrepancies between lists at the earlier stages, it follows that where there are more displacements early on, matches in rank ordering further down the list become less likely. For the lowest knowledge ranking levels, the level of correspondence peters out to hardly any correspondence at all (3%–5%) (see more on this below).

Overall, this data indicates that frequency rankings are highly discrepant from knowledge rankings, except for a small number of relatively well-known lemmas. Where precision of 500 or less is desirable for pedagogical purposes (see the following section in this chapter), the results suggest that frequency rankings have limited value in reflecting learner knowledge, at least at a form-recall level of mastery. Although this comparison of rank orders is not a predictive model, the observations here concur with findings from (a much smaller study) by Dunn (2014) which indicated, using an inferential model, that word frequency explains less than 13% in the variation of word knowledge among Hungarian teenage learners of English.

Of course, this does not mean that frequency lists are not useful for pedagogy. Rather, it highlights how they can best be used. Frequency lists are very good at indicating the vocabulary which users will come across in discourse, and which words are relatively common, and which are not. As such, they are good indicators of what vocabulary people need to know to operate in a language. What they cannot show is what vocabulary users actually know. For that, users need to be tested on their knowledge, as in the *Vocabulary Challenge*. We know that language is largely learned from exposure, with more frequent words typically being learned earlier than less frequent words (Ellis, 2002, 2006). But this frequency-learning causality is not always robust, and many factors can override it, e.g., whether words are explicitly taught in classes, learner preference, and a word's intrinsic difficulty. With the empirically-based KVL knowledge lists (and others such as Brysbaert et al., 2020), we now have much better information about the likelihood of particular words being known or not. Practitioners can now use frequency-based and knowledge-based lists in conjunction, weighting their respective information based on whether the pedagogical purpose is prescriptive (i.e., which words learners need to know, thus prioritising frequency lists) or descriptive (i.e., which words learners are already likely to know, thus prioritising knowledge lists). Knowledge lists have the additional value of indicating words which are, in general, more likely to be known by learners from different language backgrounds. This means that frequency lists should not be used in isolation as proxies for describing probable learner knowledge of vocabulary.

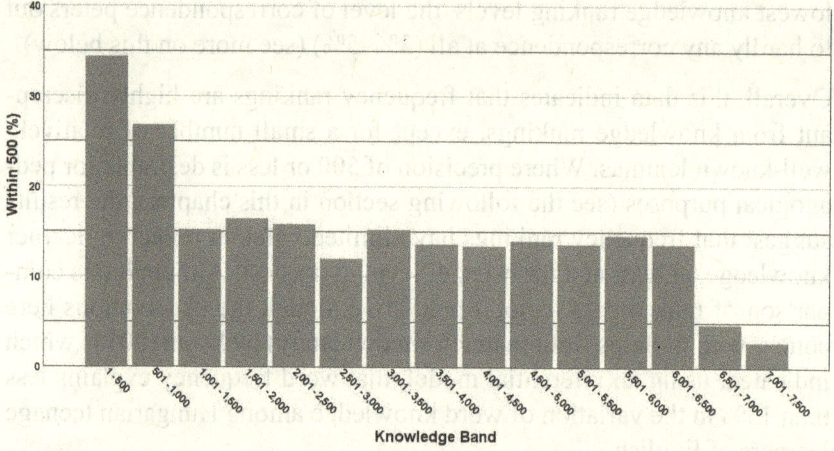

Figure 7.4: *Percentage of frequency ranks within ±500 of knowledge ranks (Spanish results)*

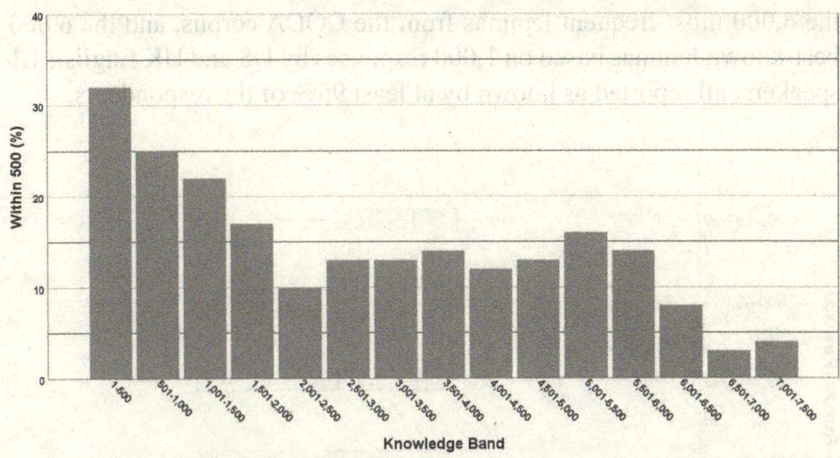

Figure 7.5: Percentage of frequency ranks within ±500 of knowledge ranks (German results)

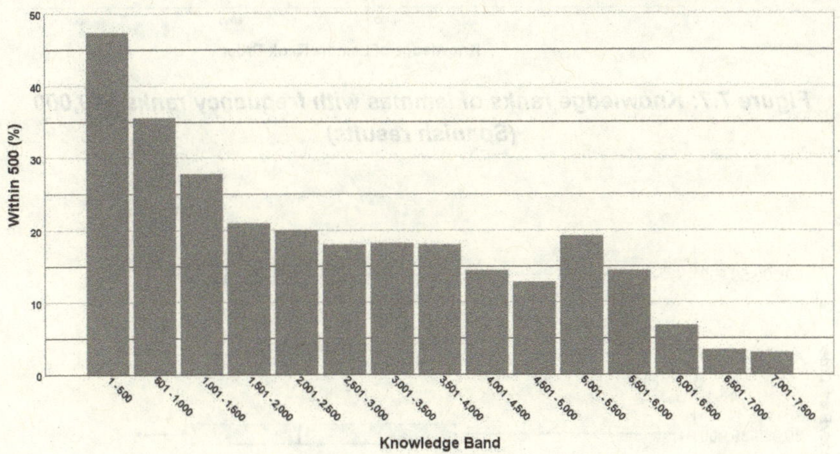

Figure 7.6: Percentage of frequency ranks within ±500 of knowledge ranks (Chinese results)

7.3   Knowledge–frequency correspondence

7.3.1 Knowledge of low-frequency lemmas

The word selection procedure for inclusion in the KVL prioritised both high-frequency lemmas and well-known lemmas (as determined by Brysbaert et al.'s (2016a) study); the selection process is described in detail in Chapter 2. The two sources of input both comprised 6,000 words:

the 6,000 most-frequent lemmas from the COCA corpus, and the 6,000 best-known lemmas based on 1,000 responses by US and UK English-L1 speakers, all reported as known by at least 95% of the respondents.

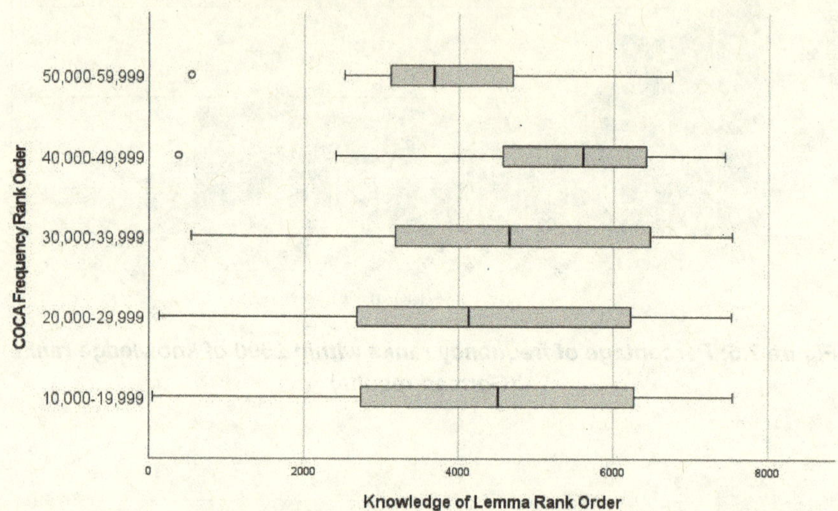

Figure 7.7: Knowledge ranks of lemmas with frequency ranks >10,000 (Spanish results)

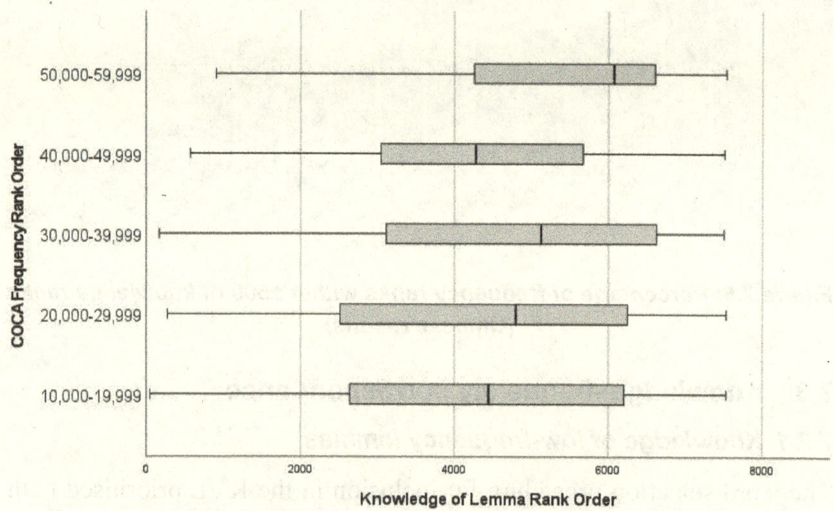

Figure 7.8: Knowledge ranks of lemmas with frequency ranks >10,000 (German results)

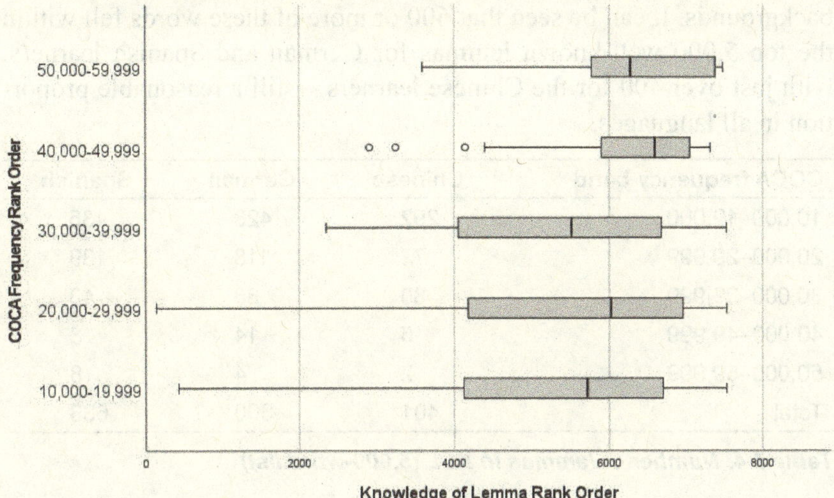

Figure 7.9: Knowledge ranks of lemmas with frequency ranks >10,000 (Chinese results)

There was a large overlap between these two lists since many of the well-known lemmas were understandably also very frequent; however, some of the Brysbaert et al. lemmas had surprisingly low frequencies. In fact, 1,105 of these well-known lemmas had COCA frequency rankings of over 10,000. Figures 7.7 to 7.9 present box and whisker plots to show the distribution on the knowledge rankings of these lower-frequency items.

The first point to make is that we were well justified in including the Brysbaert et al. data when building our candidate list as Figures 7.7–7.9 clearly show that many of these lower-frequency lemmas fell within the well-known category. From these box plots, it can also be seen that there is a distinction between the pattern of knowledge of these lower-frequency lemmas for the Chinese learners, as compared to the German and Spanish learners. For the Chinese learners, the distribution of knowledge rankings for each 10K word frequency band is much more skewed towards the right-hand side of the plot than for German and Spanish. This indicates that these low-frequency words are less likely to be very well-known by the Chinese learners than by learners from either of the other two language backgrounds.

Table 7.4 gives a breakdown of the numbers of these low-frequency words that appear in the KVL for each language, which reinforces the distinction between the knowledge of low-frequency words amongst Chinese learners, and those from German- and Spanish-speaking backgrounds. It can be seen that 600 or more of these words fell within the top 5,000 well-known lemmas for German and Spanish learners, with just over 400 for the Chinese learners – still a reasonable proportion in all languages.

COCA frequency band	Chinese	German	Spanish
10,000–19,000	292	428	435
20,000–29,999	72	118	139
30,000–39,999	30	36	43
40,000–49,999	5	14	8
50,000–59,999	2	4	8
Total	401	600	633

Table 7.4: Number of lemmas in KVL (5,000-word list)

Looking in some more detail at examples of these very well-known lemmas with lower frequencies, we see for Spanish learners that words such as *bye* (knowledge rank = 48; frequency rank = 19,365), *latex* (86; 14,244), and *hotdog* (279; 28,606) fall into this category. For the German learners, examples include: *bingo* (46; 15,845), *demo* (68; 12,698), and *paintball* (173; 34,597). Moving down the knowledge ranking continuum, we find similar patterns at the 5,000 knowledge level for both Spanish (*sensationally*: 4,924; 42,321; *sweating*: 4,932; 17,550; *passionately*: 4,939; 10,349; *snowfall*: 4,943; 14,268) and German (*diagnostics*: 4,914; 19,626; *motorcycle*: 4,929; 34,784; *anonymously*: 4,930; 15,040; *battleship*: 4,991; 13,747). The Chinese group produced considerably fewer well-known low-frequency lemmas. Examples include *superman* (139; 24,022), *dreamer* (424; 12,071), and *storybook* (495; 16,974).

In summary, these findings show there is a clear difference between the cognate and non-cognate languages, which indicates that the influence of cognateness often overrides that of frequency (see below). Having made this observation, it is of interest as to *why* these lemmas are so well known by the cognate respondents. For the Spanish speakers, nearly all the lemmas in Table 7.5 (47/56, 84%) are either cognates or loanwords with very similar spellings to the target English lemmas. Similarly, in the German data 57/69 (83%) are cognates or loanwords (Table 7.6). But even these high figures might be slight underestimations. Whether the lemma was listed as a cognate/loanword in Tables 7.5–7.7 depended on whether the translations given on the test prompt written by the item writers was similar in spelling to the English target lemma. However, the item writers were instructed not to use a cognate translation if a non-cognate word or translation could be used instead without confusion (see Appendix 1). For four of the lemmas nominally listed as non-cognate/non-loanword in Table 7.5, there exist perfectly usable Spanish translations that have essentially the same spelling as the corresponding English lemmas: *hotdog/el hotdog*, *superman*, *iceberg/el iceberg*, and *zombie/el zombi*. If we reclassify these as cognates/loanwords, we end up with a total of 51/56 (91%). For the German data, it would be 58/69 (84%).

Being a non-cognate language, unsurprisingly there were only two loanwords in the Chinese data (Table 7.7): *jeep/jípǔchē* and *bingo/bīn gē yóuxì*. So, the cognate and non-cognate languages behaved conversely. All three language groups knew some low-frequency lemmas much better than the frequency would predict. For the Spanish and German speakers, some of these lemmas were non-cognate, but the vast majority contained formal similarities. For the Chinese speakers, a few of the lemmas were cognates, but the vast majority were not.

English lemma	Knowledge rank	Frequency rank	Spanish cognate/loanword?
bye	48	19,365	NO adiós
latex	86	14,244	YES látex
elastic	132	12,097	YES elástico
kiwi	136	23,419	YES kiwi
Euro	170	10,449	YES Euro
karate	202	15,162	YES karate
karma	211	18,823	YES karma
karaoke	240	17,417	YES karaoke
hotdog	279	28,606	NO perrito caliente *[el hotdog]
federation	293	10,557	YES federación
superman	368	24,022	NO superhombre *[superman]
kickboxing	384	49,370	YES kickboxing
zebra	385	14,397	YES cebra
tango	415	12,477	YES tango
dreamer	422	12,071	NO soñador
jaguar	433	20,099	YES jaguar
cloudy	446	10,472	NO nuboso/nublado
calculator	477	11,833	YES calculadora
astrology	524	22,794	YES astrología
bingo	526	15,845	YES bingo
acrobatic	536	23,616	YES acrobática/o
patriot	539	12,431	YES patriota

ninja	546	18,418	YES ninja
preposition	548	30,419	YES preposición
pitbull	554	51,738	YES pitbull
surname	565	16,307	NO apellido
paintball	591	34,597	YES paintball
superhero	600	18,468	YES superhéroe
geology	618	11,752	YES geología
telegram	655	12,580	YES telegrama
topless	657	17,113	YES topless
shampoo	669	10,319	YES champú
watermelon	694	11,221	NO sandía
pixel	697	10,608	YES píxel
violinist	710	14,167	YES violinista
sushi	735	11,845	YES sushi
gladiator	733	23,987	YES gladiador
activation	756	13,360	YES activación
iceberg	762	10,219	NO gran masa de hielo flotante *[el iceberg]
brownie	775	14,105	YES brownie
bisexual	792	12,842	YES bisexual
tsunami	805	11,213	YES tsunami
unicorn	809	18,136	YES unicornio
neutron	868	10,394	YES neutrón
zombie	877	13,470	NO muerto viviente *[el zombi]
bikini	881	10,303	YES bikini
aerobics	884	12,579	YES aeróbicos
finalist	922	10,418	YES finalista
collage	934	11,407	YES collage
panoramic	939	15,925	YES panorámico
mozzarella	943	15,056	YES mozzarella
unreal	962	12,934	YES irreal
subculture	963	13,172	YES subcultura
subtitle	972	11,919	YES subtítulo
adverb	975	28,655	YES adverbio
paranormal	984	24,854	YES paranormal

Note: * indicates a lemma which did not have a cognate/loanword prompt on the test, but for which one in square brackets does exist.

Table 7.5: Lemmas within the best-known 1,000 knowledge level with frequency ranks above 10,000 (Spanish data)

English lemma	Knowledge rank	Frequency rank	German cognate/loanword?
bingo	46	15,845	YES bingo
demo	68	12,698	YES demo
webcam	70	29,992	YES webcam
tango	109	12,477	YES tango
spam	115	13,081	YES spam
booking	172	15,009	NO buchung
paintball	173	34,597	YES paintball
highland	176	11,965	NO hochland
geology	249	11,752	YES geologie
snowman	265	19,019	NO schneemann
karate	281	15,162	YES karate
eyeliner	282	23,274	YES eyeliner
Euro	286	10,449	YES Euro
baker	342	10,366	YES bäcker
jogging	355	15,499	YES joggen
hotline	393	13,881	YES hotline
surfer	429	11,869	YES surfer
bodybuilder	433	22,075	YES bodybuilder
elastic	450	12,097	YES elastisch
sushi	472	11,845	YES sushi
blogger	478	16,589	YES blogger
milkshake	484	26,030	YES milchshake
brainstorm	508	21,649	YES brainstorming
dreamer	509	12,071	NO träumer
shampoo	554	10,319	NO haarwaschmittel *[shampoo]
bye	558	19,365	NO tschüss
streaming	577	44,360	YES streaming
zebra	587	14,397	YES zebra
disco	613	10,816	YES diskothek
watermelon	614	11,221	YES wassermelone
android	654	21,449	YES android
hotdog	657	28,606	YES hotdog
bikini	676	10,303	YES bikini
cobra	678	20,577	YES kobra
daydream	680	17,097	NO tagtraum

superman	690	24,022	YES superman
handball	692	26,304	YES handball
delta	699	12,219	YES delta
stylist	707	11,537	YES stylistin
kissing	736	13,494	YES küssen
adverb	745	28,655	YES adverb
hacker	747	10,520	YES hacker
remix	758	34,301	YES remix
fireball	763	15,158	YES feuerball
panorama	769	13,456	YES panorama
snowboard	772	17,864	YES snowboard
bulldog	774	20,939	YES bulldogge
zombie	796	13,470	YES zombie
stopped	809	20,580	YES gestoppt
motherless	811	30,501	YES mutterlos
cloudy	832	10,472	NO wolkig
blocked	836	15,459	YES blockiert
karma	847	18,823	YES karma
snowball	861	14,081	NO schneeball
troll	871	11,577	YES troll
streaming	877	30,064	YES streaming
caramel	876	14,900	YES karamell
airbag	885	20,359	YES airbag
teamwork	889	12,126	NO teamarbeit
kickboxing	891	49,370	YES kickboxen
panda	914	15,238	YES panda
gladiator	917	23,987	YES gladiador
pitbull	918	51,738	YES pitbull
biker	922	10,357	NO motorradfahrer
copied	971	40,809	YES kopiert
latex	987	14,244	YES latex
simulator	988	13,337	YES simulator
workbook	994	20,560	NO arbeitsbuch
ketchup	997	12,011	YES tomatenketchup

Note: * indicates a lemma which did not have a cognate/loanword prompt on the test, but for which one in square brackets does exist.

Table 7.6: Lemmas within the best-known 1,000 knowledge level with frequency ranks above 10,000 (German data)

English lemma	Knowledge rank	Frequency rank	Chinese cognate/loanword?
superman	139	24,022	NO 超人
hotdog	267	28,606	NO 热狗，红肠面包
dreamer	424	12,071	NO 做梦的人，梦想家
storybook	495	16,974	NO 故事书
panda	520	15,238	NO 熊猫
unfriendly	580	15,565	NO 不友好的，不友善的
jeep	637	11,201	YES 吉普车 *[jípǔchē]
blackboard	713	13,765	NO 黑板
kindly	737	10,921	NO 友善地，和善地，亲切地
lunchtime	834	11,821	NO 午餐时间，午饭时间
snowball	945	14,081	NO 雪球
bingo	968	15,845	YES 宾戈游戏 *[bīn gē yóuxì]
cloudy	976	10,472	NO 阴的，多云的

Note: * indicates a lemma which did not have a cognate/loanword prompt on the test, but for which one in square brackets does exist.

Table 7.7: Lemmas within the best-known 1,000 knowledge level with frequency ranks above 10,000 (Chinese data)

There were relatively few high-knowledge, low-frequency lemmas which were common across the language groups. This suggests that the L1 and/or the L1 context play an influential role as to whether a learner is likely to know these words or not. Out of a total of 1,105 of these lemmas, only 24 (2%) were common between the Spanish and German speakers in Tables 7.5 and 7.6. Given that there were only 13 high-knowledge, low-frequency lemmas in the Chinese data, it is not surprising that there are few common lemmas between the Chinese and Spanish speakers (5) and Chinese and German speakers (7). There were only five lemmas common among the three languages combined. The relatively low frequencies of these lemmas (10,000+) mean that their acquisition is probably not driven mainly by frequency of exposure, although it is very possible that any individual person's exposure might be higher than the COCA frequency counts would indicate (e.g., lovers of bingo). Also, the small numbers suggest that knowledge of high-knowledge, low-frequency lemmas was not primarily caused by their being intrinsically easy, at least for the Spanish and German speakers. Rather, the vast majority seem to be driven by cognateness. As we will expand upon in

Chapter 8, it seems clear that formal similarity, whether stemming from cognateness or being a loanword, can lead to much better knowledge than frequency would predict.

Common lemmas: Spanish–German (24)

adverb	elastic	karma	superman
bikini	euro	kickboxing	sushi
bingo	geology	latex	tango
bye	gladiator	paintball	watermelon
cloudy	hotdog	pitbull	zebra
dreamer	karate	shampoo	zombie

Spanish–Chinese (5)	German–Chinese (7)	Spanish–German–Chinese (5)
bingo	bingo	bingo
cloudy	cloudy	cloudy
dreamer	dreamer	dreamer
hotdog	hotdog	hotdog
superman	panda	superman
	snowball	
	superman	

It is worth noting that the discrepancies between very high knowledge rankings and very low frequency rankings are to some degree artefacts of our research methodology. This is partly due to the limitations of our reference corpus, the COCA. In Spain, the *Euro* is the standard currency, and will surely be more frequent than the COCA (which is based on American English) indicates. But anyone with an awareness of international currencies would likely know the lemma *Euro*, even if it was not frequent in any particular corpus. Similarly, *bye* (*goodbye*) is becoming commonly used in many languages for leave-taking, and so it is not surprising that is very well known, even though the COCA frequency rank is only 19,365. The low frequency rank is largely caused by the COCA being mainly written, which causes it to underrepresent lemmas like *bye*, which are very common in spoken discourse.

7.3.2 *Less well-known high-frequency lemmas*

It is also informative to look at the disparity between knowledge and frequency rankings from the other direction: high-frequency lemmas that were not very well known. We took a sample of lemmas from the 4,900–5,000 knowledge band (i.e., relatively lesser known), which also had relatively high frequency rankings (<2,000). Tables 7.8 to 7.10 show the lemmas which met these criteria: 15 for Spanish; 14 for

German; and 6 for Chinese. Some of the frequency–knowledge discrepancies can probably be attributed to the COCA having a written bias, with lemmas like *credit, attend, attorney, model* (Spanish), *connection, sector* (German), and *senate, supreme, instruction* (Chinese) occurring often in newspapers and/or academic sub-corpora. Also, in the case of the everyday lemma *okay* (Spanish), one might posit that the respondents were more familiar with the shortened form *ok*. However, there were many other everyday lemmas that could not be explained so easily: *head, stir, tough* (Spanish), *painting, field, strength, entire* (German), and *trip* (Chinese). Some of the Spanish lemmas were particularly surprising, as cognates existed for them, although not used as prompts on the *Vocabulary Challenge* test.

English lemma	Knowledge rank	Frequency rank	Spanish cognate/loanword?
head	4,902	935	NO dirigir
credit	4,903	1,126	NO financiación *[crédito]
rely	4,918	1,867	NO depender
stir	4,920	1,909	NO remover
attend	4,934	1,169	NO asistir *[atender]
limit	4,936	1,352	NO restringir *[limitar, limitarse]
attract	4,937	1,877	NO atraer
attorney	4,957	1,070	NO abogado
eventually	4,961	1,107	NO finalmente
okay	4,962	1,647	NO vale
attitude	4,968	1,156	NO postura
aim	4,974	1,941	NO apuntar
injury	4,980	1,558	NO lesion
model	4,983	504	NO maqueta *[modelo]
tough	4,995	1,013	NO difícil

Note: * indicates a lemma which did not have a cognate/loanword prompt on the test, but for which one in square brackets does exist.

Table 7.8: Lemmas with lower knowledge rankings (4,900–5,000) but with high frequency ranks (<2,000) (Spanish data)

English lemma	Knowledge rank	Frequency rank	German cognate/loanword?
board (n)	4,900	667	NO Brett, Diele *[board]
require	4,907	446	NO erfordern
sort (n)	4,924	836	NO art *[sorte]
painting (n)	4,926	1,057	NO bild, gemälde
connection	4,940	1,425	NO zusammenhang
vast	4,944	1,975	NO gewaltig, riesig
predict	4,950	1,618	NO vorhersagen
sector	4,967	1,984	NO bereich *[sector]
field (n)	4,968	439	NO wiese, weide *[feld]
topic	4,969	1,870	NO thema
strength	4,971	1,279	NO kraft
entire	4,974	869	NO gesamt, ganz
combine	4,980	1,452	NO etw mit etw verbinden *[kombinieren]
complete (v)	4,981	1,209	NO etw fertigstellen, zu Ende bringen *[komplett]

Note: * indicates a lemma which did not have a cognate/loanword prompt on the test, but for which one in square brackets does exist.

Table 7.9: Lemmas with lower knowledge rankings (4,900–5,000) but with high frequency ranks (<2,000) (German data)

English lemma	Knowledge rank	Frequency rank	Chinese cognate/loanword?
particular	4,911	949	NO 具体的（某一种或某一人），特别的
senate	4,946	1,112	NO 参议院
trip	4,952	963	NO 旅行
supreme	4,982	1,623	NO 至高的，至上的
instruction	4,992	1,568	NO 指示，命令
reveal	4,998	928	NO 揭露，披露

Table 7.10: Lemmas with lower knowledge rankings (4,900–5,000) but with high frequency ranks (<2,000) (Chinese data)

One possible explanation could be that the low knowledge rankings were caused by test items that were misleading in some way. We checked such items with L1 speakers. In the German list, for example, we found that only two items were questionable: the test item for *painting* was problematic as it strongly elicited *picture*, which although not having the correct number of letters, still seemed to distract respondents from the correct answer *painting*. However, on the whole it was found that the test items were sound and so the higher-frequency lemmas in Tables 7.8 to 7.10 were simply not known as well as might be expected based on frequency, again illustrating the knowledge–frequency disconnect highlighted in this chapter. These tables have important pedagogic value as they indicate the words on a frequency-based vocabulary syllabus that might go untaught but require more attention. (Note that we did find some other misleading test items in subsequent analyses; see the discussion in the following section.)

Another possible explanation for some of the discrepancies is that the frequency count for a lemma in COCA includes all the different meanings of a lemma (e.g., *model* [n] in the fashion industry, and *model* [n] of a car or train), whereas in the test, only one of the lemma meanings (the most frequent) is tested. This possibility was not investigated, but it would be an interesting area for further study.

In short, it must be recognised that all attempts to assess knowledge of the target lemmas are mediated by items. The conclusions reached regarding word knowledge are therefore contingent on the quality of the items. This is the reason behind the exhaustive improvements made at the development stage (see Chapters 4 and 5). As with any research, the results are dependent on the instrument used for collecting data, and the potential that some of the items did not function as well as hoped is an acknowledged limitation of the KVL. To account for this, in instances where there was room for doubt, we have left the knowledge rankings intact based on the (potentially faulty) data, but indicate in the KVL spreadsheets that the rankings are uncertain, and that accurate rankings are likely to be higher. We also include these uncertain lemmas in a separate list (*Supplementary List C: KVL lemmas that are uncertainly ranked*) in the User Manual which can be found online (www.britishcouncil.org/exam/aptis/aptis-expertise/knowledge-based-vocabulary-lists-kvl).

In recognition of this uncertainty, we carried out a more qualitative analysis of some words that intuitively appeared mis-ranked; this is reported in the next section.

7.4   Examination of individual lemmas that intuitively appeared mis-ranked

7.4.1 *Lower-frequency lemmas that were better known than might be expected from frequency*

A solely statistical analysis can often miss important information; it is also valuable to carry out a manual analysis to check that the results make sense. In the case of the KVL, this involved checking the ranking of all lemmas to identify any that seemed oddly placed. We first looked for lower-frequency lemmas that were well known. Since cognateness has already been shown to be the cause of many cases of frequency–knowledge mismatches, this search focused on non-cognate words. This was largely an intuitive process, but we still felt it was useful to discover any systematic problems with the research results or any lemmas that may have been mis-ranked due to poorly performing test items, especially ones where inadvertent cues in the prompt may have given away the answers. The results of this subjective perusal of oddly placed items are given in Tables 7.11 to 7.13, including the test prompts and their English translations.

Close inspection of the test items in Tables 7.11 to 7.13 did not yield any obvious problems with the items themselves. Thus, it was concluded that there was no reason to think that they did not simply represent the relatively good knowledge of these lemmas by respondents. However, four factors could potentially explain why these lemmas were known better than their frequency figures would have suggested. Firstly, all items contain contextual information that the respondents are able to use when deciding their answers. In some of the cases in Tables 7.11 to 7.13, this contextual information may have been particularly helpful.

English lemma	Knowledge rank	Frequency rank	Spanish test prompt example sentence	Test prompt – English translation
German (adj)	7	1,833	Mi mejor amigo es alemán y vive en Berlín.	My best friend is German and lives in Berlin.
winner	15	1,926	El ganador del partido recibirá un trofeo.	The winner of the match will receive a trophy.
homeless	380	3,372	Hay mucha gente sin hogar en el mundo occidental.	There are many homeless people in the western world.
German (n)	432	3,189	A pesar de ser alemana de nacimiento, ha vivido en Menorca casi toda la vida.	Despite being a German by birth, she has lived in Menorca almost all her life.
surname	565	16,307	Tenemos el mismo apellido pero no somos familia.	We have the same surname but we are not family.
van	946	3,551	Tiene un furgoneta que usa para trasladar las herramientas.	He has a van that he uses to move tools.
swimmer	1,060	8,301	El estilo preferido del nadador es el mariposa.	The preferred style of the swimmer is the butterfly.
fireball	1,258	15,158	Primero se oyá la explosión y despuís se viá una enorme bola de fuego.	First the explosion was heard and then a huge fireball was seen.
keyword	1,287	18,204	La palabra clave cuando estás aprendiendo un idioma nuevo es paciencia.	The keyword when you are learning a new language is patience.
snowball	1,428	14,081	Los niños me tiraron una bola de nieve.	The children threw a snowball at me.
spam	1,444	13,081	No abrí el correo electrónico sospechoso porque parecía no deseado.	I did not open the suspicious email because it seemed like spam.
freestyle	1,556	12,628	Participó en la carrera de estilo libre en la competención de natación la semana pasada.	She/he raced/participated at the freestyle race in the swimming competition last week

ambassa-dor	1,582	4,561	Este señor es el embajador de las Islas Filipinas.	This man is the ambassador of the Philippine Islands.
rename	1,732	9,439	Después de la caída de la URSS el nuevo regimen decidió cambiar el nombre de muchas calles de Moscú.	After the fall of the USSR the new regime decided to rename many streets in Moscow.
unsigned	2,000	21,157	El certificado está sin firmar así que no me vale.	The certificate is unsigned so it's not worth it.
reborn	2,068	16,138	Lamentablemente creo que los movimientos racistas en nuestro país estén renacidos.	Unfortunately I believe that racist movements in our country are reborn.
underworld	2,085	13,387	La película trata de la vida en el submundo criminal el siglo pasado.	The film is about life in the criminal underworld of the last century.
fireworks	2,333	7,961	Al final de la fiesta habrá un espectáculo de fuegos artificiales en la plaza.	At the end of the party there will be a fireworks show in the plaza.
hairless	2,348	21,025	Se quedó sin pelo después del tratamiento médico.	He became hairless after medical treatment.
countdown	2,371	15,255	La cuenta atrás para las vacaciones ya ha empezado.	The countdown to the holidays has already started.
diving	2,388	12,891	Le gusta mucho practicar el buceo en el Pacífico.	He really likes diving in the Pacific.
neon	2,402	8,122	El parpadeo de los tubos de luz fluorescente de repente empezá a marearme.	The flickering of neon tubes suddenly made me dizzy.
unwashed	2,818	20,651	Había unos platos sin lavar en la pila.	There were some unwashed dishes in the sink.

Table 7.11: Lemmas up to the 3K level which intuitively seem to be ranked too high in terms of knowledge (Spanish data)

English lemma	Knowledge rank	Frequency rank	German test prompt example sentence	Test prompt – English translation
reading	96	1,586	Das Lesen ist wirklich ihr liebstes Hobby.	Reading is really her favourite hobby.
booking	172	15,009	Die Hotelbuchung wurde storniert.	The hotel booking has been cancelled.
rainbow	270	7,549	Hast du den wunderbaren Regenbogen gestern gesehen?	Did you see the wonderful rainbow yesterday?
caller	326	5,089	Der Anrufer wollte anonym bleiben.	The caller wanted to remain anonymous.
reader	440	1,272	Die Geschichte fesselt den Leser mit spannenden Dialogen und turbulenten Verfolgungsjagden.	The story captivates the reader with exciting dialogues and turbulent car chases.
dreamer	509	12,071	Du bist ein Träumer!	You are a dreamer!
nickname	586	6,171	Mein Spitzname lautet "Steffi".	My nickname is "Steffi".
timeless	638	9,945	Seine Werke besitzen zeitlose Gültigkeit.	His works have timeless validity.
passport	969	6,322	Ich muss meinen Reisepass verlängern.	I need to renew my passport.
running	991	3,273	Vom Helikopter aus konnte man Herden von laufenden Giraffen und Gazellen sehen.	Herds of running giraffes and gazelles could be seen from the helicopter.
worldwide	1,103	4,497	Ihre Firma hat weltweit über 4,000 Mitarbeiterinnen.	Your company has more than 4,000 employees worldwide.
drinkable	1,184	30,606	Das Getränk ist trinkbar.	The drink is drinkable.
kidnapping	1,308	7,803	Alle Zeitungen berichteten über die Entführung des Kindes.	All newspapers reported on the kidnapping of the child.
handmade	1,325	10,464	Die Tasche ist handgefertigt.	The bag is handmade.
playroom	1,363	21,890	Ein eigenes Spielzimmer wurde im Erdgeschoss bereits eingeplant.	A separate playroom has already been planned on the ground floor.
keyword	1,377	18,204	Lüge mich nie an, Ehrlichkeit ist das Schlüsselwort.	Never lie to me, honesty is the keyword.

unknown	1,654	2,842	Aus unbekannten Gründen zog er sich aus dem Berufsleben zurück.	For reasons unknown, he retired from professional life.
waitress	1,877	6,479	Die Kellnerin ließ sehr lange auf sich warten.	The waitress took a long time to arrive.
member-ship	1,880	3,104	Er hat eine Mitgliedschaft beim Fitnessstudio abgeschlossen.	He signed up for a gym membership.
faceless	1,906	16,515	Die Familie bahnte sich geduldig ihren Weg durch die gesichtslosen Massen.	The family patiently made their way through the faceless crowds.
nightmare	1,988	3,612	Das Kind hatte einen bösen Albtraum.	The child had a bad nightmare.
overheat	2,065	24,189	Wir müssen anhalten, der Automotor ist überhitzt.	We have to stop, the car engine has overheated.
congratu-late	2,123	8,516	Die Familie gratulierte dem Sohn zur bestandenen Führerscheinprüfung.	The family congratulated the son on passing his driving test.
over-heated	2,290	17,835	Der überhitzte Motor musste ausgetauscht werden.	The overheated engine had to be replaced.
ironing	2,312	21,812	Das Bügeln der Hemden macht mir keinen Spaß.	Ironing the shirts is not fun for me.
wherever	2,581	3,738	Wir können uns treffen wo auch immer du willst.	We can meet wherever you want.
laundry	2,785	4,988	Mein Vater macht die Wäsche und meine Mutter kocht.	My father does the laundry and my mother cooks.
expected	2,820	4,340	Der zu erwartende Erfolg blieb aus.	The expected success did not materialize.
inhabitant	2,963	5,991	Die Gemeinde hat zirka 15 000 Einwohner.	The municipality has around 15,000 inhabitants.
surname	2,970	16,307	Wie lautet dein Familienname?	What's your surname?

Table 7.12: Lemmas up to the 3K level which intuitively seem to be ranked too high in terms of knowledge (German data)

English lemma	Knowledge rank	Frequency rank	Chinese test prompt example sentence	Test prompt – English translation
winner	364	1,926	谁会是今年布克奖的获胜者？	Who will be the winner of this year's Booker Prize?
superstar	435	7,120	每一个歌手都有成为超级巨星的梦。	Every singer has a dream of becoming a superstar.
Latin	531	2,542	我从未去过拉丁美洲。	I have never been to Latin America.
moonlight	537	8,086	他们在月光下散步。	They walked in the moonlight.
exchange (v)	553	4,180	我们互换了电话号码。	We exchanged phone numbers.
exchange (n)	579	1,518	1) 双方进行了人质的交换。2) 信息与想法的交流十分重要。	1) The two parties exchanged hostages. 2) The exchange of information and ideas is very important.
educate	626	3,052	他们教育孩子毒品的危害性。	They educate children about the dangers of drugs.
Interview (v)	630	2,268	我们面试了五位应聘者，最终选择了两位。	We interviewed five candidates, and finally selected two.
swimmer	649	8,301	他想成为职业的游泳运动员。	He wants to be a professional swimmer
aloud	681	5,765	老师让后排的学生大声回答问题。	The teacher asked the students in the back row to answer the questions aloud.
homeless	701	3,372	战争让许多人无家可归。	The war left many people homeless.
super-market	797	4,726	许多人选择去超市采购水果蔬菜。	Many people choose to go to the supermarket to purchase fruits and vegetables.

fox	821	7,586	他在草丛上发现一只白狐狸。	He found a white fox in the grass.
location	842	1,437	我们选定了新家的地点。	We have chosen the location of our new home.
rewrite	863	7,762	老师要求她重写这篇文章。	The teacher asked her to rewrite the article.
overnight	939	4,787	如果你无处可去，你可以呆在我家过夜。	If you have nowhere to go, you can stay at my house overnight.
snowball	945	14,081	他们互相扔着雪球。	They throw snowballs at each other.
romantic	951	3,154	她总想象浪漫的求婚场景。	She always imagined romantic marriage proposals.
wallpaper	1,001	10,018	我不喜欢深色的墙纸，贴在家里太沉闷了。	I don't like dark wallpaper, it is too dull to stick it at home.
dentist	1,089	6,386	我的父亲是牙医。	My father is a dentist.
elder	1,098	4.088	老师是年长我十岁的人。	The teacher is ten years older than me.
keyword	1,103	18,204	请提供论文的五个关键词。	Please provide five key words for the paper.
logic	1,189	3,492	我跟不上演讲者的逻辑。	I can't keep up with the speaker's logic.
fruitcake	1,200	24,095	她用蓝莓和草莓做了水果蛋糕。	She made a fruit cake with blueberries and strawberries.
under-ground	1,238	5,401	公司的两栋楼之间有一个地下通道。	There is an underground passage between the two buildings of the company.
broadcast (v)	1,298	4,841	丘吉尔向英国人民广播了与德国开战的消息。	Churchill broadcast the news of war with Germany to the British people.
under-water	1,357	9,303	我们开展了水下的测量工作。	We carried out underwater survey work.

German (adj)	1,386	1,833	奥地利是一个德语国家。	Austria is a German-speaking country.
rename	1,390	9,439	列宁格勒被重新命名为圣彼得堡。	Leningrad was renamed St. Petersburg.
fireball	1,417	15,158	他被一团火球击中。	He was hit by a fireball.
fluent	1,650	12,244	他能够说流利的意大利语。	He can speak fluent Italian.
recharge	1,680	14,328	人生中我们有时需要关闭系统，重新充电，然后再次开始。	Sometimes in life we need to shut down the system, recharge it, and start again.
faceless	1,693	16,515	传说中有一种无脸的鬼怪。	There is a faceless ghost in the legend.
van	1,923	3,551	我们雇了一辆送货车运送钢琴。	We hired a delivery van to transport the piano.
earth-quake	2,066	4,295	地震造成多人伤亡。	The earthquake caused many casualties.
unwashed	2,130	20,651	丈夫总把一堆未洗的碗筷丢在洗碗池边，这让她十分恼火。	Her husband always throws a pile of unwashed dishes by the sink, which makes her very annoyed.
hairless	2,247	21,025	真正无毛发的犬种是很少的。	Really hairless dog breeds are rare.
diving	2,447	12,891	我参加了潜水课程。	I took a diving course.
heart-broken	2,552	19,173	工党败选的消息让他心碎。	He was heartbroken at the news of the Labor Party's defeat.
unsigned	2,555	21,157	他把这份未签名的报告递交总统审阅。	He submitted the unsigned report to the pres-ident for review.

unofficial	2,572	9,454	这只是一个非官方的通知：真正的合作方案会在周一正式下发。	This is just an unofficial notice: the real cooperation plan will be officially issued on Monday.
unre-corded	2,573	31,307	双方的谈话是未经记录的，因此我们也无从了解谈话内容。	The conversation between the two parties is unrecorded, so we have no way of understanding the content of the conversation.
inactive	2,598	14,039	一些动物在冬季并不活跃。	Some animals are inactive in winter.
unedu-cated	2,634	16,340	有多少未受教育的选民投票给他？	How many uneducated voters voted for him?
fingerprint	2,642	20,749	警察根据犯罪现场的指印确定了凶手。	The police identified the murderer based on fingerprints at the crime scene.
fireworks	2,748	7,961	我们在新年观看了烟花。	We watched fireworks in the New Year.
over-heated	2,854	17,835	天气太热，因此车的引擎过热了。	The weather is too hot, so the car's engine is overheated.
motherless	2,862	30,501	他自幼是个没有母亲的孩子。	He has been motherless since he was a child.
disadvan-tage	2,912	43,228	生活在乡村的不利因素是生活的不便。	The disadvantage of living in the country is the inconvenience of life.

Table 7.13: Lemmas up to the 3K level which intuitively seem to be ranked too high in terms of knowledge (Chinese data)

Secondly, the corpus frequency of many lemmas simply did not mirror the frequency of vocabulary input experienced by ESL learners. A good example from the German data is *reading*, which is typically learned quite early in ESL classes, and used very often thereafter. Another example is *booking*, as booking.com is a very popular website in German-speaking countries. Similarly, we can look to Brysbaert et al.'s (2020) conclusions that many well-known words are important elements in the world of ESL learners and are related to their personal experiences. Lemmas like *earthquake, fireworks, homeless, snowball, spam, supermarket, superstar,* and *winner* could easily be seen as falling into this category. For lemmas like these, corpus frequency does not appear to be a good indication of typical learner exposure and use.

A third factor is what might be called 'easy derivations'. Learners are likely to know very basic words like *call, dream,* and *drink*, and so very transparent derivations like *caller, dreamer,* and *drinkable* may not be that difficult to construct from familiar and regular morphological rules.

The fourth factor is that some lemmas were direct translations of L1 words. Examples from German include *weltweit = worldwide* and *Spielzimmer = playroom*, and from Spanish *keyword = palabra clave* and *snowball = bola de nieve*. For compound words like these, if learners knew the translation equivalents for the component words, they were sometimes able to produce the longer compound combinations, even though those compounds were not particularly frequent.

Often these factors worked in conjunction. For example, Spanish learners might know *swimmer* because they can easily derive it from *swim*, and *swim* in turn is probably known better than frequency predicts because it is a common verb that students learn in the topic 'hobbies', which appears quite early in the learning process. Another example is *hairless*. In Spanish, it is a direct translation (*hair = pelo, less = sin →
sin pelo*), but it is also an easy derivative (adding *-less* to mean 'without'). Overall, the lemmas in Tables 7.11 to 7.13 are simply additional evidence that learner knowledge often has a weak relation to corpus frequency.

7.4.2 Higher-frequency lemmas that were not as well-known as might be expected

Another stage of analysis involved looking for systematic problems in lemmas that were not known as well as would be expected despite their relatively high frequency. We examined lemmas from knowledge ranks 5,000 to 7,532 identifying those which intuitively seemed as if they should be known better than their knowledge ranking indicated. It was important to discover any lemmas which missed the 5,000 cut-point, but perhaps should have been included. The results are shown in Tables 7.14 to 7.16, with a comparative analysis in Table 7.17. (We also report *not*, *okay*, and *tough* which we found at #4,874, #4,962, and #4,995 respectively.) These results could flag items that were potentially problematic in terms of misleading respondents into wrong answers when they actually knew the target lemmas. Let us first consider the Spanish responses (Table 7.14).

The *Vocabulary Challenge* web application recorded every participant's response to every test item. Thus, it was possible to examine the responses for patterns which caused incorrect answers (note that the responses were all anonymous). Table 7.14 summarises the results of an analysis of the 22 lemmas which looked surprisingly poorly known going by intuition and frequency. For many lemmas, the majority of incorrect responses were accounted for by non-response. In cases where the test items proved to be sound, presumably the Spanish respondents simply did not know the target lemma, and the test items were successful in showing this lack of knowledge. For example, the prompt for *loss* often elicited *lose* and *lost*. The prompt clearly indicated the noun *loss*, so the results suggest that the respondents had some difficulties with derivative knowledge for this lemma, a common weakness of ESL learners (Schmitt & Zimmerman, 2002). Interestingly, they also suggest that the lack of knowledge is orthographic rather than semantic. The respondents sometimes also demonstrated a lack of a clear understanding of the semantic difference between the target word and alternatives. For example, the prompt for *onto* clearly indicated this lemma (*Por favor, coloca los libros sobre el segundo estante* = Please put the books onto the second shelf). Regardless, 55% of the Spanish respondents who missed the item wrote *over*, even though they were explicitly instructed in the prompt that this was not the correct answer. The fact that they did illustrates the confusion learners have between *onto* and *over* (and other related words such as *on, upon, above*) as Spanish only has one word, *sobre*, for all of these concepts.

English lemma	Knowledge rank	Frequency rank	Spanish test prompt example sentence	Test prompt – English translation
not	4,874	28	Negativo voy a clase hoy, me encuentro mal.	I am not going to class today, I feel bad.
okay	4,962	1,647	¿Me quieres acompañar a la fiesta? Vale.	Do you want to come with me to the party? Okay.
tough	4,995	1,013	Escalar el monte Everest es sumamente difícil.	Climbing Mount Everest is extremely tough.
topic	5,042	1,870	El tema no entra dentro del Ã¡mbito de este curso.	The topic is not within the scope of this course.
hurt	5,084	1,141	La lluvia podría dañar la cosecha, me temo.	Rain could hurt the crop, I'm afraid.
most	5,160	144	¿Cual era el libro que más te gustaba de pequeña?	What was the book you liked the most when you were little?
remove	5,222	877	Uso detergente para eliminar las manchas.	I use detergent to remove stains.
tight	5,249	3,425	Se tapó los oídos y cerró los ojos firmemente.	He covered his ears and closed his eyes tight.
onto	5,337	927	Por favor, coloca los libros sobre el segundo estante.	Please put the books onto the second shelf.
super	5,527	2,667	Este grupo de pop es absolutamente genial.	This pop group is absolutely super.
drug	5,537	461	Le recetó un medicamento en el centro de rehabilitación.	He prescribed a drug at the rehab centre.
loss	5,543	788	La pérdida de valores es un problema para la sociedad occidental.	Loss of values is a problem for western society.
near	5,951	4,167	Mi cumpleaños está próximo, sólo quedan dos días.	My birthday is near, there are only two days left.

plain	5,978	3,575	La instrucción siempre tiene que ser clara y sencilla.	Instruction always has to be clear and plain.
major	5,970	444	Por suerte, el terremoto no causó daño importante.	Fortunately, the earthquake did not cause major damage.
nature	6,122	696	Es natural que sientas miedo.	It is natural that you feel fear.
attack	6,168	1,542	El delincuente le quiso asaltar con un cuchillo.	The criminal wanted to attack him with a knife.
very	6,383	1,206	La comunicación está en la naturaleza misma del lenguaje.	Communication is in the very nature of language.
public (n)	6,881	859	El palacio ya está abierto a los ciudadanos para visitas.	The palace is already open to the public for visits.
public (adj)	6,934	333	La campaña ha incrementado el conocimiento popular de los problemas.	The campaign has increased public awareness of the problems.
chief	7,023	1,450	La causa principal del problema es la falta de comunicación.	The chief cause of the problem is lack of communication.
mostly	7,317	1,328	Nuestra atmósfera está compuesta principalmente de nitrógeno.	Our atmosphere is mostly comprised of nitrogen.
grand	7,362	2,251	La boda fue un evento francamente impresionante con muchos invitados.	The wedding was a frankly grand event with many guests.
off	7,455	387	Hay que mantenerse fuera del césped, no lo piséis.	You have to stay off the grass, don't step on it.

Table 7.14: Lemmas beyond the 5K level which intuitively seem to be ranked too low in terms of knowledge (Spanish data)

Sometimes the dominant response was a specific error. *Okay* appeared to be known to a degree where the spelling was partially learned, but not to the level where fully correct spelling could be produced (i.e., often misspelled as *okey*). As the criterion used in the KVL was the ability to accurately produce the fully correct spelling, the test showed the respondents' inability to do this.

Unfortunately, sometimes the errors were caused by misleading item prompts. *Hurt, most, super, drug, near, nature, public (n), public (adj), mostly, grand,* and *off* were all found to have alternative answers which, although perhaps not quite as appropriate as the target lemma, were nonetheless semantically possible. An example is the item *near*, which often elicited the answer *next*. There were also cases where a prompt (e.g., *grand*) was answered with a much more general and higher-frequency synonym (*great*). In designing the test items, we gave the initial letter and fixed the number of blanks (e.g., g _ _ _ _) to largely avoid this kind of problem. We also explicitly excluded possible alternatives when we could foresee problems (by indicating 'Not *XXX*'). Despite this, a few cases like *grand/great* still remained on the *Vocabulary Challenge*. This illustrates the difficulties in a prompt always constraining responses to the desired answers.

There were also items that appeared to be completely misleading: *not, tight,* and *nature*. We found that the example sentence for *not* was a direct translation from an English sentence, which proved to be very unnatural in Spanish, and was not grammatically correct (*Negative I am going to class today, I feel bad*). *Nature* was prompted with *Es natural que sientas miedo* (= *It is natural that you feel fear*). This prompt actually elicits *natural* or *normal* instead of *nature*, and indeed more than twice as many respondents gave these misdirected responses (*natural/normal*) compared to the key (*nature*). After all of our careful piloting and revising of test items, it was very unfortunate to find faulty items like this, but with 7,679 items in total, probably inevitable that a few would prove flawed.

Lemmas based on misleading test items that received knowledge rankings of over 5,000 (and thus missed making the KVL) are indicated on *Supplementary List D: Lemmas that potentially could have been placed on the KVL* at the end of the User Manual. This includes lemmas from all three language groups. The manual explains that lemmas on this list may have made the KVL if they had better test items. This lack of separation between the difficulty of the lemma and the difficulty of the test item is one of the limitations of the study, but not one that was possible to avoid without including a large number of item prompts for each lemma, an approach that was considered but unfortunately impractical to implement owing to resource limitations.

To gain further insight into the patterns observed for these lemmas which were relatively difficult for the Spanish respondents, another avenue was to examine the German and Chinese respondents' answers to items targeting the same lemmas. In most cases, the German and Chinese respondents had proportionally fewer incorrect responses than the Spanish respondents. This would suggest that the relatively poor performance for these lemmas (compared to intuition/frequency) was mainly limited to the Spanish cohort. This means that the lemmas were either simply more difficult for the Spanish respondents than the German or Chinese respondents, or there was potentially a problem with the Spanish prompt (such as the above example of *nature*). In some cases, the German and/or Chinese respondents also gave many incorrect/missing responses. It could therefore be concluded that these lemmas were relatively difficult not just for the Spanish respondents, but also for one or both of the other language groups.

In cases where responses were given, a parallel reason sometimes appeared across all three languages, (i.e., misspelling of *okay*, derivative confusion between *loss/lose/lost*), which suggests a common lack of knowledge across the language groups. But in a few cases, items which could potentially elicit more than one semantically appropriate response (*onto/over, near/next, mostly/mainly, grand/great, off/out*) showed that the difficulty in writing adequately constrained prompts extended across the three language groups. The full interlanguage comparison of these words is presented in Appendix 6. Overall, this comparison showed that most of the lemmas from Table 7.14 were mainly difficult for the Spanish group, or that a lack of spelling/derivational/semantic knowledge made them challenging for all groups. Most test item problems were restricted to the Spanish test, or had their greatest effect there. There was no indication that the relatively poor Spanish performance on these items extended widely to the German and Chinese groups. Therefore, we consider the lemmas which were poorly known by the German respondents (Table 7.15) and Chinese respondents (Table 7.16) without replicating the full interlanguage analysis; a description of the patterns of incorrect/lacking responses to these lemmas is given in Appendix 7 (German) and Appendix 8 (Chinese).

Table 7.15 shows lemmas that might have been expected to be known better by German respondents, based on frequency and researcher intuition.

There was always the possibility that this could have been caused by prompts which were vague or misleading. But upon inspection, most of the prompts were fine, and so the conclusion must be that German learners simply find these lemmas difficult to produce.

Sometimes the difficulty was caused by the complexities of translating words and concepts between English and German. For example, there is not a truly good translation for *sorry*, as it is used frequently in German in different ways. Also, adverbs like *clearly* and *simply* are difficult to translate with equivalent meaning senses. *Become* is a case of false cognates, where *bekommen* means 'to get' rather than 'to develop into something', and so it is inherently difficult. In these cases, the lack of clear L1–L2 equivalents seems to make the L2 words more difficult to learn.

Some lemmas were less common synonyms of more common ones. Potentially respondents did poorly on lemmas like *store, particularly,* and *charge* because they became focused on lemmas that are more common in L2 English in Germany and Austria (*shop, especially, fee*).

There are also a number of 'category' words which are high-frequency in the majority of corpora used in corpus studies (e.g., BNC and COCA), but are not necessarily salient for learners. These are usually abstract words, such as *condition, issue, action, method, performance, project,* and *approach*. The flexibility of these category words means they are widely used in discourse, even though their meaning constantly shifts depending on the surrounding context, making them potentially harder to learn. The high frequency of conceptually indeterminate words like these may be another reason why frequency and knowledge do not always match up well.

Difficulty was also caused by our desire to avoid cognates in the test prompts whenever possible (see Chapter 5). The results for lemmas like *position, method, section,* and *strategy* would surely have been better if the test items used the common German cognates as prompts (*position, methode, sektion, strategie*). However, the relatively low knowledge rankings show that the lemmas are not so easy if the cognate input is not available. We suspect that cognate lemmas like these would be understood if read, where the English form is available in the text and the cognate similarities are relatively obvious (e.g., *involve→involvieren*). But in production, where the L1 cognate form is not present to prompt the learner, cognates like these appear to be more difficult to recall and produce than might be expected.

Earlier in this chapter, we reported that many lemmas were known better than corpus frequency would have predicted because the frequencies of those lemmas simply did not mirror the much greater frequency of occurrence that would be experienced by ESL learners in the real world. Here, the opposite was occasionally true. Lemmas like *thus* and *approach* (n) are far more frequent in written texts (e.g., academic material and newspapers) than they are in the language environment of the typical EFL learner, and so it is not surprising that lemmas like these were not known as well as frequency would predict.

Finally, we found a small number of items (12) that could potentially have been misleading for respondents. The prompt was generally not incorrect, but the phrasing awkward: e.g., the example sentence for *afraid* translated to *I'm afraid I won't catch the train again* rather than a more prototypical sentence, such as *I am afraid of spiders*. Other items were potentially difficult due to verb tense. For example, the lemma *break* was embedded in the sentence, *He threw stones at the window and it broke*. The item for *move* (n) is another example of a non-optimal prompt. The German translation for *She has carefully planned her next moves* was *Sie hat ihre nächsten Schritte genau geplant*. Unfortunately, the translation *Shritte*, while correct, may have triggered *steps* for many German EFL learners. These issues remain only speculations, because the data was collected anonymously, without the option to follow up on test responses to determine how much the prompts misled or inhibited the respondents. It is also worth reiterating that these minor issues appear to have affected only a small fraction of items.

The Chinese responses in Table 7.16 show some of the same causes for lower than expected knowledge rankings as in the Spanish and German analyses. For example, many of the errors for *stretch* (46%) were misspellings, suggesting that many respondents were familiar with the lemma, but simply did not know how to spell it correctly. Confusion with derivatives also played a part. *Simply* was often answered with *simple*, which is semantically correct, but the incorrect word class. *Simply* was also sometimes answered with *solely*, a near-synonym. This happened with a number of other lemmas, e.g., *dirt→dust, grand→great/giant, simply→solely,* and *onto→over*. Unfortunately, as with the Spanish and German data, we also found several test items that were misleading. For example, the prompts for *proud, lose, freeze, might,* and *clear* also suggested other possible answers (*pride, lost, frozen, maybe,* and *clean* respectively).

Lemma	Knowledge rank	Frequency rank	German test prompt example sentence	Test prompt – English translation
afraid	5,012	1,404	Ich befürchte, dass ich den Zug nicht mehr erwischen werde.	I'm afraid I won't catch the train again.
grab	5,004	1,482	Er schnappte sich das Geld und lief davon.	He grabbed the money and ran away.
position	5,052	512	Nehmen Sie als erstes eine bequeme Körperhaltung ein.	First, take a comfortable position.
middle	5,059	989	Das Buch ist in der mittleren Schublade.	The book is in the middle drawer.
explain	5,092	480	Die Angestellte erklärte dem Kunden geduldig, dass sie ihm das Geld nicht rückerstatten kann.	The clerk patiently explained to the customer that she could not refund the money.
beyond	5,097	746	Jenseits des Flusses lag ein kleines Dorf.	Beyond the river, there was a small village.
condition	5,120	629	Die Bauarbeiter untersuchen den Zustand des alten Hauses.	The construction workers examine the condition of the old house.
occur	5,142	756	Laut Polizei ereignete sich der Unfall gegen 16 Uhr.	According to the police, the accident occurred at around 4 pm.
issue	5,167	248	Ich möchte über dieses Thema jetzt nicht mehr diskutieren.	I do not want to discuss this issue anymore.
deal	5,156	674	Er kümmert sich um die Autoversicherung.	He deals with the car insurance.
skill	5,160	822	Jeder kann hier sein Können unter Beweis stellen.	Everyone can put their skills to the test here.
lie	5,195	751	Er liegt auf dem Sofa.	He is lying on the sofa.

thus	5,200	744	Sie ist die älteste Tochter und folglich Anwärterin auf den Titel.	She is the eldest daughter and thus a contender for the title.
very	5,227	1,206	Das ist genau das Buch, nach dem ich gesucht habe!	This is the very book I've been looking for!
action	5,310	502	Es ist eine sofortige Maßnahme notwendig.	Immediate action is required.
method	5,316	999	Für die Herstellung von Kissen wird ein traditionelles Verfahren verwendet.	A traditional method is used to make pillows.
dish	5,334	1,945	Gib das Obst in die Schale und stell sie auf den Tisch.	Put the fruit in the dish and place it on the table.
particular	5,529	949	Gibt es bestimmte Themen, die ihr noch nicht verstanden habt?	Are there particular topics that you haven't understood yet?
performance	5,560	675	Sie ist vor der ersten Vorführung sehr nervös.	She is very nervous before the first performance.
project	5,592	534	Bei diesem Vorhaben haben wirklich alle Dorfbewohner mitgearbeitet.	Really all of the villagers worked on this project.
section	5,593	819	Auf diesem Abschnitt ist die Straße derzeit ziemlich glatt und eisig.	This section of the road is currently pretty slippery and icy.
spot	5,643	1,232	Das ist ein richtig ruhiger Ort, wo man sich gut entspannen kann.	It's a really quiet spot where you can relax.
concern	5,671	717	Ihr könnt euch beruhigen, es besteht kein Anlass zur Sorge.	You can calm down, there is nothing to concern you.
store	5,675	700	Warst du schon in dem neuen Geschäft, das sie am Wochenende eröffnet haben?	Have you been to the new store they opened over the weekend?

break	5,783	494	Er warf Steine gegen das Fenster und es zerbrach.	He threw stones at the window and it broke.
present	5,798	818	Sie überreichte die Auszeichnungen an die jungen Sportler und Sportlerinnen.	She presented the awards to the young athletes.
likely	5,824	624	Der wahrscheinlichste Grund für sein Nichterscheinen ist, dass er verschlafen hat.	The most likely reason he didn't show up is because he overslept.
official	5,847	526	Der Regierungsbeamte geht bald in Pension.	The government official is about to retire.
particularly	5,959	781	Seine Bemühungen waren besonders hilfreich.	His efforts have been particularly helpful.
charge	6,086	924	Man muss eine kleine Gebühr entrichten, um hier parken zu können.	You have to pay a small charge to park here.
specific	6,112	980	Man muss die Antworten in einer bestimmten Reihenfolge angeben.	You have to give the answers in a specific order.
lose	6,125	283	John hat seinen Haustürschlüssel verloren.	John lost his front door key.
clearly	6,351	847	Er hat offenbar gelogen.	Clearly he lied.
major	6,375	444	Die Jungunternehmer haben einen bedeutenden Beitrag geleistet.	The young entrepreneurs have made a major contribution.
become	6,415	139	Der Himmel wurde dunkel. Viele Wolken zogen auf.	The sky became dark. Many clouds came up.
simply	6,431	583	Die Aufgabe ist einfach zu schwierig.	The task is simply too difficult.
strategy	6,435	845	Sie muss sich für die Verhandlung eine gute Herangehensweise zurechtlegen.	She has to come up with a good strategy for the negotiation.

sorry	6,467	1,207	Über den Verlust, den sie erleben mussten, war ich sehr traurig.	I was very sorry about the loss they suffered.
move	6,603	1,403	Sie hat ihre nächsten Schritte genau geplant.	She has carefully planned her next moves.
standard	6,615	806	Die Lehrerin ist mit dem Niveau der Leistungen in dieser Klasse noch nicht ganz zufrieden.	The teacher is not yet completely satisfied with the standard of performance in this class.
approach	6,633	750	Wir brauchen einen alternativen Zugang um das Problem zu lösen.	We need an alternative approach to solve the problem.
involve	7,306	656	Das neue Projekt beinhaltet sicherlich sehr viel Arbeit.	The new project certainly involves a lot of work.

Table 7.15: Lemmas beyond the 5K level which intuitively seem to be ranked too low in terms of knowledge (German data)

Lemma	Knowledge rank	Frequency rank	Chinese test prompt	Test prompt – English translation
trip (n)	4,952	963	我始终记得我们去意大利的旅行。	I always remember our trip to Italy.
stir	5,062	1,909	她若有所思地搅着咖啡。	She stirred the coffee thoughtfully.
pride	5,174	2,818	母亲把女儿当作她的骄傲。	The mother regarded her daughter as her pride.
lose	5,370	283	我弄丢了我的钥匙。	I lost my keys.
dirt	5,396	2,754	洗衣粉能洗去衣服上的污垢。	Washing powder can wash away the dirt on clothes.
stretch	5,402	1,925	我不停抻这件毛衣，想让它恢复原来的大小。	I kept stretching this sweater, trying to restore it to its original size.
grand	5,583	2,251	我从没见过如此宏伟的宫殿。	I have never seen such a grand palace.
might (v)	5,711	175	1）我可能会来。2）一切都可能在未来发生。	1) I might come. 2) Everything might happen in the future.
simply	5,800	583	1)这不过是因为低温把水管损坏了。2)这仅仅是个时间问题。	1) This is simply because the low temperature damaged the water pipe. 2) This is simply a matter of time.
freeze	5,893	2,824	天太冷，湖面结冰了。	It is too cold and the lake is frozen.
clear (v)	5,889	1,904	1)他清了清喉咙。2)请在离开时清空桌子。	1) He cleared his throat. 2) Please clear the table when you leave.
onto	6,253	927	1)他把买来的东西倒到桌子上。2)她从火车下到站台上。	1) He poured the things he bought onto the table. 2) She got off the train onto the platform.

chief	6,420	1,450	这里当下的主要问题是交通拥挤。	The chief problem here is traffic congestion.
plain	6,512	3,575	1)我听不懂这些专业术语，请用白话再说一遍。2)他就要被辞退了，这是个明白的事实。	1) I don't understand these technical terms. Please say it again in plain language. 2) He is about to be fired. This is a plain fact.
loss	6,573	788	银行卡的遗失给我带来许多麻烦。	The loss of the bank card caused me a lot of trouble.
true	6,828	492	1)这是一个真实的故事。2)判断题的答案为"正确"。	1) This is a true story. 2) The answer to the true or false question is "true".
false	7,051	2,532	判断题的答案为"错误"。	The answer to the true or false question is "false".

Table 7.16: Lemmas beyond the 5K level which intuitively seem to be ranked too low in terms of knowledge (Chinese data)

Tables 7.14 to 7.16 show the item analyses of lemmas which intuitively seemed to be ranked too low in terms of knowledge, leading to the supposition that the test prompts might be misleading. A comparative analysis highlighted lemmas for the three language groups to check for noticeable discrepancies. Of course, each of the three language groups would often know any particular lemma to a greater or lesser degree. But much of this was caused by cognateness, and the highlighted lemmas in the three tables did not include cognates. Therefore, if the results from two language groups were somewhat similar, but those of the third language very different, careful analysis of the item testing for the third language was undertaken. For example, a clear case of this was the lemma *true*. It is a very common, essential, and widely used lemma, and we would expect it to be well-known by all three language groups. For Spanish and German respondents, it ranked 676 and 909 respectively, but for Chinese respondents, it only ranked 6,828. This indicated that either: (1) the Chinese respondents simply did not know *true* very well, which seems unlikely; or (2) there was a problem with the test item on the Chinese version of the *Vocabulary Challenge*.

We usually found that surprisingly low knowledge rankings were either mixed or consistently low across the three language groups. For example, we might expect that the lemma *grand* would be relatively well-known. However, the knowledge rankings were relatively low for all three groups (Spanish 7,362; German 7,263; Chinese 5,583), thus suggesting the reality that *grand* is simply not known very well, rather than that all the test items were performing poorly.

Using this comparative information in conjunction with the analyses in Appendices 6, 7, and 8, we determined that a small number of test items were faulty or misleading, which meant the KVL knowledge rankings based on those items were unreliable. In total, 13 Spanish items, 12 German items, and 13 Chinese items fell into this category. These are indicated by shading in Table 7.17. The unreliable rankings were beyond the 5,000 level, and so these lemmas did not make the respective KVL. Our item analyses suggested that the item prompts misled the respondents in a way which underestimated their actual knowledge, so it can be assumed that accurate rankings would be higher if the test items functioned properly. Unfortunately, we had no way of knowing what the accurate knowledge rankings would be, or even if they would move below the 5,000 threshold to make the KVL. As noted above, to acknowledge this issue, we created *Supplementary List D: Lemmas that potentially could have been placed on the KVL* in the User Manual which can be found online (www.britishcouncil.org/exam/aptis/aptis-expertise/knowledge-based-vocabulary-lists-kvl). These lemmas could not be reliably ranked, and may belong in the respective KVL at some undetermined ranking.

Lemma	Spanish rank	German rank	Chinese rank	Spanish–German difference	Spanish–Chinese difference	German–Chinese difference
action	3,651	5,310[a]	1,123	1,659	2,528	4,187
afraid	2,894	5,012[b]	1,800	2,118	1,094	3,212
approach (n)	5,256	6,633	4,672	1,377	584	1,961
attack (v)	6,168	2,668	2,387	3,500	3,781	281
become	2,774	6,415	585	3,641	2,189	5,930
beyond	3,055	5,097	4,641	2,042	1,586	456
break (v)	2,058	5,783	3,557	3,725	1,499	2,226
charge (v)	4,364	6,086	2,887	1,722	1,477	3,199
chief (adj)	7,023	7,314	6,420	291	603	894
clear (v)	4,141	3,830	5,889	311	1,748	2,059
clearly	4,469	6,351	1,597	1,882	2,872	4,754
concern (v)	4,145	5,671	5,275	1,526	1,130	396
condition (n)	3,933	5,120	2,682	1,187	1,251	2,438
deal (v)	2,355	5,156	1,454	2,801	901	3,702
dirt	2,167	2,337	5,396	170	3,229	3,059
dish (n)	3,845	5,334	1,024	1,489	2,821	4,310
drug (n)	5,537	226	1,324	5,311	4,213	1,098
easy (adv)	7,075	306	1,075	6,769	6,000	769
explain	4,513	5,092	710	579	3,803	4,382
false	4,384	1,305	7,051	3,079	2,667	5,746
freeze (v)	3,602	4,321	5,893	719	2,291	1,572
grab	4,873	5,004	4,413	131	460	591
grand	7,362	7,263	5,583	99	1,779	1,779
hurt (v)	5,084	1,258	1,186	3,826	3,898	72
involve	5,381	7,306	4,529	1,925	852	2,777
issue (n)	3,823	5,167	1,913	1,344	1,910	3,254
lie (v)	5,816	5,195	4,422	621	1,394	773
likely (adv)	4,520	5,824	4,196	1,304	324	1,628
lose	2,378	6,125	5,370	3,747	2,992	755

loss	**5,543**	4,649	**6,573**	894	1,030	1,924
major (adj)	**5,970**	6,375	3,936	405	2,034	2,439
major (n)	6,655	**2,334**	5,751	4,321	904	3,417
method	6,996	**5,316**	2,191	1,680	4,805	3,125
middle (n)	2,337	**5,059**	910	2,722	1,427	4,149
might (v)	3,393	2,483	**5,711**	910	2,318	3,228
most	**5,160**	376	197	4,784	4,963	179
mostly	**7,317**	2,016	**3,960**	5,301	3,357	1,944
move (n)	5,680	**6,603**	1,908	923	3,772	4,695
nature	**6,122**	180	730	5,942	5,392	550
near (adj)	**5,951**	7,414	373	1,463	5,578	7,041
not	**4,874**	13	1,876	4,861	2,998	1,863
occur	3,987	**5,142**	1,884	1,155	2,103	3,258
off	**7,455**	2,771	2,812	4,684	4,643	41
official (n)	5,931	**5,847**	4,465	84	1,466	1,382
okay	**4,962**	1,354	3,944	3,608	1,018	2,590
onto	**5,337**	4,095	6,253	1,242	916	2,158
particular	5,810	**5,529**	4,911	281	899	618
particularly	5,630	**5,959**	5,178	329	452	781
performance	2,122	**5,560**	2,356	3,438	234	3,204
plain (adj)	**5,978**	6,530	**6,512**	552	534	18
position (n)	4,234	**5,052**	1,672	818	2,562	3,380
present (v)	6,821	**5,798**	4,250	1,023	2,571	1,548
pride (n)	4,338	5,043	**5,174**	705	836	131
project (v)	7,494	**5,592**	7,404	1,902	90	1,812
public (adj)	**6,934**	1,319	774	5,615	6,160	545
public (n)	**6,881**	1,910	1,420	4,971	5,461	490
remove	**5,222**	4,157	2,782	1,065	2,440	1,375
section (n)	6,153	**5,593**	3,745	560	2,408	1,848
simply	2,497	**6,431**	**5,800**	3,934	3,303	631
skill	2,069	**5,160**	497	3,091	1,572	4,663
sorry	3,405	**6,467**	173	3,062	3,232	6,294
specific	5,484	**6,112**	4,151	628	1,333	1,961
spot (n)	3,896	**5,643**	6,456	1,747	2,560	813
standard (n)	6,079	**6,615**	1,947	536	4,132	4,668
stir (v)	4,920	4,154	**5,062**	766	142	908

store (v)	4,136	**5,675**	3,302	1,539	834	2,373
store (n)	4,138	**5675**	2,693	1,537	1,445	2,982
strategy	6,896	**6,435**	3,685	461	3,211	2,750
stretch (v)	4,821	4,293	**5,402**	528	581	1,109
stretch (n)	7,215	4,287	**4,587**	2,928	2,628	300
super	**5,527**	2,443	1,661	3,084	3,866	782
thus	5,148	**5,200**	3,623	52	1,525	1,577
tight (adv)	**5,249**	3,510	1,663	1,739	3,586	1,847
tough	**4,995**	5,679	2,439	684	2,556	3,240
trip (n)	1,663	2,852	4,952	1,189	3,289	2,100
true	676	909	6,828	233	6,152	5,919
very (adj)	**6,383**	**5,227**	4,411	1,156	1,972	816

a. Bold type indicates the language group in which the lemma was noticed as being potentially intuitively mis-fitting. In some cases, the same lemma was initially flagged in two languages.

b. Shading indicates an item that was found to be questionable

Table 7.17: Comparison of knowledge ranks of three language groups for higher-frequency lemmas that were not as well-known as might be expected

7.5 Conclusion

In comparing the KVL and the frequency lists for the analyses reported in this chapter, the key point is that frequencies derived from corpora are surprisingly poor at predicting learner knowledge of vocabulary, at least at a form-recall level of mastery. The correlations between knowledge ranks and frequency ranks were very modest (0.224–0.402), and the various tables and graphs in this chapter paint a picture of marginal correspondence. A relatively low percentage of lemmas were predicted to within a rank of ±500 or ±1,000, and not many more than half of the lemmas were predicted at the very loose criterion of ±2,000.

The analyses in this chapter clearly show that corpus-derived frequencies should not be used as a proxy for learner knowledge. There are many factors which could lead to this knowledge–frequency disconnect. In the next chapter, we further explore cognateness, an important factor in the context of this study. This emphasises the usefulness of lists based on the actual testing of language learners. The KVL used a form-recall level of testing, and so would seem to be an obvious candidate if the pedagogical purposes relate to a productive level of vocabulary mastery. If the pedagogical purposes relate to a receptive knowledge of mastery, the Brysbaert et al. (2020) list is a good recent possibility. The KVL may also prove to be useful for indicating knowledge ranking of receptive knowledge. This remains to be demonstrated by future research (see Chapter 11). There are, of course, other lists which may indicate learner vocabulary knowledge to various degrees (although usually not based on direct testing), and Chapter 9 discusses some of these in more detail.

CHAPTER 8
EFFECTS OF COGNATENESS ON KVL RANKINGS

From the beginning of the project, we suspected that cognates/loanwords would have a large impact on our findings, especially for the Spanish and German data. Research shows that cognates and loanwords are more easily learned (or at least recognised) by L2 learners than words that are non-cognates/non-loanwords.

> *Cognates are recognized, learned, and translated faster than non-cognates . . . especially when these items are high frequency in the L1 and low frequency in the L2.*

> – Helms-Park & Dronjic, 2013, p. 2

For reviews of cognate effects, see Helms-Park & Deonjic (2013) and Otwinowska & Szewczyk (2017). Some cognate research has been carried out on Spanish learners of English, which is logical because there are over 20,000 cognates between Spanish and English (Montelongo et al., 2010). For example, Bravo et al. (2006) analysed 86 key words found in US primary school science curricula (e.g., *infirm, ecology*) and found that 66 (77%) were Spanish cognates (*enfermo, ecología*). Only 2 (2%) were false cognates. Similarly, German has a great deal of orthographic, phonologic, and morphological similarity with English (Banta, 1981), both being Germanic languages. For Spanish, Hall (2002) explored the degree to which Spanish-L1 speakers studying English could derive knowledge of unknown cognates in comparison to unknown non-cognates. The participants were shown 30 English nonwords. Half of the nonwords looked like cognates (e.g., *campanary, cognate with Spanish *campanario* = bell tower), and the other half were nonwords that did not share any formal features with Spanish words (e.g., *thrimble*, not similar to any Spanish word). The participants claimed to recognise more cognate nonwords than non-cognates and were more consistent in assigning proposed meanings to those cognate nonwords. Hall concluded that learners are sensitive to formal similarities between L1 and L2 words and will assign meaning to L2 items based on overlap in form.

In addition to Spanish, cognate research has been carried out in many other languages. For example, in two studies in the Netherlands, Dutch participants learned cognates and non-cognates of Italian (Lotto & de Groot, 1998) and English (de Groot & Keijzer, 2000). In both studies, cognates had better scores and faster response times in comparison to non-cognates. Young Italian-L1 speakers in two age groups were shown German and English cognates/non-cognates three times (Tonzar et al., 2009). Both 9-year-olds and 13-year-olds remembered the L2 forms of a greater number of cognates. In a different study, after one exposure and three practice attempts, Japanese university students made average relative gains of 48.2% on English loanwords, but only 28.9% for non-cognates (Rogers et al., 2015). Interestingly, all of these studies used a test format similar to the one we used in our KVL test, i.e., form-recall, where the participants were required to spell out the word's form.

This learning advantage for cognates is explained by Nation (1990) as stemming from a lower learning burden. He suggests the similarity in L1–L2 form and meaning reduces the amount of knowledge required to learn those aspects of word knowledge, which facilitates the learning process. The form overlap also provides stronger cues for retrieval (de Groot & Keijzer, 2000). Often the form similarities are rather obvious, with Ishikawa & Rubrecht (2008) finding that around 80% of English cognates appearing in a small corpus of Japanese television programs were relatively transparent in form and meaning. Indeed, many cognates have only minor differences in spoken and written form and convey the same meanings (e.g., Spanish–English: *león/lion, nacional/national, aeropuerto/airport*; German–English: *hund/hound, abstrakt/abstract, preis/price*).

Despite this, learners may fail to recognise cognates in context. L2 cognates bearing less orthographic overlap with L1 counterparts can remain unnoticed (Dressler et al., 2011) but even the most closely related cognates are often not recognised by language learners. For example, fifth- and sixth-grade Hispanic learners of English sometimes failed to recognise the relationships between everyday Spanish words and English cognate counterparts (García, 1991). With similar young learners, Nagy et al. (1993) found that they all underused their knowledge of Spanish to grasp cognate words in English (although there was great variation), but that recognisability increased with L2 lexical proficiency and age. In Poland, 122 university students were given a list of Polish–English cognates and false cognates (which varied according to orthographic similarity), as well as non-cognate controls, and were asked to translate them into Polish (i.e., meaning recall) (Otwinowska & Szewczyk, 2017).

As with other studies, cognates were known better than non-cognates, but false cognates were known *worse* than non-cognates. This shows the cognitive difficulty of false cognates (often called *false friends)*, which look like they are interpretable through the L1, but which in fact are completely misleading (e.g., English *coin* = money, but French *coin* = corner). But the most interesting part of the study showed that the more similar the cognates' orthography, the easier they were to learn, with more proficient learners being better able to benefit from the cognateness.

These studies highlight the need for explicit instruction on cognates, especially during the early stages of L2 acquisition and especially among young children. Fortunately, it appears that cognate training can be effective. Tréville (1996) found that cognate instruction helped beginner-level English-speaking university students of French to identify cognates and infer their grammatical properties. Importantly, the instruction also included manipulating cognates morphologically and semantically. Similarly, Perhan (2008) found that Ukrainian undergraduates who had completed a range of tasks requiring manipulation and processing of English cognates outperformed students who were simply exposed to these cognates in reading passages. Interestingly, the 'explicit instruction' students were able to generalise their knowledge of cognates to English items that they had not previously encountered. Thus, instruction including active engagement with cognates unsurprisingly seems more effective than instruction focusing merely on recognition skills.

8.1   Cognates in the KVL Spanish data

Based on this literature review, there was every reason to believe that the knowledge of English lemmas by Spanish learners would be affected by cognates and loanwords (hereafter referred to as just 'cognates'). To examine this more directly, we looked at the best-known 50 lemmas to gauge the effect of cognates; 20 of these were cognates, as shown in Table 8.1. In many cases, the similar cognate spellings to English appear to explain why some lemmas with relatively lower-frequency rankings were known so well (e.g., *jet*, the second best-known lemma, but with a frequency ranking of 3,163). We also looked further down the knowledge rankings at the 3,000–3,100 level in Table 8.2 to explore the relationship among the relatively less well-known lemmas. Similarly, we see some lemmas that appear to benefit from cognateness: *duplicate/duplicar, millionaire/millonario,* and *architecture/arquetectura*. Without the benefit of think-aloud protocols or interviews with the respondents, it is impossible to state unequivocally that the high knowledge ratings were the direct result of cognateness. However, as noted throughout our analyses, it seems clear that cognateness is a cause of some of the divergence of the knowledge and frequency rankings.

While Tables 8.1 and 8.2 are strongly illustrative of our point, this is not the complete picture. In the data, there were numerous examples of lemmas which were known worse (or not much better) than the frequency rankings would predict, despite their cognateness: e.g., *mark/marcar* (frequency: 1,689; knowledge: 1,614), *tribe/tribu* (2,966; 3,088), *evolve/evolucionar* (2,838; 3,083), and *organic/orgánico* (3,089; 3,104). Cognateness can clearly promote knowledge, but it is not automatic or fool-proof. As the research shows (e.g., Dressler et al., 2011; Rogers et al., 2015), learners, especially lower-level ones, often do not recognise or benefit from cognates. Thus, it seems that the value of cognates is idiosyncratic to some extent, with some cognates being known much better than frequency would predict, but others not.

English lemma	Spanish translation	Knowledge rank	Frequency rank	Frequency–knowledge difference
jet	jet	2	3,163	3,161
zoo	zoológico	4	6,371	6,367
radio	radio	11	905	894
no	no	12	93	81
human	humano	13	399	386
hour	hora	14	272	258
hero	héroe	17	1,922	1,905
family	familia	18	147	129
day	día	19	90	71
acid	ácido	20	3,259	3,239
atomic	atómico	22	5,498	5,476
federal	federal	24	493	469
my	mi	25	44	19
clinic	clínica	31	2,404	2,373
religion	religión	34	1,387	1,353
atom	átom	36	5,238	5,202
fruit	fruta	38	1,668	1,630
air	aire	41	370	329
class	clase	44	431	387
expert	experto	49	900	851

Table 8.1: Cognates from best-known 50 lemmas compared to their frequency ranks (Spanish results)

English lemma	Spanish translation	Knowledge rank	COCA frequency rank	Frequency–knowledge difference
duplicate	duplicar	3,017	9,434	6,417
venture	aventurar	3,031	5,296	2,265
millionaire	millonario	3,036	6,868	3,832
trap	trampa	3,043	4,061	1,018
architecture	arquetectura	3,054	3,533	479
phoenix	fénix	3,059	26,947	23,888
minimum	mínimo	3.062	4,422	1,360
collector	recolector	3,062	4,006	944
flamingo	flamenco	3065	22,488	19,423
Christian	Cristiano	3,068	3,186	118
Caribbean	Caribeña	3,075	5,598	2,523
evolve	evolucionar	3,083	2,838	−245
colleague	colega	3,087	1,523	−1,564
tribe	tribu	3,088	2,966	−122
cellular	celular	3,092	5,869	2,777
clinical	clínico	3,098	2,600	−498
volcano	volcán	3,099	6,406	3,307

Table 8.2: Cognates from 3,000–3,100 knowledge ranks compared to their frequency ranks (Spanish results)

Additionally, in some cases it is not possible to separate the cognateness effect from the frequency effect. For example, *day/diá* is the 90th most frequent lemma, and this high frequency almost certainly explains the high knowledge ranking (#19) to some degree. Similarly, we have *no/no* (93rd, #12). We see this with other cognates in Table 8.1 as well (e.g., *family/familia, my/mi, air/aire,* and *class/clase*). It is impossible to partial out the relative contributions to knowledge of cognateness vs frequency in these cases, and it is probably safest to assume that both have some effect. However, both de Groot & Keijzer (2000) and Lotto & de Groot (1998) found that frequency had a very small effect compared to the effects of cognateness in their studies, which suggests that cognateness might also have the stronger influence in our data.

Our data also shows cases where non-cognates are known much better than frequency would predict, and some examples of highly-known non-cognate lemmas are shown in Table 8.3. It is difficult to find a systematic explanation. English is now the international *lingua franca* (Seidlhofer, 2005), and is used in most countries to greater or lesser extents; the influence of English on the web, cinema, and music is undeniable, and in some parts of the world, especially Scandinavia and northern Europe, it is extremely strong (Kuppens, 2010; Peters, 2018; Sylvén and Sundqvist, 2012). Basic English words like numbers (*one*), pleasantries (*please*), and essential concepts (*love*) are now oft-used loanwords in many languages. It is thus not surprising to see these loanword lemmas being well-known. Interestingly, other less essential English words were also known well by the Spanish respondents (*dance, orange, book, sing, beach*), and we can only speculate that these concepts are important in the respondents' lives, and for some reason are salient in English as well as Spanish. This is similar to Brysbaert et al.'s (2020) conclusion that some English words are well-known to L2 learners because they are 'important elements in the world of English L2 learners' (p. 1) and are 'related to experiences English L2 students are likely to have' (p. 4).

Another possible explanation for frequency–knowledge divergence is that the COCA corpus underrepresents daily (largely oral) vocabulary such as that shown in Table 8.3 because of its written bias. To explore this, we looked up the frequency rankings for the SUBTlex–US, a corpus consisting of 51 million words of American movie and television subtitles. The SUBTlex–US better represents daily conversational language, and Brysbaert & New (2009) found that frequencies from the SUBTlex–US better accounted for human psycholinguistic processing than previous corpora, such as the BNC. In the last column of Table 8.3, we calculated frequency–knowledge rank differences using the SUBTlex–US figures. We found that these frequency–knowledge differences were generally smaller compared to the COCA differences, but not always. From this small sample of basic English lemmas, it appears that the SUBTlex–US frequency figures correspond to Spanish learner knowledge slightly better than the COCA figures. Even so, the correspondences are still not particularly robust, with few lemmas having a difference of 500 or less, and half (10/20) not even within 1,000. Thus, regardless of which corpus frequency figures were used, frequency still does not seem to be a good predictor of knowledge.

English lemma	Spanish translation	Knowledge rank	COCA frequency rank	COCA frequency–knowledge rank difference	SUBTlex–US frequency–knowledge rank difference
orange	naranja	5	3,296	3,291	2,440
German	Alemán	7	1,833	1,826	1,852
book	libro	8	241	233	518
one	uno	9	837	828	46
winner	ganador	15	1,926	1,911	1,872
shoe	zapato	26	1,427	1,401	1,890
beach	playa	27	1,947	1,920	1,167
love	amour	28	579	551	96
please	por favor	47	1,168	1,121	81
sing	cantor	125	1,014	889	649
finger	dedo	149	1,043	894	1,506
carrot	zanahoria	182	4,641	4,459	7,941
sunny	soleado	197	4,913	4,716	5,007
butter	mantequilla	252	2,418	2,166	2,355
cry	llorar	301	1,355	1,054	773
married	casada	350	1,615	1,265	69
pool	piscina	400	1,570	1,170	980
beer	cerveza	451	1,912	1,461	525
unhappy	infeliz	510	4,761	4,251	2,541
danger	peligro	531	1,551	1,020	936

Table 8.3: Non-cognates with large frequency–knowledge differences (Spanish results)

In the case of low-knowledge/high-frequency lemmas (see Tables 7.14 to 7.16), the prompts generally did not give any clues regarding the word class. This must surely be one of the factors which led to the lower knowledge levels. Nevertheless, for some of the lemmas, a cognate does exist in Spanish, although it was not used in the prompt on the test (4/15, 27%). Given the relatively low knowledge rankings, this existence of a (non-prompt) L2 cognate/loanword did not seem to have a great effect in helping the respondents show their knowledge. This is in direct contrast to cases where a cognate/loanword was given directly in the prompt, which often led to high knowledge rankings, giving rise to the speculation that it was not the existence of the cognate/loanword that made lemmas easier to answer correctly, but rather that the cognate/loanword appeared in test prompts. If so, we would need to interpret the test results cautiously in cases where the cognate/loanword appeared in the prompt. It may be that such lemmas are known only to the degree of learners being able to produce the written form by scaffolding onto a cognate or loanword which is available somewhere in the input. That is, not all of the lemmas ranked as well-known may be freely available to the learner upon demand.

The question is whether respondents were able to answer the *Vocabulary Challenge* by simply inserting the Spanish prompt translation into answer blanks on the test, even if they did not actually know the English word. We do not have direct evidence to know either way, although undoubtedly this sometimes did happen. However, to answer these items correctly they still had to recognise that the cognate prompt was a good match with the given first letter and number of blanks in the answer, which shows some degree of form-similarity awareness. This is the kind of awareness which could allow them to transfer L1 cognates to L2 usage situations in the real world. This is a specific issue for a very limited number of lemmas. The Spanish translation prompt ended up being exactly the same spelling as the correct English answer for only 101 test items of the best-known 5,000 lemmas. This was only 2% (101/5,000) of the items overall. The table in Appendix 9 describes these exact cognate items. (There were many other non-exact cognates not included in this analysis, e.g., *act/actuar, liquor/licor, subjective/subjetivo*.)

While Appendix 9 indicates that the knowledge rankings are almost always higher than frequency rankings would predict (with three exceptions), the results are not straightforward. In some cases, the well-known English lemmas have frequency–knowledge differences which are relatively small, and so the knowledge rankings are in line with what frequency would predict. In other cases, the lemmas have a very high frequency (e.g., <1,000), which means that they had a good chance of being known anyway from substantial exposure (e.g., *radio, social, cultural*). In all these cases, it would seem likely that the learners for the most part knew the lemmas, rather than just gaming the test by inserting the English word from the Spanish cognate, but there is also a possibility that the knowledge ranks are artificially improved by learners just inserting the prompt into the answer blanks. There was undoubtedly some of each, and it is impossible to know the ratio of knowledge vs gaming.

This raised a conundrum for developing the KVL. We had no hard evidence to show that the exact-match cognate items were not working well (i.e., the respondents may well have known the cognate lemmas), and indeed the alternative scenario in which the cognate was avoided and a synonym used in its place did not necessarily alleviate the situation. Anecdotal feedback from some Spanish test-takers indicated that they struggled in cases where an obvious cognate was not used in the prompt, making the question more 'quizlike' and hard to answer. The use of cognates avoids this issue. On the other hand, some gaming of these exact-match items likely did occur, and so it makes their knowledge rankings somewhat uncertain.

In summary, there is not an easy solution to testing learners' knowledge of cognates under this test format, hence we understand that a greater degree of error may be present in the knowledge ranking of such words.

We have addressed the issue in the final KVL by flagging the relatively small number of exact-match lemmas in the Spanish KVL and German KVL with a minus sign (–) in the *Uncertain Ranking* column in the KVL spreadsheets and also recording them on a separate list (*Supplementary List E: Lemmas which may not be known as well as the KVL rankings indicate*) at the end of the User Manual (www.britishcouncil.org/exam/aptis/aptis-expertise/knowledge-based-vocabulary-lists-kvl). We explain in the User Manual that these lemmas have the possibility of being ranked higher than they should be.

8.2   Cognates in the KVL German data

Like Spanish, German is a cognate language to English, and has many word equivalents with form similarity (Schepens et al., 2013). It is thus not surprising that the results from German largely mirror the above results from Spanish. In the same way that Table 8.1 showed that many of the best-known lemmas had Spanish cognates, Table 8.4 shows that the vast majority (34) of the 50 best-known lemmas in the German group had German cognates. We also found many cognates at the 3,000–3,100 level (see Table 8.5). In fact, the cognateness seems even more pervasive in the German data than the Spanish, as illustrated by the fact that Table 8.4 is considerably longer than Table 8.1 (34 as compared to 20 lemmas with direct cognates).

This is not necessarily because the German language has a higher proportion of cognates than Spanish. It may be partly because the German item writers used more cognate translations than the Spanish item writers. But, if so, that would be because the German item writers felt they needed to use them because the only natural way to express concepts was with cognates (e.g., *pizza*). Regardless of the relative degree of cognateness between the two languages, it seems clear that cognates helped the German respondents when taking the *Vocabulary Challenge*. However, some well-known lemmas are also relatively frequent (e.g., *not, better, ball, water, six*), and of course the same caveat about frequency as discussed above regarding the Spanish data applies here, as our research methodology makes it impossible to apportion the relative influence of cognateness vs frequency (although see research by de Groot & Keijzer, 2000; Lotto & de Groot, 1998).

There were also cases where cognateness did not seem to facilitate a correct response, as the knowledge rankings were worse or not much better than the frequency rankings: e.g., *summer/sommer* (frequency: 619; knowledge: 1,025), *theory/theorie* (919; 1,524), *find/finden* (95; 2,212), *scenario/szenario* (2,773; 3,222). As with the Spanish respondents, cognateness did not always seem to aid the German respondents in producing the correct English lemma forms. So, although undoubtedly helpful, cognateness should not necessarily be seen as an easy or automatic route to an English written word form. An interesting question to follow from the KVL research project would be whether speakers of particular cognate languages find it easier to utilise cognates when learning vocabulary in their L2. We suggest this as a future research direction in Chapter 11.

The German data also had cases where non-cognates were known much better than frequency would predict (Table 8.6). In some cases, an obvious reason presents itself. For example, although *desk* is translated as *schreibtisch*, the computer term *desktop* is common in German, which makes *desk* a virtual cognate. But for the most part, the examples in Table 8.6 refer to basic concepts, for which German respondents knew the English equivalent relatively well.

In the Spanish analysis above, the SUBTlex–US corpus generally had smaller frequency–knowledge differences compared to the COCA corpus. We found the same trend with German data. Even so, we again found that the correspondences were not that strong, with few lemmas having a difference of 500 or less. This reinforces our impression that the weak frequency–knowledge correspondence is not just an artefact of our corpus choice (COCA).

English lemma	German translation	Knowledge rank	Frequency rank	Frequency–knowledge difference
bomb	bombe	1	2,002	2,001
English	Englisch	2	1,792	1,790
hungry	hungrig	4	3,202	3,198
kiss (n)	kuss	5	4,007	4,002
ice	eis	6	1,234	1,228
dance	tanzen	7	1,974	1,967
fit (adj)	fit	8	3,423	3,415
sun	sonne	9	1,237	1,228
burger	burger	11	7,385	7,374
better	besser	12	452	440
not	nicht	13	28	15
blog	blog	14	7,885	7,871
wind	wind	15	1,093	1,078
cat	katze	16	1,785	1,769
camel	kamel	17	7,059	7,042
west	westen	18	665	647
elite	elite	19	2,752	2,733
jeans	jeanshose	20	3,444	3,424
Korean	Koreanisch	21	3,546	3,525
idol	idol	22	9,584	9,562
orange (adj)	orange	24	3,164	3,140
generation	generation	25	1,027	1,002
king	könig	27	2,353	2,326
kiss (v)	küssen	28	2,316	2,288
ball	ball	29	913	884
lamp	lampe	31	3,967	3,936
football	fußball	32	1,539	1,508
person	person	34	345	302
zoo	zoo	35	6,371	6,336
six	sechs	39	424	385
water	wasser	40	226	186
invest	investieren	41	2,011	1,970
bingo	bingo	46	15,845	15,799
text (n)	text	48	1,293	1,245

Table 8.4: Cognates from best-known 50 lemmas compared to their frequency ranks (German results)

English lemma	German translation	Knowledge rank	Frequency rank	Frequency–knowledge difference
emotionally	emotional	3,005	4,694	1,689
heterosexual	heterosexuell	3,006	21,081	18,075
desktop	desktop	3,010	6,930	3,920
nephew	neffe	3,011	6,448	3,437
anger	ärger	3,015	2,377	–638
flood	flut	3,016	3,608	592
frustrating	frustrierend	3,017	6,272	3,255
privacy	privatsphäre	3,019	3,079	60
manipulative	manipulativ	3,020	14,471	11,451
nazi	nazi	3,027	5,451	2,424
integrated	integriert	3,029	4,845	1,816
meditate	meditieren	3,033	12,747	9,714
thousand	tausend	3,034	651	–2,383
dramatically	dramatisch	3,035	3,386	351
geographical	geografisch	3,037	6,813	3,776
renovation	renovierung	3,040	7,383	4,343
acceptance	akzeptanz	3,043	3,466	423
data	daten	3,048	559	–2,489
wonderfully	wonderfully	3,051	9,072	6,021
speciality	spezialität	3,060	25,770	22,710
genetically	genetisch	3,063	6,844	3,781
phoenix	phönix	3,065	26,947	23,882
hypothetical	hypothetisch	3,066	40,504	37,438
minister	minister	3,067	1,920	–1,147
choir	chor	3,069	5,391	2,322
bacterial	bakteriell	3,071	8,746	5,675
Egyptian	ägyptisch	3,072	5,578	2,506
adrenaline	adrenalin	3,081	10,688	7,607
miniature	miniatur	3,082	6,140	3,058
comment	commentar	3,085	1,367	–1,718
unprofessional	unprofessionell	3,088	21,940	18,852
variable	variable	3,090	1,872	–1,218

Table 8.5: Cognates from 3,000–3,100 knowledge ranks compared to their frequency ranks (German results)

English lemma	German translation	Knowledge rank	COCA frequency rank	COCA frequency–knowledge difference	SUBTlex–US frequency–knowledge difference
dear	liebe	26	3,359	3,333	415
dad	papa	45	1,824	1,779	180
bag	tasche	47	1,009	962	755
jump	sprung	52	4,312	4,260	969
desk	schreibtisch	55	1,665	1,610	1,404
driver	lenker	76	1,229	1,153	1,293
drum	trommel	85	4,148	4,063	4,794
dark	dunkelheit	90	2,164	2,074	747
clean	sauber	92	1,519	1,427	570
bike	fahrrad	99	2,176	2,077	2,082
mix	Mischung	131	2,875	2,744	2,942
smile	Lächeln	154	1,436	1,282	1,028
river	Fluss	174	1,331	1,157	1,039
dream	Träumen	203	2,609	2,406	423
rain	Regen	247	1,555	1,308	1,089
toy	Spielzeug	304	2,434	2,130	2,699
forever	Ewig	359	2,093	1,734	476
lover	Liebhaber	402	2,797	2,395	1,714
hunter	Jäger	457	3,049	2,592	2,380
shave	Rasieren	491	5,851	5,360	2,982

Table 8.6: Non-cognates with large frequency–knowledge differences (German results)

In the discussion of the Spanish data above, we considered items on the *Vocabulary Challenge* in which the test prompt translations were exact matches to the required English answers. The same analysis was undertaken for the German–English items. While there were 101 exact cognate items in the 5,000 best-known lemmas in the Spanish test, there were 331 in the German version (6.6%) (see Appendix 10 for full list). (The exact-match criteria did not include near-cognates like *water/wasser, lamp/lampe*.) Looking at the frequency–knowledge differences column of the table in Appendix 10, we find similar trends to that column in Appendix 9. Once again, we find most knowledge rankings higher than frequency rankings. Similar to the Spanish, there is no fixed pattern in the relationship, with a mix of results. Some well-known lemmas have a very high frequency (e.g., *person, million, in, nation, land*) and are presumably learned early in most learner's trajectories. Likewise, words like *burger, blog,* and *webcam*, although not that frequent according to COCA counts, have worked their way across the world as *lingua franca* lexical items. For other lemmas, the frequency–knowledge differences are relatively small. All of these cases do not suggest extensive gaming of the test items. However, as with the Spanish data, there are numerous cases where the knowledge rankings are much higher than the frequency rankings (e.g., *export, digital, bodybuilder, gladiator*). It is difficult to know how much of this is caused by useful learner knowledge of cognates and how much by simply inserting prompts into the answer blanks. Because we cannot be sure, we highlighted these exact-match lemmas with a minus sign (–) in the *Uncertain Ranking* column in the German KVL spreadsheet, noted this in the User Manual guidance, and included a list of these lemmas in *Supplementary List E: Lemmas which may not be known as well as the KVL rankings indicate*.

8.3   Influence of loanwords on the KVL Chinese data

In this study, the aim was to investigate a range of language types, including a non-cognate language, Chinese. Although, with the ubiquity of English globally, perhaps no language in the world is untouched by it. Thus, there are inevitably many English loanwords in Chinese. According to Zhu (2011, p. 101), there are '5,218 entries in total borrowed from English according to *Chinese Loanwords Dictionary*'. The question was whether they had an effect on the knowledge rankings. In short, the effect seemed very minimal. In contrast to the Spanish and German data, which showed widespread cognate influence, there was little loanword form-similarity effect to report for Chinese. This is probably the main reason why the statistical association between frequency and knowledge is higher for Chinese (tau = 0.402) than for the cognate languages. In Spanish and German, we found that many low-frequency lemmas fell within the best-known 1,000 knowledge level. For these, most were cognates (Spanish: 48/57, 84%; German: 57/69, 83%). For the Chinese, there were far fewer lemmas than in German (only 13), and only two of them might be considered loanwords (2/13, 15%), at least phonetically (*jeep, jípǔchē*; *bingo, bīn gē yóuxì*). Thus, it seems that loanword similarity is not an important influence in explaining the Chinese knowledge rankings, partly because there are fewer words with formal similarity, and also because the sound-form relationships are different in Chinese and English.

8.4   Dispersion of cognates in the KVL knowledge rankings

From the above analyses, recognition/knowledge of cognates clearly facilitated the Spanish and German respondents' performance on the *Vocabulary Challenge*. The question is whether this facilitation was consistent throughout the knowledge ranks, or was the major cause of the better-known vs lesser-known lemmas. There are two possibilities. The first is that the best-known lemmas were just that because they were mostly cognates, while lesser-known lemmas were predominately non-cognates. A second possibility is that cognates were spread relatively evenly through the knowledge bands, and that cognates in general were known better than they might have been if they were not cognates, but this was not the main factor in determining whether lemmas in general were well-known or not. To explore this, we sampled 100 lemmas from six stratified knowledge bands from the Spanish and German data: 1–100, 1,000–1,099, 2,000–2,099, 3,000–3,099, 4,000–4,099, and 5,000–5,099. The knowledge ranking bands show whether the sampled sets of lemmas were relatively well-known or not, and the number of cognates in each band can suggest the relative effect of cognateness on the knowledge ranking.

The results suggest a combination of the two above possibilities. Table 8.7 shows that, for the Spanish data, the percentage of cognates was relatively higher at the 1–100 and 1,000–1,099 levels, but was lower from there on. However, there is not a consistent stairstep lowering in cognate percentage across the levels. So while cognateness might explain the higher knowledge rankings up to the 1,099 level to some extent, and also the lower knowledge rankings at the 4,901–5,000 level, it does not explain the steadily lower knowledge rankings progressing though the levels. In terms of the German data, the percentage of cognates was highest for the best-known 100 lemmas, and still quite high up to the 2,000–2,099 level. After that, it gradually decreased. This suggests that the density of cognates remains quite high up to the 2,099 level, and so cognateness does not explain the lowering of knowledge progressing through this end of the table. Conversely, the lower density of cognates in the 4,000–5,000 bands suggests that the lower knowledge of the lemmas in these bands can be attributed (at least partially) to this relative lack of cognates. Taken together, the Spanish and German data seems to suggest that density of cognates does explain the knowledge rankings to some extent, but it does not seem to be the main factor in the steadily decreasing knowledge rankings across the breadth of the KVL.

Knowledge band	Number of cognates in band – Spanish data	Number of cognates in band – German data
1–100	33	60
1,000–1,099	34	35
2,000–2,099	18	39
3,000–3,099	16	27
4,000–4,099	17	17
4,901–5,000	7	11

Table 8.7: Number of cognates in knowledge band, Spanish and German (Max = 100 per band)

8.5   Conclusion

We found clear evidence that cognateness facilitated knowledge beyond the predictions derived from frequency rankings, both in the Spanish and German data. Notwithstanding, cognateness did not always help as much as might be expected, showing that the ability to utilise cognates is not automatic. This follows studies like Dressler et al. (2011), García (1991), Nagy et al. (1993), and Otwinowska & Szewczyk (2017) which have shown that cognates are often not recognised by language learners.

CHAPTER 9

COMPARISON OF THE KVL WITH ALTERNATIVE LISTS

In developing the candidate word list, information was drawn from Brysbaert et al. (2016a), which was based on a large, crowdsourced test of L1 English vocabulary knowledge. Ideally, information based on L2 respondents' knowledge would have been used, but the relevant study (Brysbaert et al., 2020) did not become available until the KVL project was in the final stages of data collection. Brysbaert et al. (2020) tested 61,851 words using a crowdsourced approach and a Yes/No test format which included nonwords to control for overestimation. They gathered data from 286,500 sessions, which yielded an average of 274 observations per word. As such, their data is an obvious set to compare against ours.

9.1   Brysbaert et al. (2020) L2 list

One key difference between the KVL and the Brysbaert et al. (2020) list (hereafter Brysbaert et al. L2 list) is the counting unit used. The KVL used lemmas (base form + inflections), while the Brysbaert et al. L2 list used a mix of units:

> The vast majority of them [the items on the list] are lemmas (the base, dictionary forms of the words). A few are irregular word inflections, such as *lice* or *been*. Inflected verb forms are included as separate entries if they are often used as nouns or adjectives. Examples are *finished, tuning* or *undeveloped*.
>
> – Brysbaert et al. (2020, p. 5)

Since most of the Brysbaert et al. L2 list items are lemmas, their figures should be largely comparable to ours. For example, the base word *address* has the following related entries in the Brysbaert et al. L2 list: *address, addressee,* and *readdress*. These are all separate lemmas, so comparing *address* (but not *addressee* and *readdress*) from the Brysbaert et al. L2 list and *address* from the KVL would be using the same counting unit and is fine because they are both based on lemmas. The same applies to *biology*: *biology, biological, biologist,* and *biologic*.

However, things are not always so neat, as the case of *move* illustrates. In the KVL (Spanish), the verb *move* has a high knowledge ranking of 239, but the noun *move* is only at 5,680. They are therefore dissimilar lexical items with very different knowledge rankings. In the Brysbaert et al. L2 list, on the other hand, there is only one entry for *move* (47) (and other related words on the list are *remove, removed, remover, mover, movers,* and *movement*). So, the single entry *move* in the Brysbaert list is more problematic to compare to the two KVL entries. In cases like this, we decided to compare the KVL entry with the nearest knowledge ranking to the Brysbaert et al. L2 list ranking, e.g., 239 vs 47. We acknowledge that this is an expedient, and that the KVL and Brysbaert L2 lists are not strictly comparable in such cases. However, this expedient applies to only a minority of cases as words with the same word form in different word classes – e.g., *move* (n) and *move* (v), *cool* (v) and *cool* (adj) – are much less common than words which do not transfer (e.g., *conviction, lonely, supreme*), and so are very much the exceptions on the lists. An indication of this is that in the analysis of the 1,000 best-known L2 words in the Brysbaert et al. list (see below), only about 20% had multiple entries in the pool of KVL lemmas. Furthermore, often the knowledge rankings for different word classes are (relatively) similar: *love* (n) 28, *love* (v) 192 (Spanish data); *hate* (n) 334, *hate* (v) 380 (German data). Overall, we felt the value in comparing the KVL and Brysbaert et al. L2 lists outweighed the limitation that they are not always fully comparable for every word on the lists.

A more important difference between the Brysbaert et al. L2 data and the KVL is the nature of the tests. Brysbaert et al. used a Yes/No test with the instruction to say yes if 'I know this word'. This is a common instruction in Yes/No tests but is rather vague, and leaves each respondent to decide for themselves the level of mastery they will use for 'knowing'. Some may only say *yes* if they know the words well and can use them in their writing and speaking. Others may say *yes* if they only have receptive knowledge and can understand the words in reading and/or listening. Still others may choose a very minimal level of mastery and say *yes* if they think they recognise the word form as something they have seen before, but without knowing anything about its meaning. So, while Yes/No tests do correlate with other tests of language proficiency (e.g., Alderson, 2005), as strictly vocabulary tests, they are difficult to interpret in terms of *how well* the words are known. It is probably best to use a conservative interpretation, and see the words as known at the lower end of mastery, that is, probably as form-recognition, or perhaps meaning-recall. In other words, at closer to a receptive level rather than a productive one. Our form-recall test, on the other hand, required respondents to produce the word form, which has been shown to be a higher and more challenging level of mastery (Laufer & Goldstein, 2004; Laufer et al., 2004). Thus, the real value of the comparison is seeing how the Brysbaert et al. L2 list of lower lexical mastery compares to the KVL of more advanced mastery.

As a first step in this comparison, we looked at very well-known words. Brysbaert et al. report that 114 words were indicated as known by *all* of their large number of respondents. Since they were known by everyone, they are the 114 easiest words in their study. In Appendix 11, we compare these words to our facility values and knowledge rankings for each of our three language groups (note that the Brysbaert et al. set includes data from more than 150 mother tongues). This shows that 103 words known by everyone in the Brysbaert et al. data were spread quite widely in terms of knowledge on the KVL. (Eleven Brysbaert et al. words did not appear on the KVL due to their being inflections or lemmas which were not included among the KVL target lemmas.) Over half were well-known based on the KVL, with facility values of 0.90 or higher (Spanish = 65, German = 77, Chinese = 55). However, some had facility values of 0.70 or less (Spanish = 18, German = 2, Chinese = 9). The mean/median facility values were: Spanish 0.85/0.93, German 0.92/0.95, Chinese 0.86/0.91. Overall, the Brysbaert et al. words were relatively well-known by the KVL respondents but were not close to being the best-known 103 lemmas.

In terms of knowledge rankings, the KVL rankings were rather dispersed. Some were within the best-known 500 lemmas (Spanish = 37, German = 39, Chinese = 36), but many were not nearly as well-known. A large number were not within the best-known 1,000 lemmas (Spanish = 43, German = 45, Chinese = 46), and some were not even within the best-known 2,000 (Spanish=20, German-25, Chinese=24). A few were not even among the best-known 5,000 lemmas (Spanish = 6, German = 2, Chinese = 2).

While all of these figures are informative, as usual, the best way to understand the relationship between the best-known Brysbaert et al.

words and the KVL lemmas is through a graphic representation – see Figure 9.1. The graph shows that the relationships between the Brysbaert et al. rankings based on their form-recognition Yes/No test and the KVL rankings based on the form-recall *Vocabulary Challenge* test are not all that close. It is true that the majority of the Brysbaert et al. words have KVL knowledge rankings below 1,000 (Spanish 58%, German 56%, Chinese 55%). However, considerably fewer are within the 500 best-known (Spanish 36%, German 38%, Chinese 35%), and only a handful are within the best-known 200 (Spanish 17%, German 14%, Chinese 18%). The plots paint a picture of an uneven relationship; many rankings match to some extent, but there are outliers of increasing discrepancy. Overall, it seems fair to say from this data that learner vocabulary knowledge at the form-recall level of mastery is not predicted very closely by knowledge at the form-recognition level, and so it does not seem possible to generalise form-recall knowledge from form-recognition tests. Alternatively, form-recall knowledge implies form-recognition knowledge, as form-recognition rankings were stronger (i.e., ≤ 114) than form-recall rankings in all but a few cases. This is congruent with the generally accepted understanding of the development of vocabulary knowledge (e.g., Laufer & Goldstein, 2004; Laufer et al., 2004).

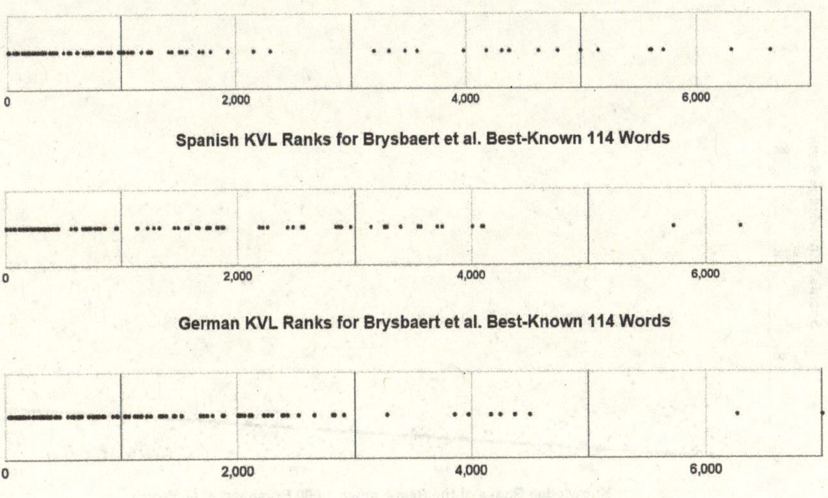

Figure 9.1: Relationship between the Brysbaert L2 list knowledge rankings and the KVL GLMM rankings (Spanish/German/Chinese data)

Moving to a larger sample of words, the next analysis compared the best-known 1,000 words from the Brysbaert et al. L2 list with their corresponding KVL knowledge rankings for the three languages. This analysis included 877 items, as the items on the Brysbaert L2 and KVL did not match up exactly, e.g., the KVL did not have lemmas with alternative US/UK spellings (*colour/color*) and the Brysbaert et al. L2 list included some inflections which the KVL did not (*children*). This comparison showed very little relationship. There were significant Kendall's tau correlations for the three languages, but they were at virtually meaningless effect levels: Spanish: 0.058 ($p<0.01$), German: 0.051 ($p<0.05$), Chinese: 0.045 ($p<0.05$). The scatterplots (Figures 9.2 to 9.4) all show a small amount of clustering around the regression line, but other than that, there essentially seems to be a random arrangement with no discernible patterning. In general, the KVL ranks (based on a form-recall test) were much lower than the Brysbaert et al. ranks (based on a form-recognition test), with only marginal clustering around the $0{\rightarrow}1,000$ slope lines. Tables 9.1 to 9.3 show that only about one-third of the words/lemmas were within ±500 in terms of knowledge rankings, and around one-quarter were not even within ±2,000. Overall, the Brysbaert et al. L2 rankings and the KVL rankings have only the weakest of relationships with each other.

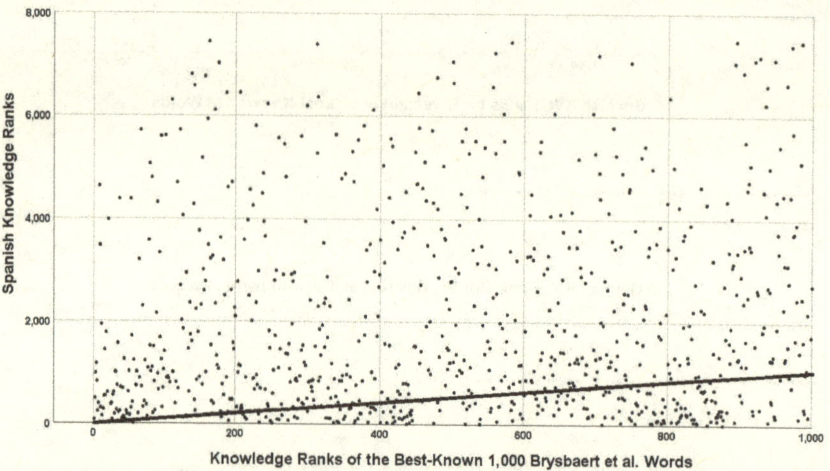

Figure 9.2: Scatterplot of the knowledge rankings of the best-known 1,000 Brysbaert et al. words and the Spanish KVL knowledge rankings

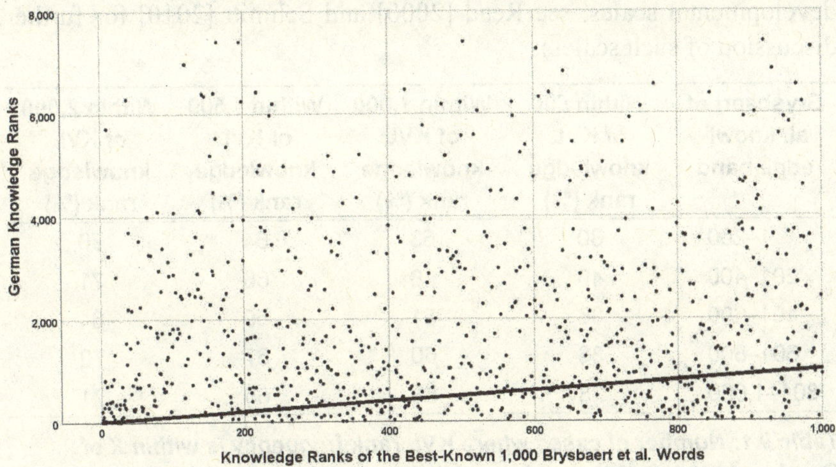

Figure 9.3: Scatterplot of the knowledge rankings of the best-known 1,000 Brysbaert et al. words and the German KVL knowledge rankings

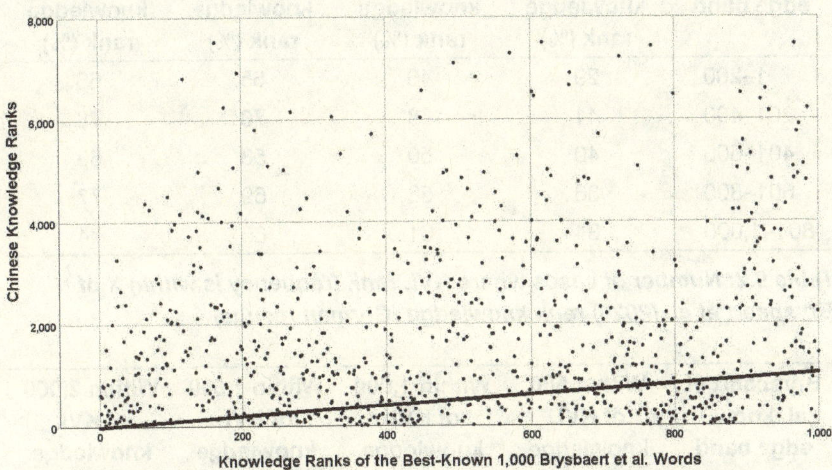

Figure 9.4: Scatterplot of the knowledge rankings of the best-known 1,000 Brysbaert et al. words and the Chinese KVL knowledge rankings

The commonly accepted view of vocabulary development is that knowledge of words begins with a receptive level of mastery and then moves on to a productive level of mastery. In the realm of testing, this conceptualisation is referred to as the *Developmental Approach* (Read, 2000). The following two examples of developmental scales illustrate the progression, albeit in quite different ways. (Note that there are several other developmental scales, see Read [2000] and Schmitt [2010] for further discussion of such scales).

Brysbaert et al. knowledge band	Within 500 of KVL knowledge rank (%)	Within 1,000 of KVL knowledge rank (%)	Within 1,500 of KVL knowledge rank (%)	Within 2,000 of KVL knowledge rank (%)
1–200	30	53	64	70
201–400	40	58	66	71
401–600	36	51	59	64
601–800	36	60	67	72
801–1,000	28	58	65	71

Table 9.1: Number of cases where KVL rank frequency is within X of Brysbaert et al. (2020) rank knowledge (Spanish results)

Brysbaert et al. knowledge band	Within 500 of KVL knowledge rank (%)	Within 1,000 of KVL knowledge rank (%)	Within 1,500 of KVL knowledge rank (%)	Within 2,000 of KVL knowledge rank (%)
1–200	29	46	55	66
201–400	41	58	70	78
401–600	40	50	58	63
601–800	36	58	69	77
801–1,000	34	61	66	74

Table 9.2: Number of cases where KVL rank frequency is within X of Brysbaert et al. (2020) rank knowledge (German results)

Brysbaert et al. knowledge band	Within 500 of KVL knowledge rank (%)	Within 1,000 of KVL knowledge rank (%)	Within 1,500 of KVL knowledge rank (%)	Within 2,000 of KVL knowledge rank (%)
1–200	28	48	62	73
201–400	43	62	73	82
401–600	42	52	62	67
601–800	43	64	74	80
801–1,000	31	60	69	75

Table 9.3: Number of cases where KVL rank frequency is within X of Brysbaert et al. (2020) rank knowledge (Chinese results)

Vocabulary Knowledge Scale (Paribakht & Wesche, 1997; Wesche & Paribakht, 1996)

I. I don't remember having seen this word before.

II. I have seen this word before, but I don't know what it means.

III. I have seen this word before, and I think it means _____. (synonym or translation)

IV. I know this word. It means _____. (synonym or translation)

V. I can use this word in a sentence: _____. (Write a sentence.) (If you do this section, please also do Section IV.)

Schmitt and Zimmerman Scale (Schmitt & Zimmerman, 2002)

A. I don't know the word.

B. I have heard or seen the word before, but am not sure of the meaning.

C. I understand the word when I hear or see it in a sentence, but I don't know how to use it in my own speaking or writing.

D. I know this word and can use it in my own speaking and writing.

If receptive knowledge does lead on to productive knowledge, then we would expect very considerable correspondence between receptive and productive mastery of target words in the L2 learner population. However, the above analyses show very limited correspondence in the knowledge rankings between Brysbaert et al.'s receptive measure and the KVL productive one.

To interpret this surprising result, we might first look at the methodologies used in the two separate studies. The first point concerns the respondent populations. The KVL focused on English L2 learners from three specific languages: Spanish, German, and Chinese. Brysbaert et al. gathered data worldwide. Their dataset included input from 286,500 sessions, of which 'only' 33,300 were from Spanish-speaking respondents (11.6%), 19,800 from German-speaking (6.9%), and 13,400 from Chinese-speaking (4.7%). Potentially, the Brysbaert et al. – KVL discrepancies are due to the respective respondents mainly coming from different language backgrounds. However, our study included three distinctive languages (a Germanic cognate language, a Romance cognate language, and a non-cognate language), yet all of the results were similar for these languages. If the factor of respondent L1 was a primary driver of the receptive-productive discrepancy, then we should have observed much greater variation among our three language groups. Yet for all three, there was very limited correspondence with the Brysbaert et al. ranking data. This indicates that the disconnect between the form-recognition knowledge rankings and the form-recall knowledge rankings are unlikely to be due to language.

A second issue concerns the different counting units of the two lists. To explore the potential effect of this, we stripped out the KVL items where there were multiple entries for a single Brysbaert et al. L2 word, e.g., Brysbaert et al. L2: *help* vs KVL: *help* (n), *help* (v); Brysbaert et al. L2: *right* vs KVL: *right* (n), *right* (adj), *right* (adv). This left 704 items. We found that the Kendall's tau correlations after stripping were virtually the same as before stripping:

Before stripping (877 items) **After stripping** (704 items)
Spanish: 0.058 ($p<0.01$)   Spanish: 0.062 ($p<0.05$)
German: 0.051 ($p<0.05$)   German: 0.064 ($p<0.05$)
Chinese: 0.045 ($p<0.05$)   Chinese: 0.073 ($p<0.01$)

This similarity suggests that the issue with counting unit is not the primary driver of the low Brysbaert et al. L2 – KVL correlations.

Another methodological point is that we looked at a limited subset of the data for our analyses in this chapter, i.e., the best-known 114 and 1,000 Brysbaert et al. words, which could potentially have skewed the results. However, the basically random scatterplots in Figures 9.2 to 9.4 give no indication that patterning would develop at the subsequent 2K–5K knowledge ranks. We sampled 50 words from the 4,900–5,000 Brysbaert et al. knowledge ranking band and found that none of the KVL rankings correlated with the Brysbaert et al. rankings for any of the three languages (all Kendall's tau results $p>0.14$). Thus, we can have some confidence in dismissing the notion that the Brysbaert et al. – KVL discrepancies are caused by our analyses of a limited set of the data, rather than the complete set of 5,000 words.

We could also look at the two tests used (the Yes/No test and the *Vocabulary Challenge* test) and conclude that the two different types of test would always give different results because they are measuring different things. While this may be true, the key issue is the *construct* being measured by the two tests. Brysbaert et al. do not clearly state what level of mastery they believe their Yes/No test captured but are clear that it is toward the less advanced end of the vocabulary knowledge continuum. The *Vocabulary Challenge* test describes the ability to correctly spell the written form of a lemma related to a known meaning. While this is not the same as full productive knowledge (i.e., the ability to produce a word accurately, appropriately, and automatically at will in one's writing when it is needed), it is clearly at a more advanced point on the continuum than the Yes/No knowledge construct. If we are interested in exploring the relationship between less/more advanced points on the receptive/productive continuum, the two tests would seem fit for purpose.

The disconnect between the Brysbaert et al. and KVL knowledge rankings might be revealing something interesting about the nature of vocabulary acquisition. Although it is clear that productive knowledge (to be read as form-recall mastery for the *Vocabulary Challenge* test) is mastered after receptive knowledge (form-recognition for the Yes/No test), it is not clear yet how the sequencing works. For example, are words that are learned first to a form-recognition level also the first to reach a form-recall level? An idealised illustration of such a lockstep progression is shown in Figure 9.5. In it, the first words to reach receptive knowledge (e.g., A, B, C) are also the first to reach productive mastery, in that exact order. That is, the sequence order reaching receptive mastery equals the sequence order reaching productive mastery.

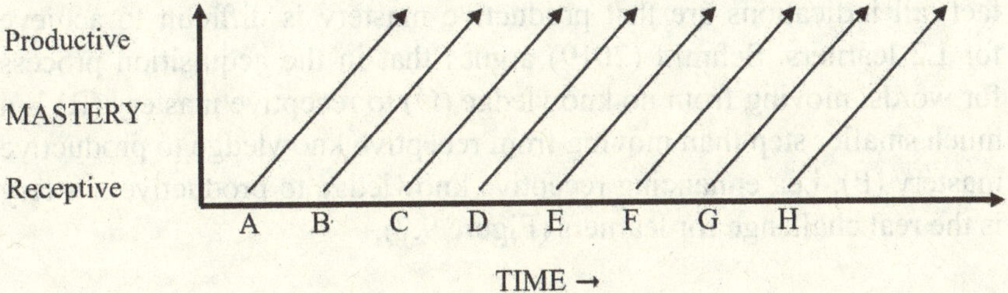

Figure 9.5: An idealised lockstep sequence order of vocabulary knowledge (contrived)

Of course, Figure 9.5 is far too systematic, and human learning behaviour is not this neat and orderly. Figure 9.6 shows some of the inevitable variation in learning trajectories, for example, as a result of teaching, materials, learner interest, and individual experiences. While words A and H develop in the systematic way illustrated in Figure 9.5, some words have plateaus and spurts in the learning rate (B, C, D) and other words have regressions before learning picks up again (E, F, G). Also, the final achievement for the words is not all the same; some words are ultimately learned to a higher level than others. This figure better illustrates the changes in learner motivation and interest, frequency in teaching materials, and the personal need for particular words, which all affect learning rate. Nonetheless, despite the variation in the trajectories of different words, they still reach productive mastery in the same lockstep order that began with receptive mastery. This represents the notion that receptive knowledge leads to productive knowledge in a relatively regular manner.

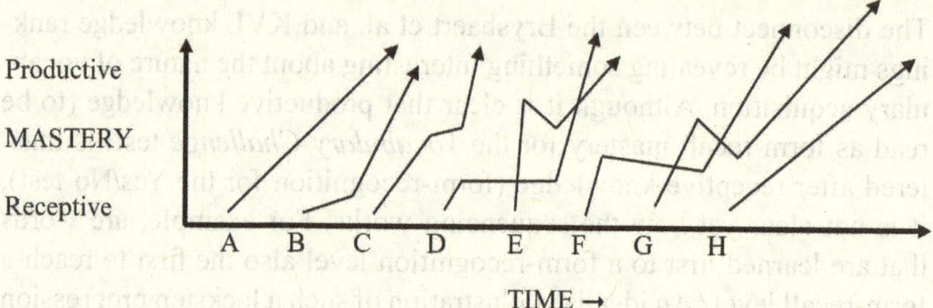

Figure 9.6: A lockstep order of vocabulary knowledge with inconstant trajectories (contrived)

However, the analyses in this chapter indicate that the progression from receptive to productive mastery does not occur in lockstep manner. In fact, all indications are that productive mastery is difficult to achieve for L2 learners. Schmitt (2019) argues that in the acquisition process for words, moving from no knowledge (Ø) to receptive mastery (R) is a much smaller step than moving from receptive knowledge to productive mastery (P), i.e., enhancing receptive knowledge to productive mastery is the real challenge for learners (Figure 9.7).

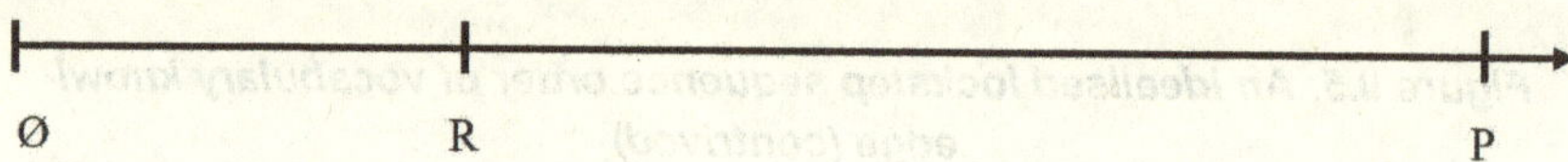

Figure 9.7: Potential acquisition of vocabulary knowledge from zero mastery to receptive mastery to productive mastery (Schmitt, 2019, p. 264)

We believe that the analyses presented here indicate a learning pattern much more like that in Figure 9.8. In it, words are learned at different rates, and with different trajectories. Some never make it to productive mastery (E). For the typical L2 learner, this is likely to be the case for many/most of the words they study. This great variation in learning trajectory means there is no close relationship between the sequence order in which a word starts at receptive mastery, and the order it finally reaches productive mastery (if it ever does).

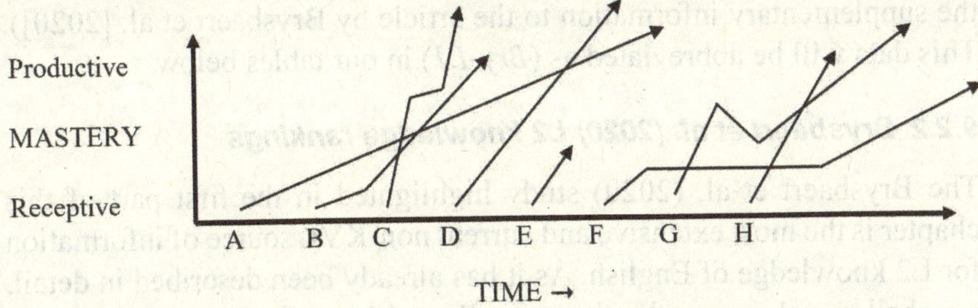

Figure 9.8: A variable sequence order of vocabulary knowledge (contrived)

9.2   Lists of vocabulary acquisition sequence and word difficulty

Chapter 8 showed that frequency is not a very good predictor of form-recognition knowledge, as a result of cognates that are specific to each L1–L2 combination. Might there be some other non-L1-specific factor which might predict form-recall knowledge better? There are a few lists which have been based on either tests of knowledge, or some conceptualisation of difficulty. These lists have used widely differing measures of 'knowing' a word and what 'difficulty' entails. Some have been based on L1 English knowledge, and some on L2 knowledge. It is interesting to compare our KVL results (based on form-recall knowledge) with a sample of these other lists of acquisition sequence/difficulty, with their various types of measure. Below is a quick survey of the other lists of knowledge/difficulty we will explore.

9.2.1   Brysbaert et al. (2016a) L1 knowledge rankings

Most of the lists have been based on L1 lexical acquisition. For our purposes, the most important is probably the Brysbaert et al. (2016a) list which we used as part of our list development (see Chapter 2). It was created using a crowdsourced self-report Yes/No test with 1,000 responses per target lemma from a variety of US and UK English-L1 respondents. The test asked respondents whether they knew the words or not, with no demonstration of knowledge (although there were nonwords included to control for overestimation). As a result, we will categorise it as a form-recognition test. The L1 knowledge rankings from this list are available in an Excel file entitled *Responses L2 English speakers to 62 thousand words.xlsx (Version: 1)* at the OFS website (https://osf.io/ gakre). In this Excel file, the pertinent column title is 'rank_L1' (this is the supplementary information to the article by Brysbaert et al. [2020]). This data will be abbreviated as (*Bry-L1*) in our tables below.

9.2.2 Brysbaert et al. (2020) L2 knowledge rankings

The Brysbaert et al. (2020) study highlighted in the first part of this chapter is the most extensive and current non-KVL source of information for L2 knowledge of English. As it has already been described in detail, we shall merely recap that it was collected by a crowdsourced Yes/No test, and so we will classify the level of mastery measured as form-recognition. There was an average of 274 observations per word, from a wide range of respondents, speaking more than 150 L1s. The largest language groups were Spanish, Hungarian, German, Polish, Dutch, and Chinese. This data will be abbreviated as (*Bry-L2*) in our tables below. The L2 knowledge ranking figures were taken from the same spreadsheet reported in the Brysbaert et al. (2020) summary above: *Responses of L2 English speakers to 62 thousand words.xlsx (Version: 1)*. In this spreadsheet, the pertinent column title is 'rank_L2'.

9.2.3 Age of Acquisition (AoA)

While the two Brysbaert et al. studies tested a very large number of words (~60,000 lemmas), other studies have involved smaller sets. Kuperman et al. (2012) worked with a still very substantial 30,121 lemmas from the SUBTlex–US corpus. But instead of asking whether the participants *knew* the words on a 362-lemma list sampled from the overall lemma population, the instructions required the participants to indicate the age (in years) at which they thought they had *learned* the words. The instructions specified that by learning a word, 'we mean the age at which you would have understood that word if somebody had used it in front of you, EVEN IF YOU DID NOT use, read, or write it at the time' (Kuperman et al., 2012, p. 980). If participants did not know a word, they were instructed to enter the letter 'x'. We would inter-pret this level of self-report mastery as meaning-recall. Although the research instrument was relatively long, it only took about 20 minutes to complete. To encourage participation, respondents were paid a nom-inal fee, e.g., $1.81 for a fully completed list. The 1,729 participants all lived in the US, varied widely in age and education, and, except for 43 non-English monolinguals or multilinguals, all spoke English as their L1. The age of acquisition figures were calculated as the numer-ical mean of the acquisition ages listed by all the participants (usually 18–22) who responded to a lemma. This is a relatively small number of respondents, which was probably inevitable given the very large numbers of lexical items being investigated. AoA studies with more constrained word sets can have larger N numbers, e.g., a Portuguese AoA study with 1,749 target words had a mean of 48 participants per word (Cameirão & Vicente, 2010).

It is unclear how well people can accurately report the age at which they learned a word. It would be better to actually observe when words were first produced, but this is only possible with very small children and their very limited vocabularies. For example, the MacArthur-Bates Communicative Development Inventories (MB-CDIs) relate when parents report words first being uttered by their toddlers (https://mb-cdi. stanford.edu/).

Nevertheless, the control words in the Kuperman et al. data correlated highly (0.93) with age of acquisition data collected from University of Bristol undergraduate students (Stadthagen-Gonzalez & Davis, 2006). Furthermore, a study exploring the AoA of 299 words across 25 languages generally found Spearman correlations of between 0.70 and 0.90 between languages (Łuniewska et al., 2016). While these correlations do not directly confirm the accuracy of the AoA ratings, at least it appears that different groups of participants tend to give similar AoA results for words. To the extent the respondents were accurate in their self-reporting, the AoA figures can be seen as representing the sequence of acquisition of English vocabulary. The L1 AoA figures were taken from the spreadsheet *File for Regression Analysis L1 and L2 Ranks.xlsx* on the OFS website (https://osf.io/gakre). In this spreadsheet, the relevant column title is 'AoA-L1'.

There have been fewer AoA studies looking at L2 acquisition. A recent one dealing with Chinese learners of English was useful as Chinese was one of our three language groups. Wang & Chen (2020) elicited AoA responses from 24 Chinese university students for 1,835 words. In our analyses, we took the AoA figures from their supplementary materials spreadsheet, *A Database of Chinese-English Bilingual Speakers: Ratings of the Age of Acquisition and Familiarity*, using the column titled 'L2AoA'. This L2 AoA data is labelled 'AoA-L2' below, although it must be remembered that it is only from Chinese speakers.

9.2.4 *The Living Word Vocabulary (LWV)*

Another way to gauge the sequence of acquisition is to test participants of various ages to see when they learn particular words. This approach was taken by Dale & O'Rourke (1981). Over 25 years, they tested US students on 44,000 words and their various meanings at school grades 4, 6, 8, 10, 12, 13 (freshman university), and 16 (4th year university). At least 200 students were tested for each word. When a threshold of 67% of the students in a year answered the word correctly on the test, it was considered learned by that school year. If the threshold was not reached, higher years were tested until it was achieved. If the threshold was reached with a high percentage, lower years were tested to see if it could be achieved earlier. Students were tested with short three-option multiple-choice items such as the following:

entymon	**(a)** study of insects	**(b)** figure of speech	**(c)** a root word
macho	**(a)** cruel	**(b)** speed	**(c)** manly
actual	**(a)** a kind of act	**(b)** busy	**(c)** real

Multiple-choice tests are prone to test-taking strategies and guessing (Gyllstad et al., 2015) and a three-option test has a 33% chance of correct answers on pure guesses. However, Dale & O'Rourke's 67% threshold is probably high enough to avoid even a substantial amount of guessing to have led words to be misplaced as to year classification. Since the three options are meanings, we would categorise the degree of mastery that this test measures as meaning-recognition. The LWV results are reported in Dale & O'Rourke (1981), from which the year classifications were taken for the following analyses.

9.2.5 English Vocabulary Profile (EVP)

A research effort headed by the then University of Cambridge ESOL Examinations (now Cambridge Assessment English) attempted to define the Common European Framework of Reference for Languages (CEFR) levels of English vocabulary (and other linguistic aspects). They were largely interested in productive vocabulary, i.e., determining when words were used by learners as indicated by learner corpora. The corpus they used was the Cambridge Learner Corpus (CLC), which consisted of the written English produced by examinees when taking tests of the Cambridge English examinations suite (i.e., from the Key English Test through to the Certificate of Proficiency in English). The subset of the CLC used for the project amounted to about 26 million words. While use of the CLC generated a good-sized corpus of learner English, an unfortunate by-product is that the data always had a bias towards 'test-taking language', which can be quite different from the language produced in daily language use. Also, quite often, test items are discrete-point, and require answers that are not particularly contextualised. Tests will also be limited in the amount and type of language they can elicit, and the CLC does not have any spoken language component. Furthermore, examinees are usually stressed and under pressure to perform quickly and accurately, and so it is unsurprising that their test output might not mirror the language they produce in non-exam situations. The English Vocabulary Profile (EVP) results are tied to one suite of tests from Cambridge Assessment English, and it is arguable how well any set of tests or measures can represent the overall CEFR levels. For example, the Global Scale of English from Pearson Publishers (see the following section) has many words at different CEFR levels than the EVP.

The research team attempted to broaden the learner corpus beyond the CLC. The EVP website (www.englishprofile.org/wordlists/evp-faqs) states that the following sources were used in the compilation of the EVP:

- wordlists from leading coursebooks, readers' wordlists, and the content of vocabulary skills books
- the Cambridge English Corpus, which was used to investigate first language frequency
- the Vocabulary Lists for the KET and PET examinations, which have been in use since 1994 and have been regularly updated to reflect language change and patterns of use
- the Cambridge English Lexicon, which was based on the intuitions of author Roland Hindmarsh
- reviewers, outside experts, and users have given their advice on levels based on their classroom experience, with changes made as a result.

While these sources could certainly improve the EVP, it is unclear to what degree the EVP is still based on the CLC data, and to what extent it has been modified by these alternative sources of information. Ultimately, the EVP is bound to still have biases resulting from its largely exam-based sources of information. More information on the development and use of the EVP can be found in the three volumes of the *English Profile Journal* (www.cambridge.org/core/journals/english-profile-journal/all-issues#).

Interestingly, the unit of measure in the EVP is word meaning, and not a grammatical counting unit (such as lemma or word family). Thus *foot* (body part) is a different item than *foot* (measurement) on the EVP, even though they would be typically counted as belonging to the same lemma or word family. This is a great advantage, as different meanings like these are typically learned at different stages of vocabulary development, e.g., *foot* (body part) = EVP A1, while *foot* (measurement) = EVP B1. The CEFR ratings for word meanings are provided on an interactive website (www.englishprofile.org/wordlists/evp), and the EVP ratings for the analyses below are taken from this site.

9.2.6 *Pearson Global Scale of English (GSE)*

Pearson Publishing has developed tools for ranking the difficulty of various English linguistic aspects on a common scale, i.e., the Global Scale of English – *GSE*, including vocabulary and grammar. As with the EVP, the unit of measure is word meaning. However, the GSE CEFR ratings do not always agree with those from the EVP, as the GSE has *foot* (body part) as <A1, and *foot* (measurement) as B2.

To rank the word meanings, the Pearson research team started by building a frequency list, based on input from three diverse corpora: the *Longman Corpus Network* (330 million words), *ukWaC* (2 billion words constructed by trawling the web), and the spoken component of the *COCA* (90 million words). They took the most frequent words from each corpus and combined them into a list of around 20,000 lemmas. The separate meanings for these lemmas were identified, totalling about 37,000. Then a panel of 10 teachers (out of a pool of 19) rated the meanings on a usefulness scale of 1–5.

1. **Essential** items are the words/phrases that learners would want to acquire first. They are essential for basic communication.
2. **Important** items are words/phrases that become necessary at a next stage; they are still very common. They are perhaps a little more detailed or a little more specific in their meaning.
3. **Useful** items are words/phrases that expand the user's vocabulary enabling more detailed and specific language use.
4. **Nice to have** items are for users to express themselves accurately and precisely.
5. **Extra** is for items that some language users will use occasionally but they are not needed for everyday communication.

    – Benigno & de Jong (2017, p. 9)

The frequency and teacher ratings were combined to produce the GSE score, usually giving the highest weighting to the teacher ratings. The details of the process and suggestions of how to use the GSE are given in the pamphlet *Developing the GSE Vocabulary* (Benigno & de Jong, 2017; www.pearson.com/english/about/gse/research.html).

The GSE is a probabilistic scale, where 'knowing' a word at a given GSE level means having a 50% probability of being able to understand/use it. For example, a learner at 35 on the GSE has 50% probability of understanding/using a vocabulary item which is at that level of difficulty (35). They would have a lower probability of understanding/using words which are higher on the GSE and a higher probability of understanding/using words which are lower on the GSE. The GSE is not pegged to a certain level of vocabulary knowledge mastery, and so cannot be categorised as something like form-recognition or form-recall.

Although neither frequency nor teacher ratings of usefulness are the same as word difficulty or sequence of acquisition, the GSE does provide a ranked order of vocabulary which has proven useful in sequencing syllabi, classroom materials, and language tests. As such, it serves as a useful proxy for difficulty/acquisition sequence and has been mapped onto the CEFR framework of increasing language proficiency. This makes it interesting to include in our analysis. GSE ratings for individual word meanings are available at the Pearson GSE Teacher Toolkit website (www. english.com/gse/teacher-toolkit/user/vocabulary?page=1&sort=gse;asc&text=accrue&gseRange=10;90&audience=GL), where the GSE ratings in the analysis were obtained.

9.2.7 *Word characteristics which affect difficulty*

In addition to the lists described above, additional factors that relate to the characteristics of the words themselves were included in our analyses. In psycholinguistic experiments, a wide range of factors have been shown to affect sensitive measures of knowing a word, such as in reaction time experiments (e.g., de Groot, 2006; de Groot & van Hell, 2005). Length of a word (*Len*) (i.e., the number of letters it contains) is one of those, with longer words generally being more difficult. We would expect this to be the case in terms of form-recall, with longer words needing more letters to be accurately rendered. Similarly, words with more morphemes (*Mor*) are generally more complex (and longer), and so should be more difficult to spell. It is easy to confuse words with similar word forms (e.g., *affect/effect, invaluable/invariable*), and so the more words in a language with similar spellings to a target word, the more likely that word will be confused with those alternatives. Sets of words with similar spellings are called *orthographic neighbours*, and Orthographic Levenshtein Distance (*OD*) is a measure to show how similar a word's spelling is to its nearest orthographic neighbours. Finally, concrete words (*Con*) are usually more imageable than abstract words and have generally been shown to be easier to learn. Although this is a semantic issue, and not directly connected to word form, it is interesting to see if such a semantic factor relates to KVL form-recall knowledge rankings. The data for all of these measures was taken from the spreadsheet *File for regression analysis L1 and L2 ranks* which is available as supplementary materials in Brysbaert et al. (2016a).

9.3 Comparison of KVL knowledge rankings with other lists of vocabulary acquisition sequence and word difficulty

We wished to compare the above lists of knowledge/difficulty with our KVL rankings. Because the lists were compiled in different ways and with different sets of target words, and most were very large, we needed to draw a sample of words which were common to each list. The main purpose was to see if any of the alternative lists could predict the form-recall knowledge as indicated by the KVL. However, as the knowledge rank orders of the Spanish, German, and Chinese KVL did not agree very well, it was not obvious which of them to use as the basis of the sample. We therefore used the L2 ranking list from Brysbaert et al. (2020) (*Bry-L2*) to sample from, because that study included a large number of participants from a range of L2s. We sampled from the best-known 5,000 items on this list, at a rate of about every 20th word (i.e., 20, 40, 60, 80, 100, 120 etc.). This returned a sample of 250 items (5%). Because we were extracting data from different lists, sometimes the word at the sample point did not exist in the other lists, and so a nearby word above or below the sample point was selected in its place. This resulted in a 250-word dataset for all lists except two. The Wang & Chen (2020) study only investigated 1,835 words, and so the AoA-L2 comparison only contained 86 common items. Being older, the LWV sometimes had meanings which were not the ones the KVL measured (e.g., the LWV listed the meaning of *spam* as canned meat, not unwanted computer messages), and so contained 234 common items.

9.3.1 *Initial analyses*

The sample was subjected to a Kendall's tau correlation analysis, and the results are illustrated in Table 9.4. Looking at the correlation matrix, we see that most of the factors are interrelated with the KVL rank orders, and with each other. The correlations range from nonsignificant (*ns*) to 0.751. The correlations between the knowledge rank orders of the three KVL language groups (Spanish, German, Chinese) with the 250-word samples show very similar correlations (0.489–0.506) to those obtained from the complete 7,532 datasets (0.454–0.505, see Chapter 6). The rank order of one language does not strongly relate to the rank order of another, but the moderate correlations between the language pairs shows that there is some degree of systematicity in the sequence that words are learned to a form-recall level of mastery across different L1, schooling, and cultural contexts.

With regard to measures which might predict form-recall knowledge, we started with form-recognition knowledge. We saw earlier in this chapter that the form-recognition knowledge rankings of the best-known 1,000 words from Brysbaert et al. (2020) correlated only extremely weakly with the KVL form-recall rankings (Spanish: 0.058, German: 0.051, Chinese: 0.045). Here we sampled from a wider range of words up to the 5,000 knowledge rankings. We found that the *Bry-L2* correlations are somewhat higher for all three languages (Spanish: 0.256, German: 0.296, Chinese: 0.369). So, over a wider range of words (at least in terms of knowledge rankings), form-recognition knowledge relates to form-recall knowledge somewhat more strongly in terms of correlation figures than indicated earlier in this chapter. However, these higher correlation figures are still very modest and perhaps even a little misleading. Figures 9.9 to 9.11 make it clear that there is so much variation that it is very difficult to say that form-recognition knowledge provides useful guidance as to form-recall knowledge. Thus, our conclusion from earlier, that form-recognition knowledge does not predict form-recall knowledge very well, still holds based on this additional analysis.

	KVL-S	KVL-G	KVL-C	Bry-L2	EVP	GSE	AoA-L2	Bry-L1	AoA-L1	LWV	Len	OD	Mor	Con
KVL-S	–	.506	.499	.256	.448	.447	.349	.096*	.410	.405	.371	.308	.349	−.168
KVL-G	.506	–	.489	.296	.450	.442	.394	.128	.349	.340	.368	.309	.373	−.177
KVL-C	.499	.489	–	.369	.547	.525	.523	ns	.446	.466	.400	.340	.374	−.112
Bry-L2	.256	.296	.369	–	.393	.367	.336	ns	.235	.245	.126	.090*	.149	ns
EVP	.448	.450	.547	.393	–	.630	.566	ns	.498	.537	.346	.300	.380	−.166
GSE	.447	.442	.525	.367	.630	–	.516	.106*	.445	.447	.396	.345	.413	−.159
AoA-L2	.349	.394	.523	.336	.566	.516	–	ns	.490	.407	.276	.251	.319	ns
Bry-L1	.096*	.128	ns	ns	ns	.106*	ns	–	.106*	ns	ns	ns	ns	ns
AoA-L1	.410	.349	.446	.235	.498	.445	.490	.106*	–	.558	.385	.329	.337	−.230
LWV	.405	.340	.466	.245	.537	.447	.407	ns	.558	–	.361	.334	.335	−.201
Len	.371	.368	.400	.126	.346	.396	.276	ns	.385	.361	–	.751	.666	−.221
OD	.308	.309	.340	.090*	.300	.345	.251	ns	.329	.334	.751	–	.555	−.210
Mor	.349	.373	.374	.149	.380	.413	.319	ns	.337	.335	.666	.555	–	−.289
Con	−.168	−.177	−.112	ns	−.166	−.159	ns	ns	−.230	−.201	−.221	−.210	−.289	–

Notes: KVL-S = Spanish, KVL-G = German, KVL-C = Chinese, Bry-L2 = Brysbaert et al. (2020) L2 knowledge ranks, EVP = English Vocabulary Profile, GSE = Global Scale of English, AoA-L2 = Wang & Chen (2020) Chinese L2 age of acquisition, Bry-L1 = Brysbaert et al. (2016a) L1 knowledge ranks, AoA-L1 = Kuperman et al. (2012) L1 age of acquisition, LWV = living word vocabulary year ratings, Len = length of word in letters, OD = orthographic Levenshtein distance to the 20 closest words, Mor = number of morphemes in word, Con = concreteness rating

Kendall's tau, all correlations $p<0.01$, except * $p<0.05$

Table 9.4: Correlations of KVL knowledge rankings and various acquisition/difficulty measures

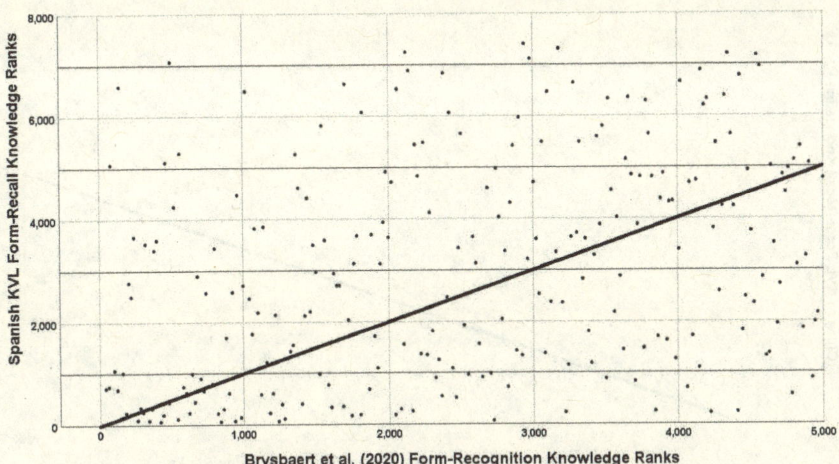

Figure 9.9: Correspondence of Brysbaert et al. (2020) form-recognition knowledge rankings and KVL form-recall knowledge rankings (Spanish data)

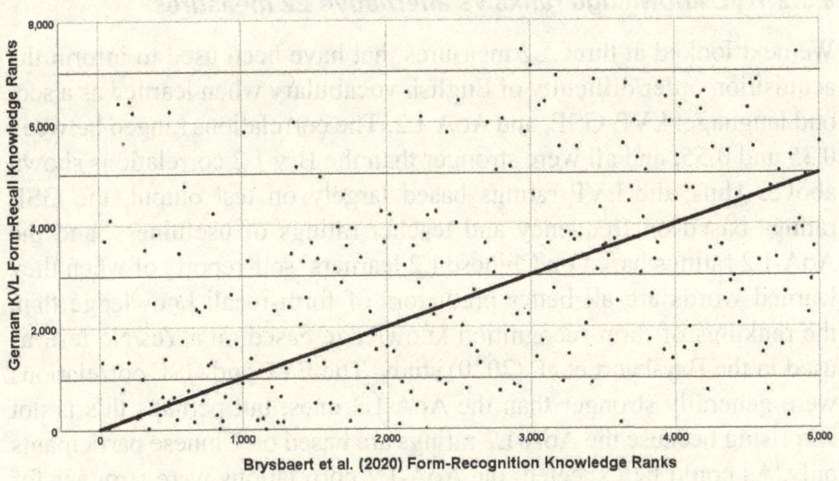

Figure 9.10: Correspondence of Brysbaert et al. (2020) form-recognition knowledge rankings and KVL form-recall knowledge rankings (German data)

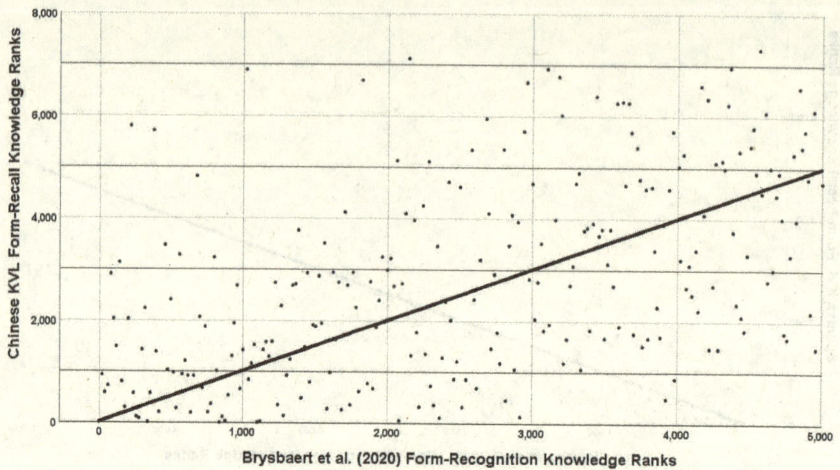

Figure 9.11: Correspondence of Brysbaert et al. (2020) form-recognition knowledge rankings and KVL form-recall knowledge rankings (Chinese data)

9.3.2 KVL knowledge ranks vs alternative L2 measures

We next looked at three L2 measures that have been used to inform the acquisition order/difficulty of English vocabulary when learned as a second language: EVP, GSE, and AoA-L2. The correlations ranged between 0.35 and 0.55, and all were stronger than the Bry-L2 correlations shown above. Thus, the EVP ratings based largely on test output, the GSE ratings based on frequency and teacher ratings of usefulness, and the AoA-L2 ratings based on Chinese L2 learners' self-reports of when they learned words are all better predictors of form-recall knowledge than the rankings of form-recognition knowledge based on a Yes/No test, as used in the Brysbaert et al. (2020) study. The EVP and GSE correlations were generally stronger than the AoA-L2 ones, but perhaps this is not surprising because the AoA-L2 ratings are based on Chinese participants only. As could be expected, the AoA-L2 correlations were stronger for the Chinese KVL group than the Spanish or German groups. The correlations were strongest for the Chinese group for all three factors. While this is explainable for the AoA-L2 factor, it is difficult to understand why the EVP and GSE factors should correlate more strongly with the Chinese group than the Spanish or German ones.

Overall, the 0.35–0.55 correlations indicate that these alternative L2 measures predict form-recall knowledge to some extent, but the relationship is not particularly strong. The scatterplots for each comparison back this up. We found that they were relatively similar, in the sense that they had too much variation to give very much of an idea of the order in which form-recall knowledge would be mastered. To illustrate this, we show the scatterplots for the three L2 measures for the German group (Figures 9.12 to 9.14).

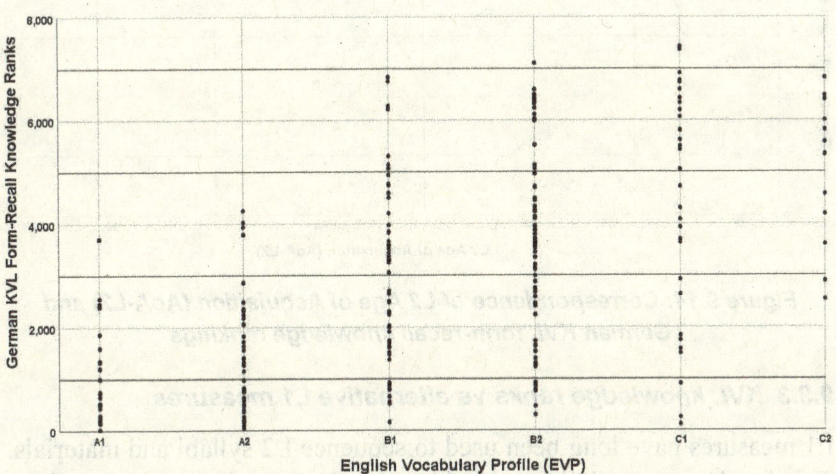

Figure 9.12: Correspondence of the English Vocabulary Project (EVP) and German KVL form-recall knowledge rankings

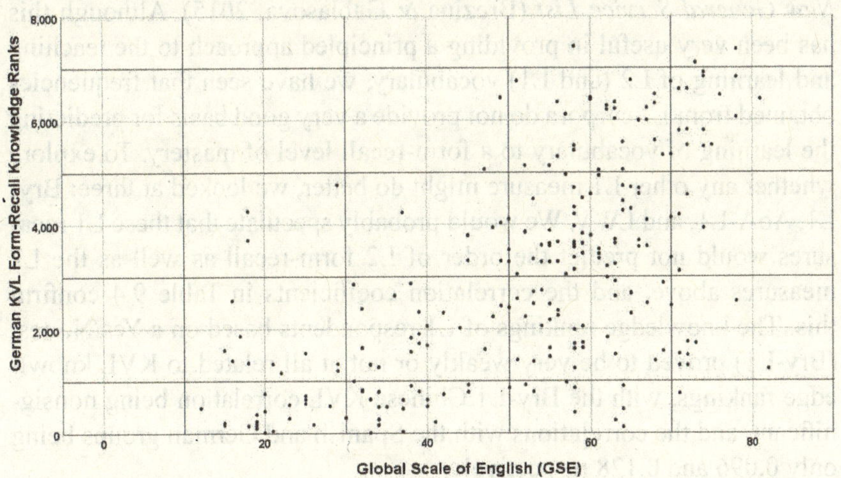

Figure 9.13: Correspondence of the Global Scale of English (GSE) and German KVL form-recall knowledge rankings

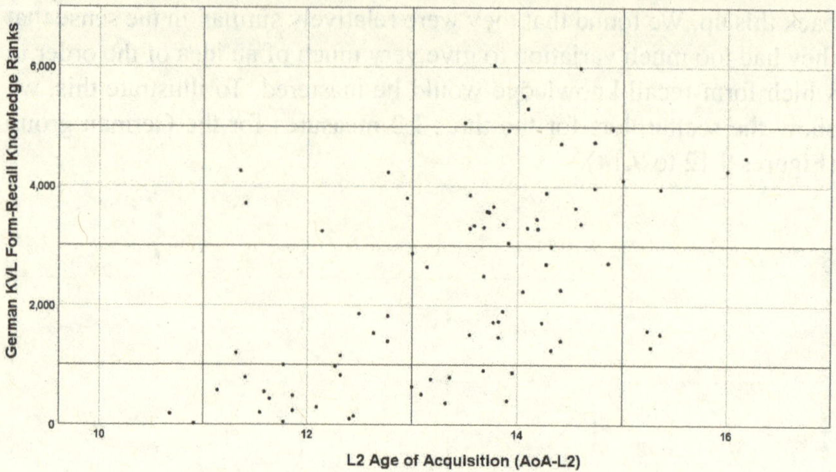

Figure 9.14: Correspondence of L2 Age of Acquisition (AoA-L2) and German KVL form-recall knowledge rankings

9.3.3 KVL knowledge ranks vs alternative L1 measures

L1 measures have long been used to sequence L2 syllabi and materials. This has been especially noticeable with frequency counts taken from L1 corpora and language materials informing ESL vocabulary and reading pedagogy, with a history stretching from before *The Teacher's Word Book of 30,000 Words* (Thorndike & Lorge, 1944), through to the current *New General Service List* (Brezina & Gablasova, 2015). Although this has been very useful in providing a principled approach to the teaching and learning of L2 (and L1) vocabulary, we have seen that frequencies obtained from L1 corpora do not provide a very good basis for predicting the learning of vocabulary to a form-recall level of mastery. To explore whether any other L1 measure might do better, we looked at three: Bry-L1, AoA-L1, and LWV. We would probably speculate that these L1 measures would not predict the order of L2 form-recall as well as the L2 measures above, and the correlation coefficients in Table 9.4 confirm this. The knowledge rankings of L1 respondents based on a Yes/No test (Bry-L1) proved to be very weakly or not at all related to KVL knowledge rankings, with the Bry-L1/Chinese KVL correlation being nonsignificant, and the correlations with the Spanish and German groups being only 0.096 and 0.128 respectively.

The other two L1 measures did somewhat better. The AoA-L1 ratings correlated with the KVL groups at 0.35–0.45 and the AoA-L1 correlation was actually higher for the Spanish group (0.410) than the AoA-L2 rating

(0.349). The year levels in the LWV correlated with the KVL groups at 0.34–0.47. Thus, the self-reporting of L1 AoA and the testing of L1 students to determine the year level of words does relate moderately to the sequence of mastering L2 form-recall. However, as with the L2 measures, there is too much variation to say that the L1 measures can provide much useful guidance as to the sequencing of form-recall mastery. This is illustrated by the scatterplots for the three L1 measures for the Spanish group (Figures 9.15 to 9.17).

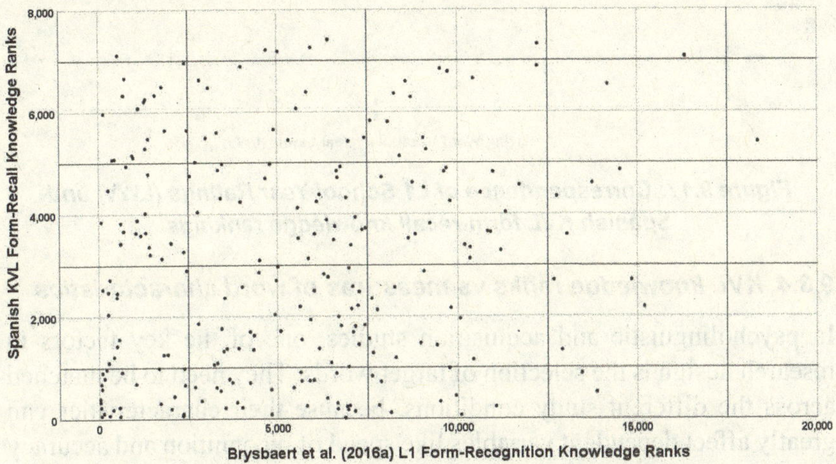

Figure 9.15: *Correspondence of L1 knowledge rankings (Bry-L1) and Spanish KVL form-recall knowledge rankings*

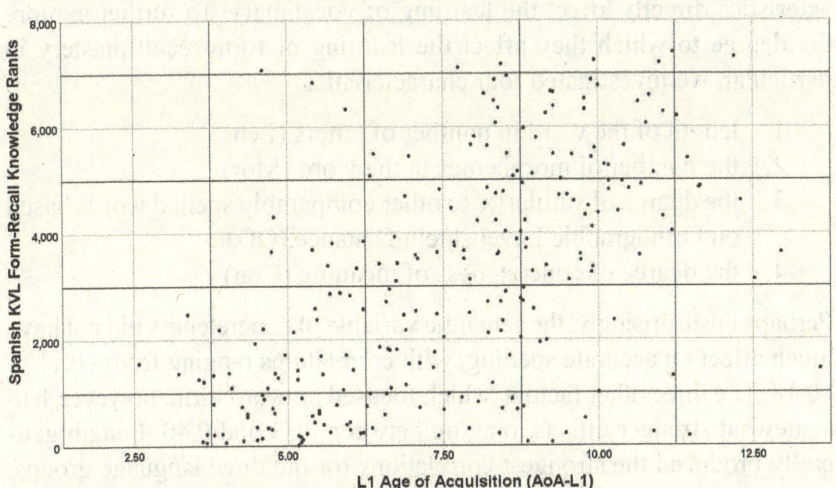

Figure 9.16: *Correspondence of L1 Age of Acquisition (AoA-L1) and Spanish KVL form-recall knowledge rankings*

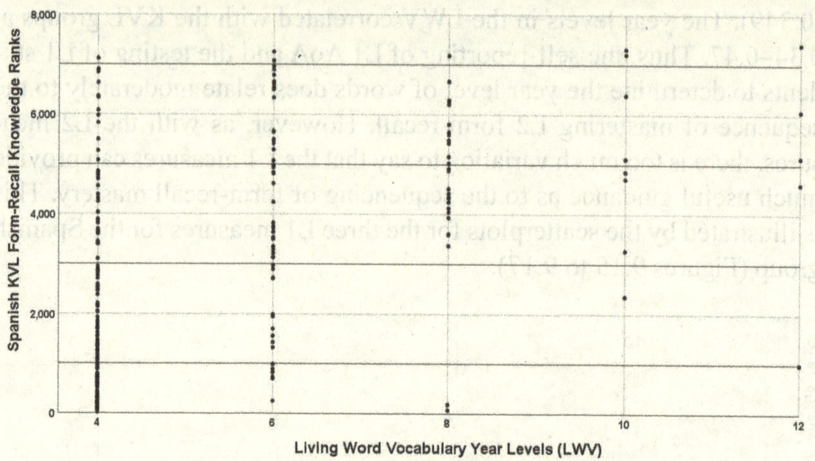

Figure 9.17: Correspondence of L1 School Year Ratings (LWV) and Spanish KVL form-recall knowledge rankings

9.3.4 KVL knowledge ranks vs measures of word characteristics

In psycholinguistic and acquisition studies, one of the key factors in research design is the selection of target words. They need to be matched across the different study conditions, because their characteristics can greatly affect dependent variables like speed of recognition and accuracy rates. For example, cognates and concrete words will usually be processed and/or learned faster and more accurately than non-cognates and abstract words (e.g., de Groot & Keijzer, 2000). Thus, many word characteristics directly affect the learning of vocabulary. To further explore the degree to which they affect the learning of form-recall mastery in particular, we investigated four characteristics:

1. length of the word in number of letters (Len)
2. the number of morphemes in the word (Mor)
3. the degree of similarity to other comparably spelled words based on Orthographic Levenshtein Distance (OD)
4. the degree of concreteness of meaning (Con)

Perhaps unsurprisingly, the semantic variable of concreteness did not have much effect on accurate spelling, with correlations ranging from –0.11 to –0.18. The three other factors, which focused on word form, however, had somewhat stronger effects, ranging between 0.31 and 0.40. Length generally produced the strongest correlations for the three language groups, with longer words being more difficult. Number of morphemes produced a similar result, but to a slightly lesser extent for the Spanish and Chinese groups; it was marginally higher for the German group. The orthographic distance also produced a moderate effect, so the ability to learn words to a form-recall level of mastery is not just contingent on a particular word's formal characteristics, but also depends on how many other words have a similar spelling in the language, and how close the correspondence is. However, the fact that these form-specific factors did not correlate more highly than 0.40 drives home the point that learning vocabulary to a form-recall level of mastery appears to be quite idiosyncratic, and difficult to predict. As before, we illustrate the lack of a strong correspondence with scatterplots, this time with the Chinese group (Figures 9.18–9.21).

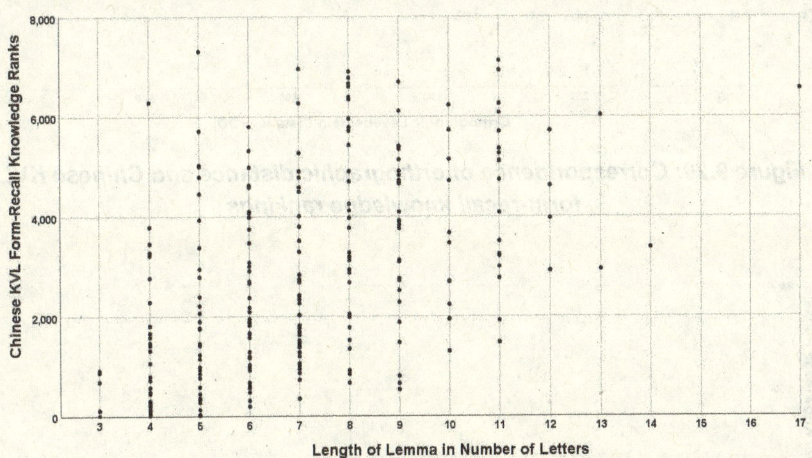

Figure 9.18: Correspondence of word length and Chinese KVL form-recall knowledge rankings

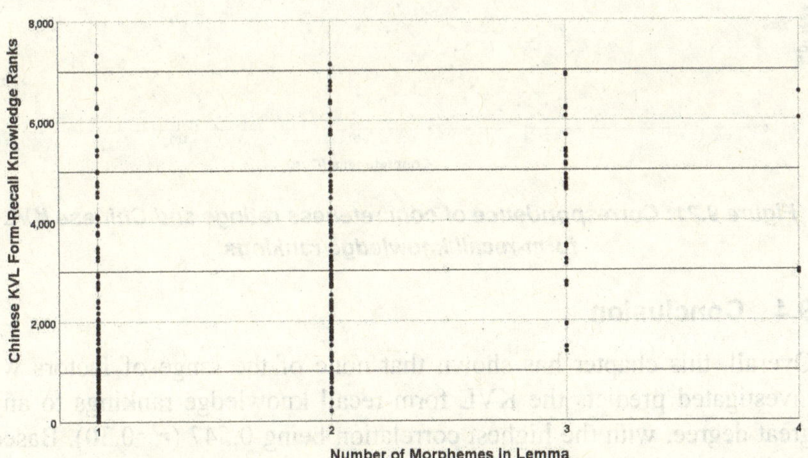

Figure 9.19: Correspondence of number of morphemes and Chinese KVL form-recall knowledge rankings

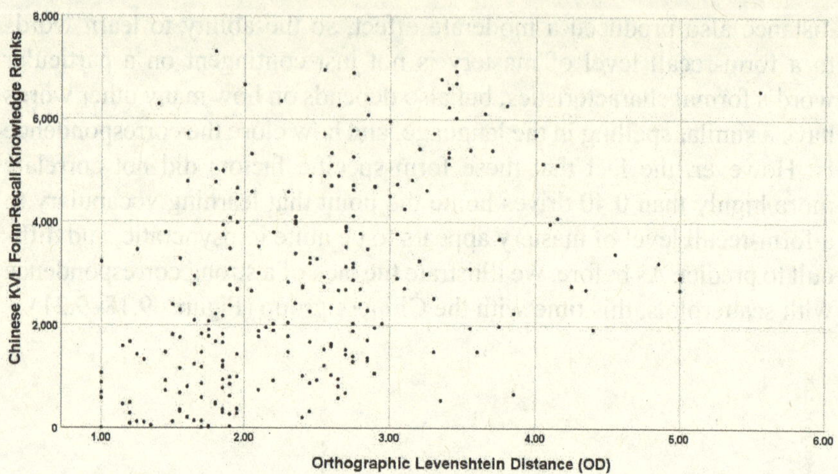

Figure 9.20: Correspondence of orthographic distance and Chinese KVL form-recall knowledge rankings

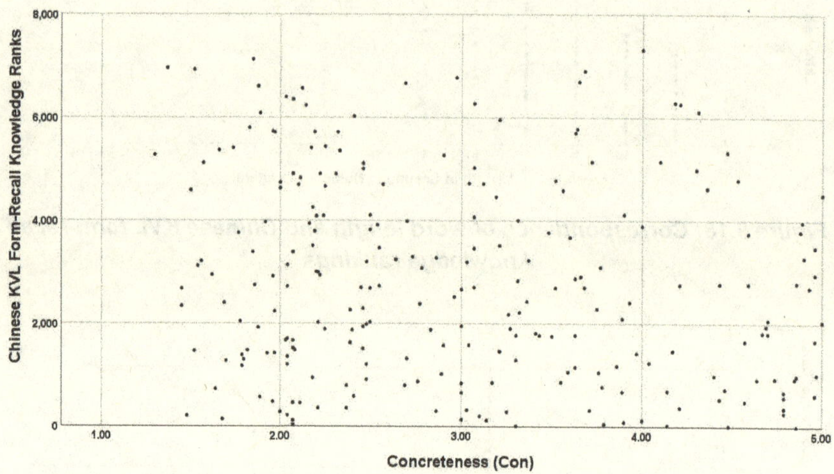

Figure 9.21: Correspondence of concreteness ratings and Chinese KVL form-recall knowledge rankings

9.4   Conclusion

Overall, this chapter has shown that none of the range of factors we investigated predicts the KVL form-recall knowledge rankings to any great degree, with the highest correlation being 0.547 (r^2=0.30). Based on this, it can be concluded that the sequence of mastery of form-meaning link is relatively unpredictable, at least by the kind of measures we examined. The reason for this likely lies in the relatively advanced nature of form-meaning mastery. Many studies have shown it is learned much later than more receptive levels of mastery (e.g., González-Fernández & Schmitt, 2019; Laufer and Goldstein, 2004; Laufer et al., 2004; Levitzky-Aviad & Laufer, 2013), and the early suggestion that there is not much of a gap between the amount of receptive and productive vocabulary one knows (e.g., Melka, 1997) is now untenable. For example, Laufer (2005) found that only 16% of receptive vocabulary was known productively at the 5,000-frequency level, and 35% at the 2,000 level. Other studies conclude that around 50% to 75% of receptive vocabulary is known productively (Fan, 2000; Laufer & Paribakht, 1998).

The present study adds further evidence of the difficulty in acquiring vocabulary to a productive level, in our case, form-recall mastery. Thus, it is not surprising that Schmitt's (2019) review of the research leads him to conclude that the interval between receptive and productive mastery is actually bigger than the one between no knowledge and receptive mastery on the developmental continuum.

So why is productive knowledge so hard to acquire? Second language acquisition (SLA) and spelling research point to a number of reasons. First, second language learners typically have trouble producing derivational suffixes in English (e.g., McLean, 2018; Schmitt & Zimmerman, 2002; Ward & Chuenjundaeng, 2009). The trouble is not the quantity of suffixes, but rather that they are partially idiosyncratic in their application (or the 'rules' are opaque). For example, the suffixes *-ion, -ment,* and *-al* all form nouns, but do not all apply to any given base form, and in each case a decision needs to be made (e.g., *refer/referion? referment? referral?*) with an additional complication being how to transform the spelling to make the suffix fit (*refer→referal? referral?*).

Second, the spelling system of English is not entirely systematic, and has numerous exceptions. For example, the sound-symbol correspondences for vowels in English are complex. There are only five written vowels (*a, e, i, o, u*) and sometimes *y* also serves as a vowel. But there are at least 14 vowel sounds in standard American English, and more in British English. So, there are numerous spellings and combinations of the written vowels to represent the various phonological sounds. For instance, the sound 'long a' /eɪ/ can be spelled as *a* (sale), *ai* (plain), *ay* (may), and *ei* (rein). Things become even more problematic with unstressed vowels (often in the middle of words), where a variety of spellings are all pronounced with a schwa /ə/, e.g., the second vowels in all of the following words are pronounced as /ə/ but spelled differently: *wom<u>a</u>n, barg<u>ai</u>n, mark<u>e</u>t, for<u>ei</u>gn, typ<u>i</u>cal, el<u>o</u>quent, nerv<u>ou</u>s, ind<u>u</u>stry,* and *bic<u>y</u>cle*. Add to that the learner quagmire of double and silent letters (*really, occasionally, knight, cane*), then it becomes obvious why English spelling is more difficult to produce (form-recall) than to recognise (form-recognition).

A third reason revolves around the amount of exposure learners typically receive and the practice they do. It is probably safe to say the average learner is exposed to much more spoken and written input than they produce themselves as output. So, they read more than they write. The relative deficit in writing practice naturally leads to slower progress in the ability to write and spell accurately. It also appears that learners must practice vocabulary productively to reach productive mastery (e.g., Laufer, 2005), and so repeated reading will usually not be enough to achieve this mastery. School systems and syllabi will vary greatly in which words they focus upon in terms of spelling, literacy, and dedicated productive practice, and so it is no wonder that learners from different contexts will also vary greatly in which words are learned to productive mastery.

In sum, it is very difficult to predict which words learners might know to form-recall mastery. Most research and lists to date have focused on levels of mastery closer to the receptive end of the knowledge continuum. This is what makes the KVL particularly valuable, as they provide one of the few evidence-based descriptions of L2 form-recall knowledge. They will not describe the learning trajectory of any particular Spanish, German, or Chinese learner of English, but they do provide useful information about how *groups* of learners from these L1s develop their productive vocabulary knowledge. As such, they have many potential pedagogic applications, as will be seen in the next chapter.

CHAPTER 10
ACCESSING AND USING THE KVL

This chapter will discuss how the KVL can be usefully employed. Just as importantly, we describe the caveats which users should be aware of, and how *not* to use the lists.

10.1 Accessing the KVL

The KVL is available online on this British Council webpage:

**www.britishcouncil.org/exam/aptis/aptis-expertise/
knowledge-based-vocabulary-lists-kvl**

Users should always check the British Council website for the current version. The first version of all three lists is KVL Version 1.00 (1 February 2022).

The main list for each language is presented in Excel spreadsheets named:

- *KVL-Spanish*
- *KVL-German*
- *KVL-Chinese*

Each spreadsheet contains information about the relative difficulty of the 5,000 lemmas included in the relevant list. There is another set of technical spreadsheets available for researchers with information about the lemmas' characteristics, and the design of the test items on which the knowledge rankings are based (*KVL-Spanish-Technical*, *KVL-German-Technical*, and *KVL-Chinese-Technical*). Descriptions of the columns in these technical spreadsheets are given on the second sheet labelled *Key*.

10.2 Uses of the KVL

The information presented in the KVL can be used for a range of applications. Following are some possibilities to illustrate the uses of the lists (while also pointing out certain limitations that need to be kept in mind while using them), but there will be many more.

- One main application will be informing the likelihood of ESL learners achieving form-recall mastery of vocabulary, as it can provide good predictions about the sequence in which learners achieve spelling control over a range of lemmas. This information should be useful for writing teachers, and test developers who assess writing ability.

- In selecting reading materials, it is often useful to grade the readings to match the abilities of learners. This is currently done by frequency profiles. However, corpus-based frequency counts are only a crude proxy for knowledge. Using the KVL should give a better idea of whether learners know the words in particular texts or not. While the KVL are based on form-recall tests, research shows that if words are mastered to a form-recall level, learners can typically also understand the words when they see them. This makes the KVL potentially suitable for reading-based applications.

- The sequencing of the KVL should provide a baseline for understanding which lemmas learners know. For example, if learners know many lemmas at the 1,000–1,500 level, there is good evidence that they will also know most of the other lemmas in that band, and in the 1–1,000 range as well. However, such assumptions would need to be constrained by what is known about the individual learners, as we have seen that vocabulary knowledge varies considerably in and across the language groups. While corpus-based frequency lists also give us similar information, the KVL are customised to each of the three language groups (Spanish, German, and Chinese speakers), and so take account of words which are relatively easy for each group due to cognateness.

- Because the KVL are language-specific, they can provide teachers with information about cases where lemmas are highly frequent, but less likely to be known by learners of a particular L1. That is, lemmas that learners might find unexpectedly difficult. Conversely, the lists can indicate lemmas, which though relatively infrequent, are likely to be known by learners because of L1 similarities. For example, *caramel* is a low-frequency lemma (#14,900), yet easy for German learners (#876 in knowledge ranking) because it is *karamell* in German.

- In testing, we often attempt to measure or discover which words learners know. To do this, we first need to build a pool of which words learners *might* know. Corpus-based frequency lists have typically been drawn upon to build this pool. However, as the frequency values from corpora do not predict knowledge of individual words very well, target words drawn from corpus-based frequency lists may not match learner knowledge very closely, which makes for inefficient and potentially misleading tests. Drawing on the KVL for pools of test words should give test developers a better chance of targeting the words on their tests to the level of their test-takers.

However, if the purpose of a test is to describe learner knowledge of words which the learners *need to know*, then corpus-based frequency lists may be a better source, as they describe which words occur most commonly in discourse. Thus, such lists may be more suitable for *prescriptive* testing purposes (learners need to know frequent words), while the KVL may be better for *descriptive* testing purposes (understanding the inventory of words learners already know).

- In psycholinguistic experiments, a range of factors affect the processing of vocabulary. This makes it crucial that target words are selected which are controlled in terms of the word characteristics that make the words easier-to-more difficult to process. Frequency of occurrence has been shown to be a robust word characteristic which affects processing. However, it does not account for cognateness, and so target words may be exceptionally easier or more difficult than a simple frequency of occurrence in a corpus might suggest for particular language groups. The KVL provides psycholinguists with a valuable alternative source of information about potential word knowledge/difficulty to use in building their experiments.

- Because vocabulary knowledge relates so strongly with virtually all aspects of language proficiency, vocabulary tests can be usefully employed as part of placement tests. The KVL can be used to select words of the proper difficulty for these placement tests.

- The KVL may also be of value in human-to-machine communication where we increasingly find automated dialogue systems in use, e.g., in automated computer, phone, or car systems. Where a user's first language is known, then communication can be tailored by including vocabulary that is likely to be known to that user.

- Ultimately, it is probably most useful for teachers, materials writers, syllabus designers, and test developers to use both KVL and corpus-based frequency lists in conjunction, as long as they understand the strengths and limitations of each type of list.

CHAPTER 11

FURTHER RESEARCH DIRECTIONS

There are several opportunities for further research that can enhance the usefulness of the KVL, increasing their potential as a valuable resource for ESL practitioners. Interested researchers are invited to pursue the ideas suggested, or other directions that they think would be beneficial or interesting.

11.1 Investigating whether learners from other languages follow the KVL sequencing, and the compilation of additional Knowledge-based Vocabulary Lists for other languages

One of the main limitations of the KVL is that they are language-specific lists. We found that sequences for the three languages did not correspond very well. In some ways, this is not surprising, as we chose three quite different languages to work with. It is possible that languages which are more similar might follow comparable KVL sequencing. For example, might speakers of Romance languages (e.g., French or Portuguese) follow the Spanish sequencing relatively closely? Or speakers of Germanic languages (e.g., Swedish or Dutch) follow the German sequencing? To explore this possibility, learners from alternative languages could be tested on a large sample of lemmas from the most relevant KVL, to determine whether their sequencing is similar to the KVL sequencing. The learners would need to be tested with the same form-recall format as used in the *Vocabulary Challenge*, ideally using translations of the actual items used on the test. If the sequencing is found to be similar, it might be possible to use the existing KVL for the new language group, either intact, or with some revision. If the sequencing is not similar, that would indicate that a new list needs to be compiled for the new language.

Hopefully, the detailed methodological descriptions in this monograph will enable researchers to replicate this research for ESL learner groups from other L1 backgrounds. To make the additional KVL comparable, the same methodology would need to be used in their creation. It is probably best to use our materials as a basis for building the new KVL tests, e.g., using the current KVL example sentences as the basis for translation would ensure maximum uniformity between various KVL tests. The test items are given in the *KVL-Technical* spreadsheets on the British Council website. Similarly, the same procedure should be followed. Once further lists are developed, comparisons between these lists should supply many answers to questions concerning the learning similarities/differences of speakers of other languages.

Researchers interested in developing additional KVL should be aware that the item-writing process (i.e., deciding on the translations and creating the example sentences) was not as straightforward as we expected. It may be better to first develop English example sentences for each lemma, which clearly show its meaning and are in the correct tense (e.g., past tense, present tense) and correct derivative form. Once these are developed, they can be translated into the prompt language. This would hopefully avoid some of the issues we had with inappropriate prompts, which later had to be rectified. However, translators/item writers will still need some flexibility so that the cultural context of the individual language translations can be utilised when appropriate. In addition, the initial piloting should carefully consider the best way to handle cognates (if applicable) in the prompts.

11.2 Determining whether the KVL also describe the sequence of acquisition for other levels of mastery

We have been conservative and interpreted the form-recall test format used in the *Vocabulary Challenge* to indicate the ability to spell a lemma correctly if its meaning is known. Based on other research (e.g., Laufer & Goldstein, 2004; Laufer et al., 2004), we also feel confident assuming that success on the test additionally implies the ability to understand a lemma when read in a text. It is possible, however, that the format may indicate a greater degree of mastery than this. For example, it is very likely that at least some of the learners who were able to answer the form-recall test items could also use the lemmas accurately and appropriately in their free writing. The question is, however, what percentage could do this? If a very large percentage, then the KVL may also be interpreted as indicating fuller productive written knowledge.

In order to explore this, we could prepare a series of writing tasks designed to encourage the use of a set of target lemmas extracted from the relevant KVL. These lemmas could then be tested with a group of learners, who would also respond to the writing tasks. Comparison between accurate use of the lemmas and accurate responses to test items could then be made. The results would indicate whether the approach does, in fact, indicate fuller productive knowledge. Similarly, the lemmas could be tested in the participants' speaking, as it would be very useful to know whether the KVL sequence also indicates oral ability. Finally, the participants could be tested for their ability to understand the lemmas in reading and listening passages, to directly explore whether the assumption (based on implication scale research) is valid that the test also indicates this.

This research strand would do much to clarify how the KVL sequencing (based on a single type of test) can be interpreted in terms of the level(s) of knowledge indicated.

11.3 Exploring the effect of cognates on the KVL sequencing in more depth

Our research has shown that cognates have a strong effect on the sequencing of lemmas at the form-recall level of mastery. However, our analysis was necessarily limited in scope. The KVL database has test score information on a large number of cognates which may provide answers to many further interesting cognate-related questions. Researchers interested in this area may wish to avail themselves of this resource.

Chapter 8 discussed how cognateness should not necessarily be seen as an easy or automatic route to an English written word form, though it should be noted that we only investigated two cognate languages, Spanish and German. It would be interesting to study other cognate languages to determine how easy it is for their speakers to utilise their L1 cognates when learning L2 English vocabulary.

11.4 Exploring the degree to which partial knowledge gives insights into the mastery of spelling

Our criterion for 'correctness' on the *Vocabulary Challenge* was the ability to spell the target lemmas accurately. Near misses were counted as incorrect (e.g., *okey* for the lemma *okay*). We chose the criterion largely because we wanted to use a measure closer to the productive/advanced end of the vocabulary knowledge continuum, so that respondents answering correctly could be assumed to know the lemmas reasonably well. However, we realised this would not capture partial knowledge below this criterion (e.g., *okey*). An interesting research direction would be to explore this partial knowledge. As part of our data collection, we have a record of all the responses to each of the 7,679 lemmas tested in the *Vocabulary Challenge*, including both correct and incorrect responses. It would be possible to interrogate the incorrect responses to determine the degree of partial knowledge which exists on the road to fully correct spelling. For example, many respondents from all three language groups answered *lose* or *lost* for the target lemma *loss*, which suggests they might have known the form-meaning link for the base verb *lose* but lacked the derivational knowledge that the noun derivative form is *loss*. Similarly, 15% of Spanish respondents' errors for *particularly* were spelling errors, even though those respondents did seem to know the word they were unsuccessfully trying to spell. Tracking the nature of the errors on the *Vocabulary Challenge* might provide interesting insights into the development nature of spelling mastery.

Researchers interested in this area can contact the British Council's Assessment Research Group for information on how to apply for access to the appropriate datasets.

11.5 Exploring how individual differences affect the KVL sequencing of lemmas

Biodata was collected from each participant before they took the *Vocabulary Challenge*. Originally, we envisioned a fairly substantial biodata section, but then had to minimise the number of questions to avoid the risk of respondents quitting the test at the outset. The final list comprised three questions: the respondent's age (10-years-old or less, 11–16, 17–23, 24 years or more); the number of years they had studied English (3 years or less, 4–6, 7–10, 10 years or more); and the number of hours a week they used English, including reading, talking, watching television, or using social networks, the Internet, or video games (Never, 1–2 hours, 3–4, 5 hours or more). Information about L1 was assumed, based on the language in which participants chose to take the quiz. Given our deadlines and constraints, we were not able to explore this biodata. However, it is highly likely that learner characteristics including age, L2 proficiency, intrinsic and extrinsic motivation to learn the language, and many others will have a significant impact on their knowledge of vocabulary. The degree to which learner characteristics affect vocabulary knowledge is an important question that interested researchers are encouraged to investigate. The biodata that we have collected might be useful to begin such an investigation. It is included in the technical datasheets. Needless to say, although we have created the knowledge KVL for Chinese, German, and Spanish learners of English, we certainly do not consider each group to be homogeneous in their knowledge of vocabulary. As the results show, there is a great deal of variation at the individual level.

11.6 How to use the KVL in learning system development

The concept of the comprehensive learning system (O'Sullivan, 2020) proposes that all elements must be in alignment if the system is to be successful. The three elements are outlined below.

1. Curriculum
   a. Formal (school-based)
   b. Informal (apps, television, music, films, etc.)
2. Delivery
   a. Teacher (selection, training, professional development, evaluation, etc.)
   b. Materials (textbooks, apps, teacher-devised, etc.)
   c. Physical space (school and classroom design)
3. Assessment
   a. Summative (judgemental)
   b. Formative (developmental)

Traditionally, educators use existing word lists when developing their language learning systems. While this approach has offered acceptable results for global standardised tests and materials that are, in effect, population- and context-agnostic (i.e., they assume that learners form a single homogeneous population), the findings from the KVL project suggest that this may not be appropriate for local system development. These 'local' systems would, it appears, benefit from a locally-specific word list. The three lists generated by the KVL project offer such a possibility for Chinese, Spanish, and German.

We feel that the lists can be used in the development of all three main elements, contributing to the curriculum, to the delivery systems and, of course, to the assessment systems. However, research is needed into the actual application of the KVL within the various elements of the learning system. Examples of this research might include the following areas:

- Identification of achievement in terms of lemmas appropriate to the various stages of the learning system. This requires the development of lexical standards for use across a broad learning system.

- Researching the link (or lack of a link) between current learning materials and the local KVL to inform future materials development.
- Exploration of the re-specification of language tests in terms of the language of the input texts and instructions.
- Evaluation of the expectations of both productive and receptive skills in local tests. Should we be looking to local KVL when it comes to assessing vocabulary usage and understanding? This also has implications for the training of AI-driven auto-scoring engines – should these be trained on locally appropriate word lists?
- Application to the area of English as a Medium of Instruction (EMI). Clearly, it is not a level playing field where learners from different backgrounds are expected to share a similar knowledge of vocabulary.

11.7 In summary . . .

In this final chapter, we have begun to consider how the KVL can contribute to research and practice in the development and understanding of language learning systems. The ideas presented here are limited by our experiences and research interests and are not in any way meant to restrict the scope of research on this approach to vocabulary list development and how the lists can be used.

APPENDIX 1

INSTRUCTIONS TO THE ITEM WRITERS

In this appendix, we reproduce the letter sent to all item writers in order to make it very clear how they were instructed to proceed with their task.

Hello Item Writers,

You will be translating English target words into Spanish/Chinese/German, and then providing a sentence context which further illustrates the meaning and usage of the target word. So that you understand how we will use your translations, they will be fit into the following test format (using Spanish as the example L1 language):

1. saber Hay que <u>saber</u> leer.

k__ __ __

     Siguiente

[English]

1. know You have to <u>know</u> how to read.

k__ __ __

     Next

The first part of the test item gives the Spanish translation of *know*, which is 'saber'. Then a simple sentence follows which helps to show that meaning sense of 'saber' in context, with the target word translation underlined. From this translation+sentence prompt, the respondents must understand that the English word we are looking for is *know*. Respondents will then spell the word in the blanks if they know it (<u>n</u>+<u>o</u>+<u>w</u>).

Key task

Therefore, your key task to create prompts which narrow down the possible answer to only the target word. With polysemy and multiple meaning senses, this is not always easy, which is why we added the context sentence, which should help you clarify the meaning (and English word) being prompted. We have also added the initial letter of the English word ('k' in this example), and the number of blanks (3 in this example) to further constrain the possible answers down to only the target word. We trust you to write clear, unambiguous translations and sentences, and give you some leeway on how to do this. In general, shorter, simpler sentences, are best, but if you need a longer sentence (or even two) to create the right prompt, then do it. Likewise, choose the method of translation that works best for that particular target word. If it is a translation equivalent, great. If a word requires a phrase or definition, then do that. Different target words will probably benefit from different approaches. In general though, as with the sentences, shorter and simpler is preferable if possible. But the overriding consideration is creating the best prompt which guides the respondents to the target English word.

Polysemy

Many English target words have multiple meanings (polysemy/homonymy). We want the three L1 tests (Spanish/Chinese/German) to be equivalent, and so it is essential that the three tests measure the same meaning sense for the target words. But which meaning sense to use? It makes sense to measure knowledge of the most common meaning sense, which is the one respondents are most likely to know and use. To decide which of the meaning senses is the most frequent, we will use the expedient of referring to learner's dictionaries, which typically have meaning senses listed in frequency order. We will primarily use two in particular: the *MacMillan English Dictionary for Advanced Learners* (2007) and the *Oxford Advanced Learner's Dictionary* (www.oxfordlearnersdictionaries.com/about/). You may also want to refer to the *Cambridge Online Dictionary* (https://dictionary.cambridge.org/). Although they may define a meaning sense slightly differently, they will typically agree on the primary meaning sense of a target word.

However, occasionally there will be a mismatch between the dictionaries, with different meaning senses being listed first. In these cases, we will refer to corpus evidence to decide which meaning sense to go with. We will use the COCA corpus on the BYU website (www.english-corpora.org/coca/). Experience to date indicates it becomes clear very quickly which meaning sense is more frequent. This is the one we will use. We can refer to the corpus in two ways. Probably the fastest and easiest is for you to refer to the COCA yourself and make the decision. (Let me know if you do not know how to use the COCA.) However, I can do the lookup for you if you wish. If there is any uncertainty, let me know, and I will make the final decision.

Again, all item writers need to use the same meaning sense, so once one translator has made the decision on 'mismatched' meaning senses, the other item writers need to use the same sense. The mechanism we will use to coordinate the translations across languages is the following. We will use a common 'Google Docs' *Disputed Spreadsheet* into which we can all enter the decisions on mismatched senses. Our Chinese translator (Xiaofan Xu) created it, so you will need to go the spreadsheet and request access to it (click on the View Only tab which brings up a box in which you ask for access). After the request, Xiaofan will grant access. All item writers will have access and will be able to make changes to the spreadsheet from online, and it will keep being the most updated version. We can all see who made what changes to which item and comment on the changes if necessary. I will also have access, for items I need to arbitrate upon (or just to do the corpus analysis). The default setting does not notify us when changes to the document are made. You might want to receive notice of any changes, go to the 'Tools' in the toolbar and select 'Notification Rules'. In this way, you can receive instant or daily notification of any changes recently made to the document.

You will enter the English target word, the contending two meaning senses, and then the one you decided upon based on corpus evidence. In practice, the item writer who is furthest down the list will be making most of the decisions, and the other item writers will merely use these decisions in their translations, which saves them time by not having to look in the COCA themselves.

Cognates

Although not so pertinent for Chinese translations, for German, and especially Spanish, we need to think about cognates. After piloting, we found the need to avoid respondents merely typing in the L1 cognate word if it is spelled the same (or almost the same) as the English target word (e.g., English *bus* = Spanish *autobús*) and getting credit for knowing the English word even though they may not. We developed some guidelines to follow to avoid this, although please remember they take second place to Key Task idea above.

1. If there is a one-word equivalent translation that expresses the meaning perfectly on its own, this is the preferred option (e.g., *cuerpo = body*)
2. If there are two words that express the same meaning, and one is a cognate, use the non-cognate word (e.g., *alojar* instead of *acomodar* = accommodate).
3. If there is only one word that expresses the particular meaning, and this word is a cognate, it is better to use a definition (e.g., *coast* = Orilla del mar, de un río, de un lago, etc., y tierra que está cerca de ella). Also, if that definition would lead to another word that starts by the same letter and is very similar in meaning but is not the word form we want to retrieve (e.g., *destruction* for *devastation*), then specify not to use that misleading word ('NOT *destruction*').

4. If two words are needed to capture the specific meaning (i.e., one word only would be misleading or not informative enough), then use both words (e.g., *chica, niña = girl*).

5. If more information than two words are needed to capture the specific meaning and retrieve the right word form, then use a definition. There might be cases where the definition has to be extended to make word form clear: e.g., *polar*: relating to the very cold regions in the north or south parts of the world. The earth rotates around the axes located in these regions.

Translations and sentences

The purpose of the sentences is to further clarify the meaning and so point to the English word we want. You can get example sentences from a number of sources. One is (https://tatoeba.org/eng/), a website that gives sentences in several languages once a word has been specified. For example, you could insert a Spanish word like *saber*, and get a sentence like *Hay que saber leer*. Because this site is open-access, you can use these sentences 'word-for-word' if you like, but you will probably want to adopt the sentences somewhat to make them simple and straightforward, but of course, the key issue is to make the sentences point to the English target word.

You can also find sentences in learner dictionaries or by doing a Google search. But if you use sentences from these sources, you need to adapt them slightly before translating so that they are not exactly the same as the originals (because of copyright issues).

Sometimes to make the meaning clear, you might have to add a little extra information. For example, for the word *account* (verb), it has to be followed by *for*, and the Chinese translator Xiaofan gave this information in the translation. This was sensible to make the verb meaning of *account* clear, but we always need to remember that the respondents need to write just the word (e.g., *account*) in the blanks on the test. So they should not be led by the prompt into thinking that they should also include words like *for*.

We have already started with Chinese translations, and some issues have come up. Our counting unit is the lemma (headword and its inflections). This means that the most frequent/common usage of the that lemma should be used, and not necessarily its 'base' or 'stem' form. For example, the word *affair*. In singular, it is an illicit romantic relationship. But much more frequent is plural *affairs*, which is used in all sorts of manner, 'settle one's affairs', or 'political affairs are a mess'. Thus, we want to define this second more common meaning sense.

Very occasionally, there are two near synonyms which have the same first letter and the same number of letters. For example, say the target word is *allege*, with a translated definition something like 'to say that someone has done something illegal or wrong without giving proof'. The respondent could very rightly answer with *assert*. In these cases, we need to explicitly state in the prompt that it is not *assert*. You can do this with an addition to the translation stating 'The answer is NOT assert'.

Spreadsheet
You will be given an Excel spreadsheet with all 7,762 English lemmas on it in one column. There are other columns with information about the words, most of which are unimportant to you. The columns which are important to you include:

Lemma: This is the target word you are translating.

Word class: This is the word class of the lemma you are translating. It is essential you translate this word class, as in many cases the same lemma form is on the list in several word classes. For example, *abuse* is listed as two separate entries, one as a noun and one as a verb. Each will need to be translated separately for its own word class, with sentences which make that particular word class clear.

Chinese/Spanish/German translation: Here is the column into which you insert the translation of the English target word. You can type it in or cut and paste if you like. You know much better than I do the best sources for your translations. Obvious places are the two learner dictionaries we are consulting for the primary meaning sense (Macmillan and Oxford). But sometimes, you might want other input, so feel free to use other sources like Webster, or online dictionaries, translators, or other. In the end, we are trusting you to produce a good translation for our purpose, but where it originally comes from is not so important to us (you might even create it yourself). But please make sure there are **no errors** (spelling or other), as your entry will not be proofread and will be automatically inserted 'as is' into our online test platform.

Chinese/Spanish/German sentence: Here is the column into which you insert the context sentence, with the translation of the English target word underlined. As with the translation above, please make sure there are **no errors** (spelling, grammar, punctuation, etc.). They will not be proofread. Also, please underline the target word translation in your context sentences, as this will help us check that the online program is underlining correctly (see Highlight column below).

<u>Highlight:</u> Since the sentences will be uploaded into our online test platform automatically, the system needs to know what words to underline as the translation. (Although in your sentences, you will underline the translation of the target word, the computer cannot read this easily, and so we need a separate column which explicitly instructs the computer what to underline. But having you underline the translations in your sentences allows us to manually check if the system is working based on the Highlight column.) For example, if the sentence were in English and the target word was *dog*, then the sentence would look like 'The <u>dog</u> chased the cat around the tree'. You give the information 'dog' in this Highlight column, telling the computer to underline *dog*. If the rendering in the sentence is exactly the same as in the translation (as I expect will be the case for most words), then simply copy and paste the translation into the Highlight column.

But sometimes, the rendering in the sentence might include more information than in the translation to make the meaning clear. For example, in order to make an informative and natural sentence, you might need to insert some words between components of the translation. For example, if the target meaning was 'big animal' then it might be necessary to use some words between definition words:

The <u>big</u> hairy <u>animal</u> ate the deer.

In this case, in the Highlight column, we need to show the computer what to highlight and what not to highlight. In this case, write the first and last words to be highlighted, then insert an asterisk (*) for anything in between that should not be highlighted:

big * animal

Another example with Japanese would look like this.

English: big dog
Translation Japanese: 大きな犬
Sentence: 今日は、<u>大きな犬</u>がいる。
Highlight: 大きな犬

So in this case, the Highlight column simply has the translation.

But here is a sentence with something between the translated word:

English: big dog
Translation Japanese: 大きな犬
Sentence: 今日は、<u>大きな太っている犬</u>がいる。
Highlight: 大きな＊犬

So in the Highlight column, you need to show where the underlining starts and stops. Then show what information in the middle should not be highlighted with an asterisk (*). In the case above, the * replaces 太っている.

<u>Comment:</u> This column is for anything you think we might need to be aware of. But since you will be liaising with me and resolving entries before they are entered and finalized, I expect this column to be nearly empty.

The Excel spreadsheet is already saved in **.xlsx format**, but make sure that this does not accidentally change. Every spreadsheet needs to be in .xslx format, as this format handles Chinese characters and diacritic markings. This means you will need to use a version of Excel 2010 or more current.

Make sure you always update the Excel spreadsheet with the date you are working. (That is, a new name for every day you work on it: *Target Words – German November 5*). Also, don't forget to **back-up** your files very regularly!

This is a lot of information, but I tried to set out everything clearly and in detail. Before you start working, I need to have a Skype session with you just to make sure you understand everything completely and are comfortable before you set off in earnest. I think that once you do a few words, everything will become very familiar and quite second nature. I will be available via email most days, and we can Skype if this is useful. You have a lot of words to translate, and I want to facilitate the process as much as possible. I am looking forward to working with you.

Best wishes, Norbert

APPENDIX 2

LIST OF OFFENSIVE WORDS REMOVED

The following words were removed from the list after the British Council vetting process.

- abortion
- alien (noun)
- alien (adjective)
- anal
- ass
- bomber
- cocaine
- condom
- erection
- erotic
- idiot
- marijuana
- masturbate
- masturbation
- orgasm
- penis
- pornographic
- pornography
- prostitute
- prostitution
- rape
- sexual
- sexuality
- sexually
- stripper
- vagina
- virgin
- virginity

APPENDIX 3

SCREENSHOTS FROM THE VOCABULARY CHALLENGE WEBSITE

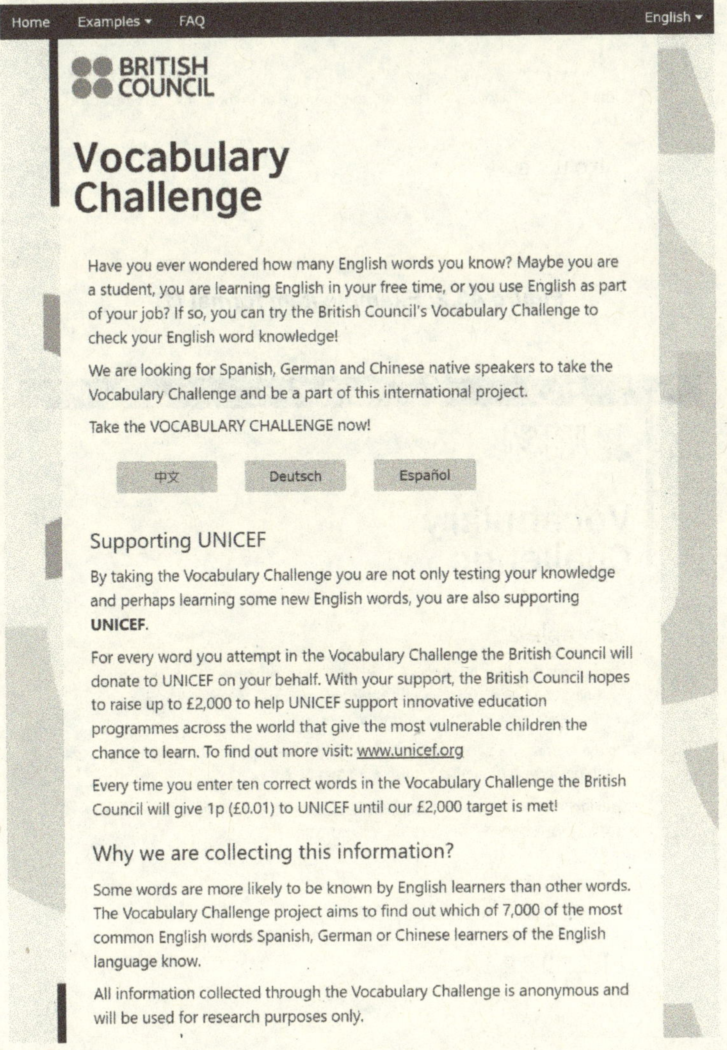

Figure A3.1: Vocabulary Challenge home page welcome message

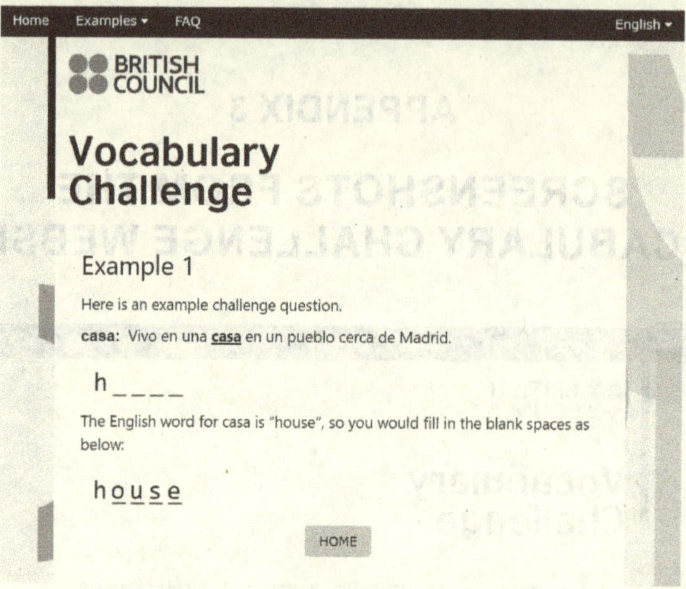

Figure A3.2: Example item format (1)

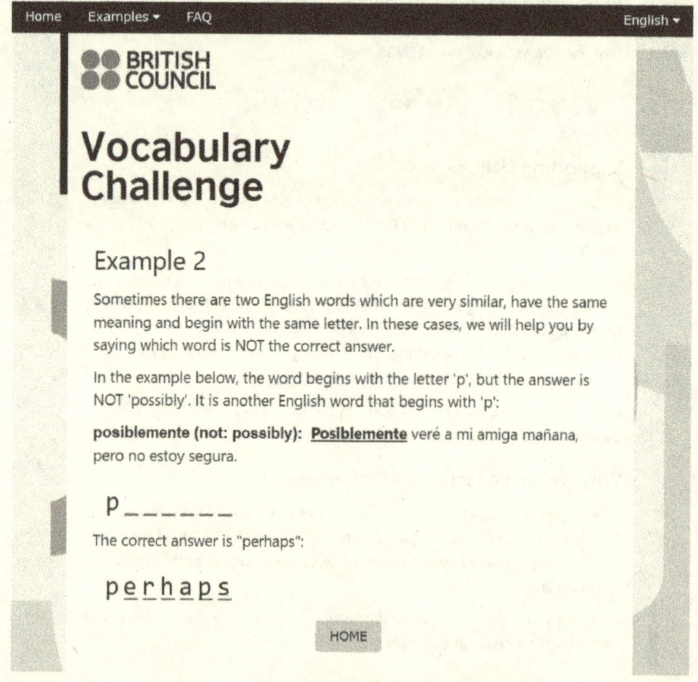

Figure A3.3: Example item format (2)

FREQUENTLY ASKED QUESTIONS

Who can take the Vocabulary Challenge?

To take the Vocabulary Challenge, you must be a native speaker of Chinese, German or Spanish.

You must be an English language learner at any stage. This could mean you are learning English at school or at university, or through a tutor or online.

You may also be a user of English, where you use English as part of your job, with family or friends, or online.

You can be any age and in any stage of education or employment.

How can I participate?

The Vocabulary Challenge is an online activity that can be accessed on smartphones, tablet computers, laptops, and desktop computers.

You can access Vocabulary challenge using any of the latest browsers, including Chrome, Firefox, Internet Explorer, and Edge.

Where should I take the Vocabulary Challenge?

The Vocabulary Challenge is designed to be taken anywhere that you can access the internet.

You can participate at home, in a library or café, as you travel or as part of a classroom activity.

Teachers may want to use the Vocabulary Challenge as an educational tool, either taken in the classroom, or set as an extra-curricular activity leading to discussions in class.

How long is the Vocabulary Challenge?

The Vocabulary Challenge is taken in rounds, each containing 10 words.

Each round can be taken at your own pace.

At the end of each round you will be given an option to continue and attempt another 10 words or end your session.

The Vocabulary Challenge shows different words each time you take it, so you can always return at another time and take the challenge again.

What type of feedback can I expect?

At the end of every round of the Vocabulary Challenge, you will be shown your score, indicating how many words you answered correctly, the correct word and spelling for any words you didn't attempt or got wrong.

You will be given an overall score when you decide to end the Vocabulary Challenge, with an option to share that score on social media.

Why are you asking for background information before I take the Vocabulary Challenge?

As well as giving you an opportunity to put your English language learning to the test, your results will provide valuable information about which words in English are easy or difficult for learners.

By asking you three short questions about your age, how long you've studied English, and how often you use English, we hope to understand more about the context in which people learn different words.

We ask a question regarding your preference for taking the Vocabulary Challenge in British or American English to make your experience as natural as possible.

All the information you provide will be anonymous and used for research purposes only.

How am I supporting UNICEF by taking the Vocabulary Challenge and will it cost me any money?

By taking part in the Vocabulary Challenge you are helping the British Council to donate to the global children's charity, UNICEF.

You will not be charged to take part in the Vocabulary Challenge and you will not have to donate to UNICEF yourself.

The British Council will donate 1p (£0.01) to UNICEF every time ten correct words are entered until we meet our £2,000 target.

What if I experience a technical problem when taking the Vocabulary Challenge?

If you experience any issues with the Vocabulary Challenge website please contact the help desk: VocabularyChallenge@britishcouncil.org

Figure A3.4: Frequently asked questions and answers (FAQs)

Bienvenido al Vocabulary Challenge.

Esta versión está diseñada para hablantes nativos de español.

Queremos conocer un poco más sobre ti. Toda la información que ingreses será anónima y se utilizará únicamente con fines de investigación.

1. ¿Cuál es tu edad en años?
○ 10 o menos   ○ 11-16   ○ 17-23   ○ 24 o más

2. ¿Durante cuántos años has estudiado inglés?
○ 3 o menos   ○ 4-6   ○ 7-9   ○ 10 o más

3. ¿Cuántas horas a la semana usas el inglés?
(Esto puede incluir leer, hablar, ver televisión o usar las redes sociales, Internet o videojuegos.)
○ Nunca   ○ 1-2   ○ 3-4   ○ 5 o más

4. Algunas palabras se escriben de manera diferente en inglés americano o inglés británico. Mira los ejemplos a continuación para saber qué ortografía usas más cómodamente.

Inglés americano	Inglés británico
Agonize	Agonise
Liter	Litre
Savor	Savour
Analog	Analogue

¿Te gustaría tomar el Vocabulary Challenge en inglés americano o inglés británico?

○ Inglés americano   ○ Inglés británico

Siguiente

Figure A3.5: Background questionnaire (Spanish language version)

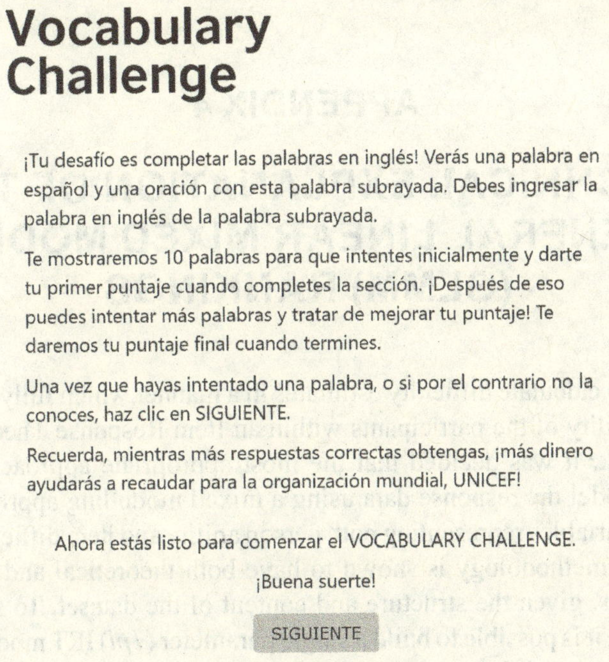

Vocabulary Challenge

¡Tu desafío es completar las palabras en inglés! Verás una palabra en español y una oración con esta palabra subrayada. Debes ingresar la palabra en inglés de la palabra subrayada.

Te mostraremos 10 palabras para que intentes inicialmente y darte tu primer puntaje cuando completes la sección. ¡Después de eso puedes intentar más palabras y tratar de mejorar tu puntaje! Te daremos tu puntaje final cuando termines.

Una vez que hayas intentado una palabra, o si por el contrario no la conoces, haz clic en SIGUIENTE.

Recuerda, mientras más respuestas correctas obtengas, ¡más dinero ayudarás a recaudar para la organización mundial, UNICEF!

Ahora estás listo para comenzar el VOCABULARY CHALLENGE.

¡Buena suerte!

SIGUIENTE

Figure A3.6: Instructions and launch page (Spanish language version)

¡Felicidades, has terminado el VOCABULARY CHALLENGE!

Tu puntaje final es 5/10.

¡Comparte tu puntuación en las redes sociales y desafía a tus amigos!

"Acabo de completar el VOCABULARY CHALLENGE. Mi puntaje fue 5/10."

Cada vez que tomes el Vocabulary Challenge, se te darán nuevas palabras para intentarlo. ¡Así que puedes tomar el desafío tantas veces como quieras!

Gracias por ser parte del **VOCABULARY CHALLENGE**!

SIGUIENTE

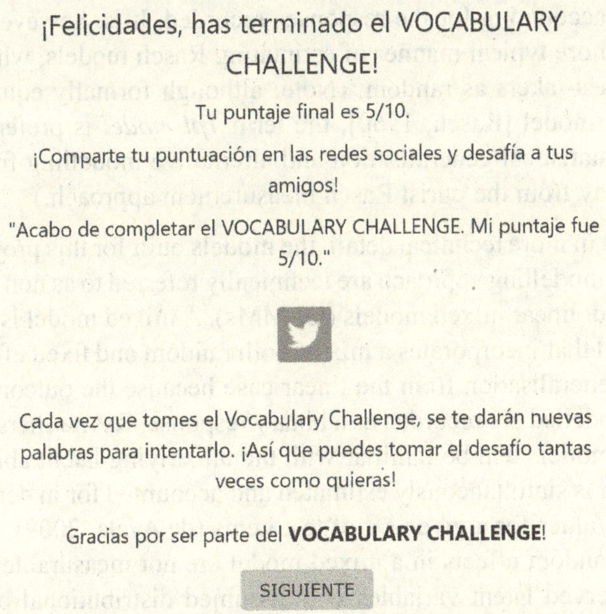

Figure A3.7: Results page (Spanish language version)

APPENDIX 4

TECHNICAL EXPLANATION OF THE GENERAL LINEAR MIXED MODEL (GLMM) RANKINGS

In order to calculate difficulty estimates in a manner which fully accounts for the ability of the participants within an Item Response Theory (IRT) framework, it was decided that the most appropriate approach to take was to model the response data using a mixed modelling approach with random variables representing both person ability and item difficulty. This statistical methodology is shown to have both theoretical and practical advantages, given the structure and content of the dataset. To start with the theory, it is possible to build a single parameter (*1pl*) IRT model within the mixed model framework, and to extend it to treat both test-takers and items as representing a random draw from a wider population (De Boeck, 2008; De Boeck et al., 2011). This, we argue, is a more accurate means of accounting for the responses recorded. It is, however, distinct from the more typical manner of estimating Rasch models, which treats only the test-takers as random. (Note: although formally equivalent to the Rasch model [Rasch, 1960], the term *1pl model* is preferred here, since the statistical generalisation and alternative modelling framework moves away from the purist Rasch measurement approach.)

To explain in more technical detail, the models built for this project using the mixed modelling approach are technically referred to as non-linear, or generalised, linear mixed models (GLMMs). A mixed model is a regression model that incorporates a mix of both random and fixed effects, and this is a generalisation from the linear case because the outcomes (item scores) modelled are recorded as a binary response. Researchers working with IRT models will be familiar with the underlying latent ability variable which is simultaneously estimated and accounted for in deriving the difficulty values for a given set of test items (de Ayala, 2009). In a similar way, random effects in a mixed model are not measurable qualities but unobserved latent variables with assumed distributional properties (Bates, 2010), i.e., commensurate with the latent variable in a 1pl model estimated using marginal maximum likelihood (Rijmen et al., 2003). In a typical 1pl IRT model, meanwhile, the difficulty estimates are commensurate with fixed effects of a mixed model, i.e., observed information which has a predicted relationship with the outcome. The difficulty estimates do not have assumed distributional properties and are considered independent from one another.

Within this GLMM framework as employed for analysing the response data in the KVL project, it was reasonably straightforward to move to the point of treating each test item as a draw from a wider population of all possible items, in addition to treating each participant as randomly selected from a wider population of English language learners from the same L1 background. In other words, to move from including a single latent variable in the model representing ability, to including two latent variables in the model, representing both ability and difficulty. These models are referred to by some researchers as *random-item IRT models* (De Boeck et al., 2011; Janssen et al., 2004). For the *Vocabulary Challenge*, this step was considered relevant, and in fact necessary, since each learner is presented with a (stratified) random sample of all possible test items when they sit down to take the Challenge. The statistical model used here, therefore, accounts more closely for the process of item allocation that occurred during the data collection in the *Vocabulary Challenge*.

In terms of the practicalities, the data could be read in long-format – i.e., each row of data representing an interaction between an individual testtaker (identified by a unique ID code) and an individual test item (again with a unique identifier). Each of these rows gives a positive piece of information about whether a given test-taker got a given item correct or incorrect, rather than accounting for a huge amount of structural missingness in a sparsely populated short-format dataset. The data was modelled using the package *lme4* (Bates et al., 2015) in the statistical software *R* (R Core Team, 2020). *lme4* is a flexible package which can handle mixed models with crossed random effects, as per the case of this data, which has non-nested random effects, i.e., *Vocabulary Challenge* items can be allocated to any and all participants in the dataset (Baayen et al., 2008).

Although it is not technically possible to derive a set of numbers called 'difficulty estimates' from the GLMMs built for this project, it is nonetheless possible to estimate a set of numeric values against each grouping factor of a random effect (in other words, for each person and each item) to indicate their relationship with the probability of a correct answer being given. While Bates (2010) concedes that it can be useful to think of them as estimates, technically they are the point at which conditional density is maximised (Bates, 2010, p. 22). These values are therefore most accurately referred to as 'conditional modes'. Additionally, because of the manner in which these are estimated, they indicate item 'easiness' as opposed to difficulty. Essentially, the only difference is that in a GLMM-specified 1pl IRT model, a positive increase in the item parameter estimate is associated with the greater probability of a correct response, while the reverse is true in traditional IRT estimation.

For the practical purposes of the KVL project, the easiness values can be interpreted as indicating the ranked probability of the learners in the target populations knowing each lemma on the candidate list. It is also possible to derive an indication of the level of precision given by these insights, by extracting the standard deviations of these conditional modes from the model (see Chapter 6). In other words, the analyses allow us to create language-specific lists which place 5,000 lemmas in the order of relative likelihood of being known by Spanish-, Chinese-, and German-speaking learners, from the lemma most likely to be known (e.g., Spanish #1: *dance*) to the 5,000th most likely to be known (Spanish #5,000: *flip*).

TECHNICAL EXPLANATION OF THE PRECISION OF THE GLMM RANKINGS

The intercept values (the point estimate we use to represent easiness in the model) assigned to each of the lemmas by the GLMM are associated with a certain degree of error. This is illustrated in Figures A5.1–A5.3, which show the 95% prediction intervals for these values (Bates, 2010, pp. 23–24). These figures show a considerable amount of information regarding the error/precision of the item 'easiness' estimates. What is notable – and totally expected from a statistical perspective – is that there is a greater degree of precision of estimates for those items that fall in the middle range of the spectrum (i.e., the range lines are shorter, showing less error). For items that are very difficult (left-hand side of the figures) and very easy (right-hand side of the figures), we see much longer lines, indicating more error and lower degrees of precision. In other words, those lemmas that fall at the extremes, i.e., those that are considerably easier or more difficult than average, are associated with a greater degree of uncertainty in their estimation. The statistical reason is that there is less information available from which to estimate the item easiness or difficulty when the major share of responses are either correct (for the easiest items) or incorrect (for the most difficult items). For example, in Figure A5.1, the four noticeably longer lines at the extreme right-hand top of the plot are for the lemmas which all Spanish respondents got correct (*city, dance, jet, zoo*).

Each of the three L1 models displays a very similar pattern in terms of precision; however, reflective of the comparatively stronger performances on average from German respondents, there are slightly wider error bars around the points showing the very easiest items on the right-hand side of the plot for the German model in Figure A5.2 compared to the other two plots.

There is less concern about the level of imprecision of the most difficult items, as these items would not make the final lists of the best-known 5,000 lemmas anyway (e.g., Spanish: the adjectives *unchallenged* and *received*). However, the easiest items merited attention. We inspected the easiest test items to ensure they were not answered correctly merely because of some flaw in the items themselves. Our analysis (see Chapter 6) showed that best-known lemmas were generally known either because they were very common words, or because they were cognates to the respondents' L1. We found no evidence that much substantial error was being caused by flaws in the test items.

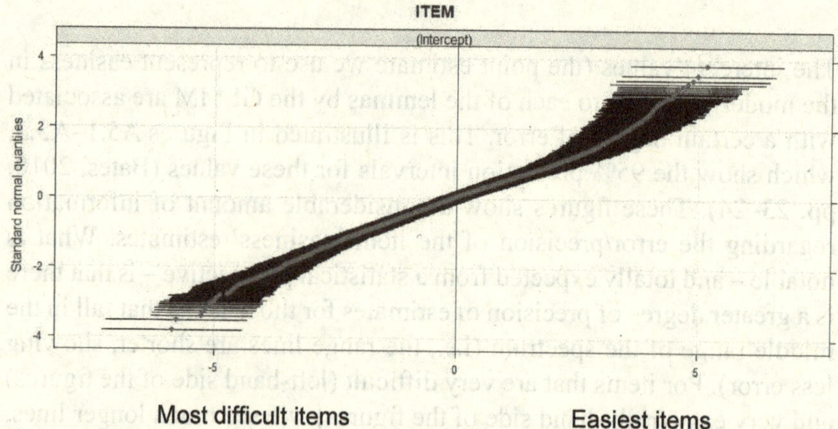

Figure A5.1: GLMM item plot – intercept estimates and associated error (Spanish)

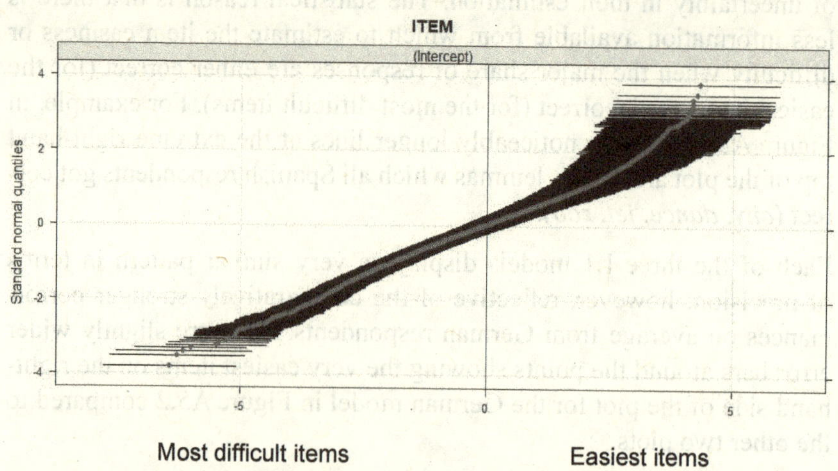

Figure A5.2: GLMM item plot – intercept estimates and associated error (German)

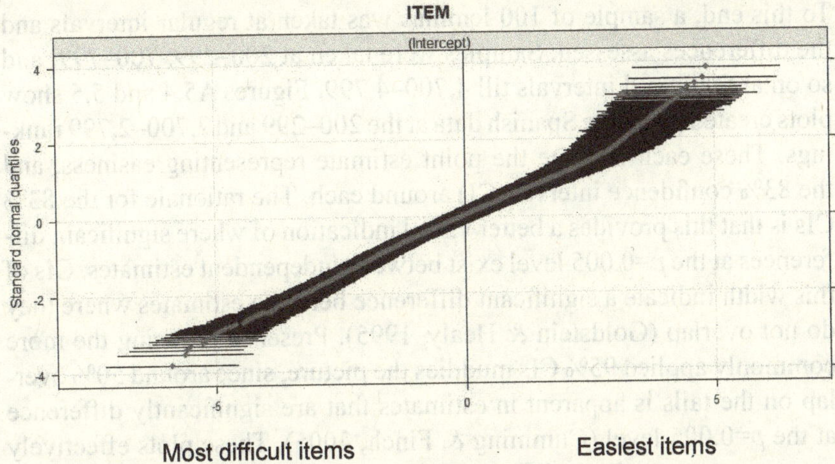

Figure A5.3: GLMM item plot – intercept estimates and associated error (Chinese)

The focal point of the KVL project was the ranking of the lemmas derived from the GLMM easiness estimates, rather than the point estimates. Inevitably, and as can be seen would be the case from Figures A5.1 to A5.3, across the full sample of lemmas there were a large number of GLMM intercept estimates that fell very close to one another, and indeed a considerable number that shared values (to the nearest three decimal places). Ultimately this meant that in creating the rank order lists, there are words that have a higher or lower rank which are not significantly more or less easy than one another as estimated by the model.

It was therefore of particular interest to find out the distance between rankings at which we could be confident of a significant difference in the easiness of two lemmas, i.e., how many lemmas on the ranking scale fall between two lemmas that are significantly different on the easiness scale. This has a practical impact on how we can interpret the rankings of the GLMMs moving forward. To investigate, we used the information described above regarding the precision of estimates from the GLMM. As can be seen from the plots in Figures A5.1 to A5.3, the slope is not linear, but rather curves more steeply at the extremes. This reflects the estimation method using a logit link function in the GLMM, and in practical terms means that there will be a greater difference between numeric estimates at the easier and more difficult ends of the scale. In order to assess how many ranks fell between significantly different estimates, we needed to account for these potential differences.

To this end, a sample of 100 lemmas was taken at regular intervals and the differences assessed. Samples were taken at 200–299; 700–799; and so on at 500-word intervals till 4,700–4,799. Figures A5.4 and 5.5 show plots created using the Spanish data at the 200–299 and 2,700–2,799 rankings. These each indicate the point estimate representing easiness, and the 83% confidence interval (CI) around each. The rationale for the 83% CIs is that this provides a better visual indication of where significant differences at the p=0.005 level exist between independent estimates. CIs of this width indicate a significant difference between estimates where they do not overlap (Goldstein & Healy, 1995). Presentation using the more commonly applied 95% CIs muddies the picture, since around 50% overlap on the tails is apparent in estimates that are significantly difference at the p=0.005 level (Cumming & Finch, 2005). These plots effectively represent a zoom-in to different ranges of Figure A5.1 (with the axes switched). It is clear that the differences between estimates for the easier items (shown in Figure A5.4) are more marked than those at the interim and more difficult end of the ranked lemmas (Figure A5.5); however the confidence bars are wider so this does not necessarily translate to narrower intervals between significantly different rankings. The number of rankings that fall between significantly different estimates at each of the sampled ranges is given in Table A5.1.

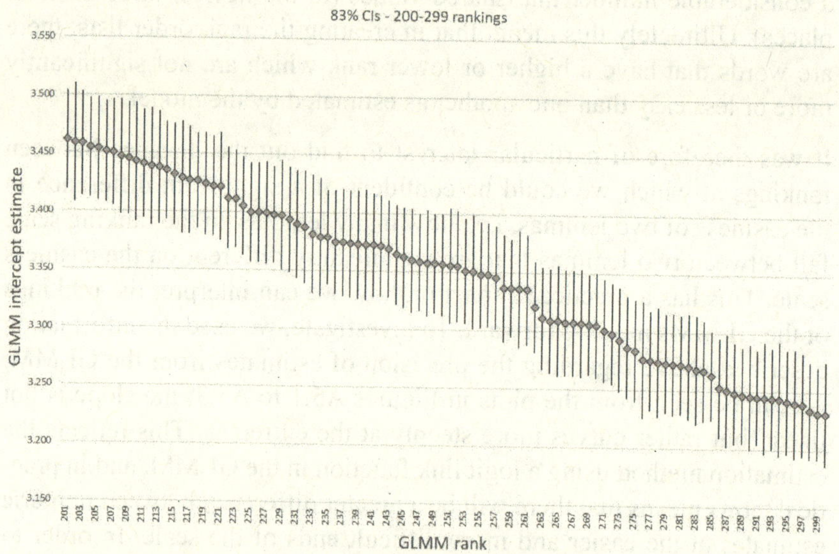

Figure A5.4: GLMM intercept estimates and 83% confidence intervals for lemmas ranked 200–299 (Spanish)

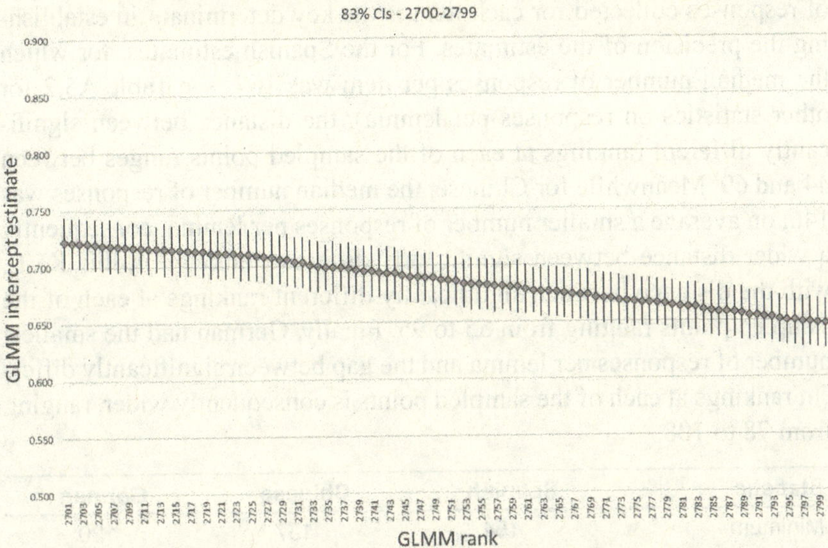

Figure A5.5: GLMM intercept estimates and 83% confidence intervals for lemmas ranked 2,700–2,799 (Spanish)

Ranking band	Number of lemmas		
	Spanish	Chinese	German
200–299	44	55	78
700–799	53	56	102
1,200–1,299	61	60	96
1,700–1,799	53	80	108
2,200–2,299	68	71	99
2,700–2,799	54	95	108
3,200–3,299	51	94	89
3,700–3,799	69	76	85
4,200–4,299	54	79	97
4,700–4,799	44	72	68

Table A5.1: Number of ranked lemmas between significantly different GLMM easiness estimates at 10 sampled points in the data

The first thing to note about these findings is that despite the comparatively lower precision of GLMM intercept estimates at the easiest end of the scale, this has relatively little impact on the number of lemmas between significantly different rankings. It is clear from looking at the comparative estimates across the three language groups that the volume of responses collected for each item is the key determinant in establishing the precision of the estimates. For the Spanish estimates, for which the median number of responses per item was 167 (see Table A5.2 for other statistics on responses per lemma), the distance between significantly different rankings at each of the sampled points ranges between 44 and 69. Meanwhile for Chinese, the median number of responses was 146, on average a smaller number of responses per lemma, consequently a wider distance between significantly different rankings in this KVL, with the distance between significantly different rankings at each of the sampled points ranging from 55 to 95. Finally, German had the smallest number of responses per lemma and the gap between significantly different rankings at each of the sampled points is consequently wider, ranging from 78 to 108.

Statistic	Spanish	Chinese	German
Minimum	154	137	120
Maximum	216	228	222
Median	167	146	125
Mean	168.01	146.88	125.11
Standard deviation	6.54	6.27	4.91

Table A5.2: Responses per lemma by language group

The results presented in Table A5.1 indicate that, for example, for the Spanish respondents, we can be confident that lemmas ranked within the 200–299 band will be statistically accurate within ±44 places. That is, we are confident from the estimates given by the statistical model that Spanish learners of English are more likely to know *hat* (#250) than *online* (#295), and less likely to know *hat* than *dog* (#205). Conversely, we would not be confident that *hat* will be better known than *eye* (#270) or lesser known than *night* (#230). However, it must be acknowledged that the KVL rankings reflect a continuum, with no clear thresholds or divisions, and so it makes sense to be cautious in how the precision of the rankings is interpreted.

Overall, for Spanish and Chinese learners these findings show that if a lemma is ranked 100 places above another lemma in one of the KVL, we can have a strong degree of confidence that a learner has a greater probability of knowing that lemma over the other lemma. For the German learners this will also broadly hold, though we would not have the same degree of confidence.

APPENDIX 6

PATTERNS OF INCORRECT/MISSING SPANISH RESPONSES TO HIGHER-FREQUENCY TARGET LEMMAS AND COMPARISON WITH GERMAN AND CHINESE RESPONSES TO THE SAME LEMMAS

Lemma	Spanish incorrect/missing responses (%)[a]	German incorrect/missing responses (%)	Chinese incorrect/missing responses (%)
not	[Total incorrect or missing responses=71][b] No response=10%[c, d] *non*=56% *nay*=10% Most errors were caused by the near-synonyms *non* and *nay* (although *non* cannot stand as an independent word in English). It would have been better if these possibilities were excluded by the prompt (NOT *non* or *nay*).	[0] No erroneous responses recorded.	[16] Only 16 erroneous responses recorded.
okay	[98] No response=10% *okey*=85%[c] Most errors[d] were caused by misspelling.	[10] *okey*=70% Most errors were caused by misspelling.	[63] *okey*=46% No response=10% Most errors were caused by misspelling.

tough	[80] No response=71% *taugh*=10% Most errors were caused by non-response.	[65] No response=65% Most errors were caused by non-response.	[40] No response=75% Most errors were caused by non-response.
hurt	[35] No response=66% Most errors were caused by non-response. The prompt proved misleading as it referred to farm crops, where *damage* would be the expected verb to refer to loss. A better example sentence would have referred to animals or humans, e.g., *hurt his arm*.	[6] Only 6 errors.	[25] No response=32% No discernible patterning.
most	[103] *more*=86% Respondents were confused between *most* and *more*. This was probably caused by the prompt being misleading, and suggesting *favourite* instead of *most*. This confusion opened the possibility of the *more* responses.	[3] Only 3 errors.	[5] Only 5 errors.
remove	[99] No response=70% *reduce*=15% Most errors were caused by non-response.	[42] No response=31% Most errors were caused by non-response.	[43] No response=53% Most errors were caused by non-response.
tight	[42] No response=52% Most errors were caused by non-response. The prompt proved misleading as the translation 'firmly' refers more to tight clothing than eyes being closed.	[71] tough=9% No response=69% Most errors were caused by non-response.	[25] No response=32% No discernible patterning.

onto	[117] No response=38% *over*=55% Respondents were confused between *onto* and *over*. Respondents were explicitly instructed in the prompt not to use *over*. The fact that they did illustrates the confusion learners have between *onto* and *over*, as Spanish only has one word for the two concepts.	[48] *over*=31% No response=40% Most errors were caused by non-response. There was some confusion of *onto/over*, even though the prompt explicitly stated 'Not *over*'.	[109] *over*=56% No response=28% Most errors were caused confusion of *onto/over*, even though the prompt explicitly stated that the answer word did not end in "r".
super	[108] No response=83% Most errors were caused by non-response. The prompt proved misleading as the translation suggested *great* rather than *super*.	[69] No response=90% Most errors were caused by non-response.	[29] No response=79% Most errors were caused by non-response.
drug	[104] No response=55% dose=18% Most errors were caused by non-response. The prompt suggested *medicine*. *Droga* in Spanish means illegal drugs, rather than legal medicines.	[2] Only 2 errors.	[20] No response=30% No discernible patterning.
loss	[106] No response=11% *lose*=33% *lost*=49% Respondents confused *loss/lose/lost*. Although semantically-correct, this appears to indicate a lack of derivative knowledge. The prompt clearly indicated the noun *loss*.	[48] *lost*=75% Respondents confused *loss* and *lost*. Although semantically-correct, this appears to indicate a lack of derivative knowledge. The prompt clearly indicated the noun *loss*.	[113] *lose*=33% *lost*=58% Respondents confused *loss/lose/lost*. Although semantically-correct, this appears to indicate a lack of derivative knowledge. The prompt clearly indicated the noun *loss*.

near	[125] *next*=93% Nearly all errors were the semantically-similar *next*. The prompt could plausibly lead to either *near* or *next*. It needed to eliminate *next* as a possible answer, i.e., 'Not *next*'.	[123] *next*=85% Nearly all errors were the semantically-similar next. The prompt *nächste* could refer to both proximity (*near/nearest*) and sequence (*next*), and so both were plausible answers. The prompt needed to eliminate *next* as a possible answer, i.e., 'Not next'.	[7] Only 7 errors.
plain	[116] No response=81% Most errors were caused by non-response.	[86] No response=81% Most errors were caused by non-response.	[117] No response=74% Most errors were caused by non-response.
major	[118] No response=54% *mayor*=19% Most errors were caused by non-response. The *mayor* errors could be cause by misspelling (j→y) or L1 transfer (*major* is *mayor* in Spanish).	[88] No response=66% Most errors were caused by non-response.	[61] No response=48% *main*=25% Most errors were caused by non-response. *Main* was a common response despite having too few letters.

nature	[120] *natura*=13% *normal*=74% Most errors were *normal*. The prompt was mis-written and led to this answer. The prompt also led to *natural* and it seems some respondents tried to type this in but ran out of available spaces.	[2] Only 2 errors.	[15] Most errors caused by misspellings of *nature*.
attack	[85] No response=55% *agress*=21% Most errors were caused by non-response. *Agress* is possibly an attempt at the verb form of *aggression*?	[13] No response=46% Few errors, and about half of these were non-response.	[31] Most errors caused by misspellings of either *assault* or *attack*.
very (adj)	[121] No response=86% Most errors were caused by non-response. Although *very* is well known in the adverb form, the adjective form is less well-known.	[53] No response=89% Most errors were caused by non-response.	[69] No response=80% Most errors were caused by non-response.
public (n)	[146] No response=8% *people*=84% Most errors were caused by the near-synonym *people*. The prompt needed to eliminate this as a possibility, i.e., 'not *people*'.	[18] Few errors of various types.	[26] *people* or misspellings thereof=54% Relatively few errors and most of those were versions of *people*.

public (adj)	[142] No response=28% *people*=31% *popla*=21% Many errors were caused by non-response. The item misled many respondents to think of *popular* (which is a cognate of the prompt), and this led to the English word *people*. *Popla* may have been an attempt to write *popular*?	[10] Only 10 errors.	[12] Misspellings of *public*=58% Most errors caused by misspellings.
chief	[142] No response=67% *cause*=21% Most errors were caused by non-response.	[106] No response=65% *cause*=13% Most errors were caused by non-response.	[113] No response=50% Most errors were caused by non-response.
mostly	[158] No response=10% *mainly*=85% Nearly all errors were the semantically-similar *mainly*. The prompt could plausibly lead to either *mostly* or *mainly*. It needed to eliminate *mainly* as a possible answer, i.e., 'Not *mainly*'.	[18] Not many errors No response=44% *mainly*=39%	[68] No response=21% *mainly*=34% There was some confusion between *mostly* and the semantically-similar *mainly*. The prompt could plausibly lead to either *mostly* or *mainly*. It needed to eliminate *mainly* as a possible answer, i.e., 'Not *mainly*'.

grand	[170] No response=21% *great*=69% Respondents were confused between *grand* and *great*. The prompt indicated *grand*, but *great* is a much higher-frequency synonym, and was plausible. The prompt needed to eliminate *great* as a possible answer, i.e., Not *great*'.	[107] No response=9% *great*=82% Respondents were confused between *grand* and *great*. The prompt indicated *grand*, but *great* is a much higher-frequency synonym, and was plausible. The prompt needed to eliminate *great* as a possible answer, i.e., 'Not *great*'.	[107] No response=18% *giant*=25% *great*=37% Respondents were confused between *grand/great/giant*. The prompt indicated *grand*, but *great* and *giant* are much higher-frequency synonyms, and were plausible. The prompt could have usefully eliminated *great* and *giant* as possible answers, i.e., 'Not *great*'.
off	[182] *out*=96% Virtually all errors were *out*. The prompt led to the lemma *out*, as only very proficient learners would know the phrasal verb usage of *off*. It would have been useful for the prompt to eliminate *out* as a possible answer, i.e., 'Not *out*'.	[21] *out*=67% Most errors were *out*. The prompt clearly indicated *off*, so it seems that respondents did not have a clear understanding of the sematic difference between the two words. It would have been useful for the prompt to eliminate *out* as a possible answer, i.e., 'Not *out*'.	[42] No response=26% *out*=60% The prompt clearly indicated *off*, so it seems that respondents did not have a clear understanding of the sematic difference between the two words. It would have been useful for the prompt to eliminate *out* as a possible answer, i.e., 'Not *out*'.

a. This column is shaded to indicate that the target lemmas were high-frequency ones on which the Spanish-speaking respondents performed surprisingly poorly (Table 7.14).

b. The 'Total incorrect or missing responses' figures are raw results. The analysis figures are given in percentages of the raw errors.

c. We only focused on main patterns, and so the total percentages do not equal 100%. The remainders consist of relatively unsystematic responses from which no patterns could be derived.

d. Technically, non-responses are not errors, but for conciseness in the table, the term *error* is used here to represent the total of 'incorrect answers+non-responses'.

APPENDIX 7

PATTERNS OF INCORRECT/MISSING GERMAN RESPONSES TO HIGHER-FREQUENCY TARGET LEMMAS

Lemma	Incorrect/missing responses (%)[a]	German test prompt example sentence	Test prompt – English translation
afraid	[Total incorrect or missing responses=53][b] No response=57%[c] Most errors[d] were caused by non-response. While not incorrect, a more prototypical example sentence (e.g., *I am afraid of spiders*) may have led to a higher score.	Ich befürchte, dass ich den Zug nicht mehr erwischen werde.	I'm afraid I won't catch the train again.
grab	[61] No response=46% *grap*=31% Most errors were caused by non-response, but with a substantial amount of misspelling.	Er schnappte sich das Geld und lief davon.	He grabbed the money and ran away.
position	[54] No response=35% *posture*=47% Many respondents replied with *posture* even though it had too few characters. The example sentence focusing on body position probably caused this.	Nehmen Sie als erstes eine bequeme Körperhaltung ein.	First, take a comfortable position.

middle	[52] No response=85% Most errors were caused by non-response.	Das Buch ist in der mittleren Schublade.	The book is in the middle drawer.
explain	[51] No response=78% Most errors were caused by non-response.	Die Angestellte erklärte dem Kunden geduldig, dass sie ihm das Geld nicht rückerstatten kann.	The clerk patiently explained to the customer that she could not refund the money.
beyond	[61] No response=36% *beside*=16% Most errors were caused by non-response.	Jenseits des Flusses lag ein kleines Dorf.	Beyond the river, there was a small village.
condition	[52] No response=71% Most errors were caused by non-response.	Die Bauarbeiter untersuchen den Zustand des alten Hauses.	The construction workers examine the condition of the old house.
occur	[50] No response=74% Various misspellings=16% Most errors were caused by non-response.	Laut Polizei ereignete sich der Unfall gegen 16 Uhr.	According to the police, the accident occurred at around 4 pm.
issue	[53] No response=60% *item(s)*=19% Most errors were caused by non-response.	Ich möchte über dieses Thema jetzt nicht mehr diskutieren.	I do not want to discuss this issue anymore.
deal	[57] No response=54% Most errors were caused by non-response. The prompt was not entirely wrong, but was misleading. A sentence using *deal* in the sense of doing business/ selling something may have resulted in a higher ranking.	Er kümmert sich um die Autoversicherung.	He deals with the car insurance.

skill	[50] No response=76% Most errors were caused by non-response.	Jeder kann hier sein Können unter Beweis stellen.	Everyone can put their skills to the test here.
lie	[56] *lay*=88% Most errors were caused by the distinction between *lie* and *lay*, which confuses even native speakers.	Er liegt auf dem Sofa.	He is lying on the sofa.
thus	[48] No response=65% Most errors were caused by non-response.	Sie ist die älteste Tochter und folglich Anwärterin auf den Titel.	She is the eldest daughter and thus a contender for the title.
very	[53] No response=89% Most errors were caused by non-response. It is difficult for German learners because German does not have an equivalent for *very* in an adjective usage.	Das ist genau das Buch, nach dem ich gesucht habe!	This is the very book I've been looking for!
action	[52] No response=81% Most errors were caused by non-response. 'Handlung' might have been a better translation for *action*.	Es ist eine sofortige Maßnahme notwendig.	Immediate action is required.
method	[55] No response=64% Most errors were caused by non-response.	Für die Herstellung von Kissen wird ein traditionelles Verfahren verwendet.	A traditional method is used to make pillows.
dish	[64] No response=80% Most errors were caused by non-response.	Gib das Obst in die Schale und stell sie auf den Tisch.	Put the fruit in the dish and place it on the table.
particular	[63] No response=67% Most errors were caused by non-response.	Gibt es bestimmte Themen, die ihr noch nicht verstanden habt?	Are there particular topics that you haven't understood yet?

perfor-mance	[61] No response=44% Trying to squeeze *presentation* into the blanks=31%.	Sie ist vor der ersten Vorführung sehr nervös.	She is very nervous before the first performance.
project	[62] No response=40% Trying to fit *plan* or *planning* into the blanks=31% The obvious prompt would have been the German 'projekt', but this was avoided because it is a cognate. This likely induced difficulty.	Bei diesem Vorhaben haben wirklich alle Dorfbewohner mitgearbeitet.	Really all of the villagers worked on this project.
section	[60] No response=50% Most errors were caused by non-response.	Auf diesem Abschnitt ist die Straße derzeit ziemlich glatt und eisig.	This section of the road is currently pretty slippery and icy.
spot	[63] No response=46% *site*=29% Most errors were caused by non-response, but *site* was semantically possible based on the example sentence.	Das ist ein richtig ruhiger Ort, wo man sich gut ent-spannen kann.	It's a really quiet spot where you can relax.
concern	[57] No response=77% Most errors were caused by non-response.	Ihr könnt euch beruhigen, es besteht kein Anlass zur Sorge.	You can calm down, there is nothing to con-cern you.
store	[59] No response=15% Various version of *shop* (*shopp*, *shops*)=71% The typical German usage is *shop*, which leads to *store* being less known.	Warst du schon in dem neuen Geschäft, das sie am Wochenende eröffnet haben?	Have you been to the new store they opened over the weekend?
break	[69] *burst*=22% *broke*=70% This was a faulty item which elicited *burst* and *broke* in addition to *break*.	Er warf Steine gegen das Fenster und es zerbrach.	He threw stones at the window and it broke.

present	[66] No response=65% Most errors were caused by non-response.	Sie überreichte die Auszeichnungen an die jungen Sportler und Sportlerinnen.	She presented the awards to the young athletes.
likely	[68] No response=76% Most errors were caused by non-response.	Der wahrscheinlich-ste Grund für sein Nichterscheinen ist, dass er verschlafen hat.	The most likely reason he didn't show up is because he overslept.
official	[66] No response=61% *officer*=17% Most errors were caused by non-response. There is a German cognate (*offiziell/offizieller*), and if this was used in the prompt, the ranking probably would have been higher.	Der Regierungsbeamte geht bald in Pension.	The government official is about to retire.
particu-larly	[68] No response=62% Misspellings=15% Most errors were caused by non-response. *Particularly* is difficult because German speakers would typically use *espe-cially* based on the German cognate *speziell*.	Seine Bemühungen waren besonders hilfreich.	His efforts have been particularly helpful.
charge	[68] No response=79% Most errors were caused by non-response.	Man muss eine kleine Gebühr entrichten, um hier parken zu können.	You have to pay a small charge to park here.
specific	[75] No response=63% Most errors were caused by non-response. The prompt *spezifisch*, probably would led to higher scores, but was avoided because it is a cognate.	Man muss die Antworten in einer bestimm-ten Reihenfolge angeben.	You have to give the answers in a specific order.

lose	[65] *lost*=94% This is a faulty item, where the example sentence led to the past form *lost*.	John hat seinen Haustürschlüssel verloren.	John lost his front door key.
clearly	[78] No response=76% Most errors were caused by non-response.	Er hat offenbar gelogen.	Clearly he lied.
major	[88] No response=66% Most errors were caused by non-response.	Die Jungunternehmer haben einen bedeutenden Beitrag geleistet.	The young entrepreneurs have made a major contribution.
become	[81] *became*=83% This is a faulty item, where the example sentence led to the past form *became*.	Der Himmel wurde dunkel. Viele Wolken zogen auf.	The sky became dark. Many clouds came up.
simply	[83] No response=13% *simple*=78% Most errors were caused by the confusion between the adverb *simply* and the adjective *simple*.	Die Aufgabe ist einfach zu schwierig.	The task is simply too difficult.
strategy	[89] No response=58% Most errors were caused by non-response. Ranking probably would have been higher if the cognate *strategie* were used in the prompt.	Sie muss sich für die Verhandlung eine gute Herangehensweise zurechtlegen.	She has to come up with a good strategy for the negotiation.
sorry	[84] No response=61% *sadly*=26% Most errors were caused by non-response.	Über den Verlust, den sie erleben mussten, war ich sehr traurig.	I was very sorry about the loss they suffered.

move	[88] No response=74% Most errors were caused by non-response. *Schritte* was perhaps not the best translation, as it could have triggered *steps* for many German respondents.	Sie hat ihre nächsten Schritte genau geplant.	She has carefully planned her next moves.
standard	[80] No response=85% Most errors were caused by non-response. Use of the cognate *standard* as the prompt would probably have led to higher scores, but was avoided because it is an exact match.	Die Lehrerin ist mit dem Niveau der Leistungen in dieser Klasse noch nicht ganz zufrieden.	The teacher is not yet completely satisfied with the standard of performance in this class.
approach	[36] No response=61% Most errors were caused by non-response.	Wir brauchen einen alternativen Zugang um das Problem zu lösen.	We need an alternative approach to solve the problem.
involve	[109] include=68% The prompt sentence elicited *include* in addition to *involve*, and being more common, *include* was the most frequent response. Without the instruction 'Not *include*' in the prompt, this turned out to be a faulty item.	Das neue Projekt beinhaltet sicherlich sehr viel Arbeit.	The new project certainly involves a lot of work.

a. The target lemmas were high-frequency ones on which the German-speaking respondents performed surprisingly poorly (Table 7.15).

b. The 'Total incorrect or missing responses' figures are raw results. The analysis figures are given in percentages of the raw errors.

c. We only focused on main patterns, and so the total percentages do not equal 100%. The remainders consist of relatively unsystematic responses from which no patterns could be derived.

d. Technically, non-responses are not errors, but for conciseness in the table, the term *error* is used here to represent the total of 'incorrect answers+non-responses'.

APPENDIX 8

PATTERNS OF INCORRECT/MISSING CHINESE RESPONSES TO HIGHER-FREQUENCY TARGET LEMMAS

Lemma	Incorrect/missing responses (%)[a]	Chinese test prompt example sentence	Test prompt – English translation
trip (n)	[Total incorrect or missing responses=45][b] *tour*=67%[c] Most errors were caused by using the near-synonym *tour*. This possibility needed to be excluded by the instruction 'Not *tour*'.	我始终记得我们去意大利的旅行。	I always remember our trip to Italy.
stir	[89] No response=66%[d] Most errors were caused by non-response. Many Chinese learners lack knowledge of English vocabulary whose Chinese counterparts are commonly used in daily life.	她若有所思地搅着咖啡。	She stirred the coffee thoughtfully.
pride	[97] *proud*=88% The prompt was faulty, as it could also be translated as *The mother is proud of her daughter*, making *proud* a viable answer.	母亲把女儿当作她的骄傲。	The mother regarded her daughter as her pride.

lose	[92] *lost*=91% Most errors were caused by using the past form *lost*. The prompt was faulty and elicited *lost* instead *lose*.	我弄丢了我的钥匙。	I lost my keys.
dirt	[101] *dust*=65% Most errors were caused by using the synonym *dust*.	洗衣粉能洗去衣服上的污垢。	Washing powder can wash away the dirt on clothes.
stretch	[67] No response=48% Various misspellings of *stretch*=46% About half of the respondents did not know *stretch* and about half appeared to know the word but could not spell it accurately.	我不停抻这件毛衣，想让它恢复原来的大小。	I kept stretching this sweater, trying to restore it to its original size.
grand	[107] *great*=37% *giant*=25% No response=18% Most errors were caused by using the near-synonyms *great* or *giant*. *Grand* for many Chinese learners means *big*. There are many words in English that indicate greatness and many learners do not know the nuances among them.	我从没见过如此宏伟的宫殿。	I have never seen such a grand palace.
might	[96] Maybe=77% The prompt in Chinese did not indicate the level of possibility, so *maybe* was also possible.	1）我可能会来。 2）一切都可能在未来发生。	1) I may come. 2) Everything may happen in the future.

simply	[91] No response= 40% *solely*=18% *simple*=21% Most errors were caused by non-response, but a substantial percentage of respondents also produced the near-synonym *solely* and the adjective form *simple* instead of the adverb form. The prompts were faulty, making *simply*, *simple* and *solely* possible.	1)这不过是因为低温把水管损坏了。2)这仅仅是个时间问题。	1) This is simply because the low temperature damaged the water pipe. 2) This is simply a matter of time.
freeze	[99] No response=12% *frozen* (or misspellings thereof)=67% The prompt was faulty and elicited *frozen* instead of *freeze*.	天太冷，湖面结冰了。	It is too cold and the lake is frozen.
clear	[104] *clean*=95% The prompts were not precise enough to eliminate *clean* as a possibility.	1)他清了清喉咙。2)请在离开时清空桌子。	1) He cleared his throat. 2) Please clear the table when you leave.
onto	[109] No response=28% *over*=56% Most errors caused by the near-synonym *over*.	1)他把买来的东西倒到桌子上。2)她从火车下到站台上。	1) He poured the things he bought onto the table. 2) She got off the train onto the platform.
chief	[113] No response=50% Most errors caused by non-response.	这里当下的主要问题是交通拥挤。	The chief problem here is traffic congestion.

plain	[117] No response=74% This item was found to be a poor translation and was thus misleading.	1）我听不懂这些专业术语，请用白话再说一遍。2）他就要被辞退了，这是个明白的事实。	1) I don't understand these technical terms. Please say it again in plain language. 2) He is about to be fired. This is a plain fact.
loss	[113] *lost*=58% *lose*=33% The prompt was faulty and *lost* was possible, but not *lose*.	银行卡的遗失给我带来许多麻烦。	The loss of the bank card caused me a lot of trouble.
true	[122] No response=73% Misspellings=8% This item was found to be a poor translation and was thus misleading.	1）这是一个真实的故事。2）判断题的答案为"正确"。	1) This is a true story. 2) The answer to the true or false question is "true".
false	[110] No response=52% This item was found to be a poor translation and was thus misleading.	判断题的答案为"错误"。	The answer to the true or false question is "false".

a. The target lemmas were high-frequency ones on which the Chinese-speaking respondents performed surprisingly poorly (Table 7.16).

b. The 'Total incorrect or missing responses' figures are raw results. The analysis figures are given in percentages of the raw errors.

c. We only focused on main patterns, and so the total percentages do not equal 100%. The remainders consist of relatively unsystematic responses from which no patterns could be derived.

d. Technically, non-responses are not errors, but for conciseness in the table, the term *error* is used here to represent the total of 'incorrect answers+non-responses'.

APPENDIX 9

LEMMAS FOR WHICH THE SPANISH TEST PROMPT WAS EXACTLY THE SAME AS THE ENGLISH TEST ANSWER (COGNATE)

Lemma	Knowledge rank	COCA frequency rank	Frequency–knowledge difference
jet	2	3,163	3,161
radio	11	905	894
no	12	93	81
federal	24	493	469
general	72	2,804	2,732
jazz	102	3,878	3,776
golf	103	1,811	1,708
club	120	1,261	1,141
kiwi	136	23,419	23,283
social	147	319	172
euro	170	10,449	10,279
hotel	195	1,003	808
karate	202	15,162	14,960
karma	211	18,823	18,612
blog	215	7,885	7,670
mineral	227	4,627	4,400
karaoke	240	17,417	17,177
civil	249	1,051	802
taxi	261	5,215	4,954
continental	272	9,132	8,860
digital	280	2,371	2,091
metal	341	1,579	1,238

suite	370	4,770	4,400
kickboxing	384	49,370	48,986
virus	388	2,717	2,329
nazi	406	5,451	5,045
tango	415	12,477	12,062
hardware	417	4,050	3,633
capital	431	1,062	638
jaguar	433	20,099	19,666
ballet	454	6,646	6,192
yoga	474	8,018	7,544
terminal	492	5,849	5,357
fax	496	5,800	5,304
literal	503	7,842	7,339
campus	500	2,070	1,570
bingo	526	15,845	15,319
piano	533	3,320	2,787
ninja	546	18,418	17,872
vodka	547	8,547	8,000
pitbull	554	51,738	51,184
paintball	591	34,597	34,006
industrial	612	1,923	1,311
polar	614	6,894	6,280
mental	623	1,589	966
topless	657	17,113	16,456
oral	670	3,905	3,235
hockey	675	4,388	3,713
autism	685	9,396	8,711
chocolate	695	2,652	1,957
colonial	698	3,343	2,645
sushi	735	11,845	11,110
cultural	748	933	185
radar	753	4,825	4,072
natural	771	715	−56
brownie	775	14,105	13,330
bisexual	792	12,842	12,050
tsunami	805	11,213	10,408

invisible	827	3,841	3,014
instrumental	870	5,722	4,852
bikini	881	10,303	9,422
molecular	896	6,408	5,512
cable	920	2,013	1,093
detector	926	5,540	4,614
liberal	931	4,620	3,689
collage	934	11,407	10,473
mozzarella	943	15,056	14,113
experimental	987	3,480	2,493
homosexual	1,079	6,890	5,811
panda	1,189	15,238	14,049
bacterial	1,269	8,746	7,477
conceptual	1,275	5,585	4,310
knockout	1,281	14,158	12,877
crisis	1,295	1,208	−87
reactor	1,346	6,402	5,056
multimedia	1,446	7,483	6,037
electoral	1,501	5,140	3,639
microchip	1,513	18,319	16,806
heterosexual	1,541	21,081	19,540
multicultural	1,574	6,891	5,317
safari	1,695	14,294	12,599
eclipse	1,794	7,743	5,949
delta	1,842	12,219	10,377
casino	1,848	4,363	2,515
softball	1,885	8,280	6,395
disco	1,905	10,816	8,911
fiscal	1,998	3,662	1,664
editorial	2,140	5,059	2,919
trauma	2,334	4,870	2,536
pasta	2,352	4,538	2,186
plasma	2,386	8,412	6,026
dimensional	2,577	19,609	17,032
variable	2,568	1,872	−696
amnesia	2,808	15,542	12,734

altar	2,881	5,731	2,850
diabetes	2,929	4,121	1,192
cobra	3,105	20,577	17,472
canal	3,384	5,454	2,070
bravo	3,416	38,479	35,063
portal	4,005	9,418	5,413
propaganda	4,210	5,913	1,703

APPENDIX 10

LEMMAS FOR WHICH THE GERMAN TEST PROMPT WAS EXACTLY THE SAME AS THE ENGLISH TEST ANSWER (COGNATE)

Lemma	Knowledge rank	Frequency rank	Frequency–knowledge rank difference
fit	8	1,353	1,345
burger	11	7,385	7,374
blog	14	7,885	7,871
wind	15	1,093	1,078
elite	19	2,752	2,733
idol	22	9,584	9,562
orange	24	3,296	3,272
generation	25	1,027	1,002
ball	29	913	884
person	34	345	311
zoo	35	6,371	6,336
text	48	1,293	1,245
virus	51	2,717	2,666
volleyball	53	8,037	7,984
tennis	60	3,101	3,041
million	64	222	158
rose	65	3,390	3,325
demo	68	12,698	12,630
blind	69	2,733	2,664
webcam	70	29,992	29,922
in	72	6	−66
global	73	1,111	1,038

motel	79	5,309	5,230
film	82	593	511
fan	83	1,210	1,127
export	86	5,361	5,275
ritual	91	3,427	3,336
pilot	93	1,782	1,689
ring	94	1,684	1,590
suite	101	4,770	4,669
uniform	102	3,062	2,960
tango	109	12,477	12,368
workshop	110	3,149	3,039
spam	115	13,081	12,966
orange	122	3,164	3,042
planet	123	1,597	1,474
atom	132	5,238	2,706
neon	136	8,122	7,986
golden	137	1,831	1,694
ego	138	4,820	4,682
modem	147	5,582	5,435
modern	159	1,047	888
warm	162	1,360	1,198
nation	171	412	241
paintball	173	34,597	34,424
outfit	178	4,440	4,262
wild	183	1,296	1,113
hotel	190	1,003	813
agent	197	1,021	824
pc	198	3,072	2,874
hobby	199	6,648	6,449
digital	227	2,371	2,144
organ	242	3,417	3,175
pony	245	8,507	8,262
bar	259	992	733
sand	266	2,219	1,953
land	280	566	286
karate	281	15,162	14,881

eyeliner	282	23,274	22,992
euro	286	10,449	10,163
arena	318	3,616	3,298
single	325	5,905	5,580
server	328	6,343	6,015
gas	337	1,024	687
garage	339	3,229	2,890
ski	348	5,548	5,200
hand	352	174	−178
pizza	366	3,948	3,582
album	378	2,229	1,851
sensor	391	4,983	4,592
hotline	393	13,881	13,488
steak	401	4,678	4,277
yoga	415	8,018	7,603
operation	420	827	407
minute	421	308	−113
surfer	429	11,869	11,440
bodybuilder	433	22,075	21,642
browser	439	9,907	9,468
hit	445	2,222	1,777
winter	449	1,248	799
gold	455	1,260	805
ideal	456	2,832	2,376
arm	458	491	33
element	460	1,216	756
comic	466	5,335	4,869
massage	467	7,158	6,691
hamburger	469	7,608	7,139
sushi	472	11,845	11,373
blogger	478	16,589	16,111
networking	490	9,561	9,071
popcorn	495	9,017	8,522
patient	496	572	76
cousin	500	2,730	2,230
moment	506	369	−137

video	511	1,110	599
baseball	533	1,377	844
festival	538	3,723	3,185
dollar[a]	553		
mailbox	555	9,191	8,636
online	562	3,515	2,953
streaming	577	44,360	43,783
jazz	578	3,878	3,300
shuttle	580	3,840	3,260
zebra	587	14,397	13,810
tradition	600	1,247	647
international	601	500	−101
internet	603	1,471	868
spray	604	4,457	3,853
scanner	608	8,335	7,727
drama	611	2,647	2,036
budget	633	1,055	422
taxi	635	5,215	4,580
laptop	637	5,941	5,304
fitness	646	3,379	2,733
terminal	651	5,849	5,198
computer	652	589	−63
android	654	21,449	20,795
hotdog	657	28,606	27,949
thriller	658	8,808	8,150
design	664	835	171
bikini	676	10,303	9,627
museum	683	1,732	1,049
information	685	314	−371
minus	686	8,792	8,106
depression	687	2,107	1,420
superman	690	24,022	23,332
handball	692	26,304	25,612
tourist	694	2,410	1,716
delta	699	12,219	11,520
norm	713	3,410	2,697

system	719	191	−528
alpha	722	6,811	6,089
post	735	2,161	1,426
name	739	298	−441
adverb	745	28,655	27,910
hacker	747	10,520	9,773
remix	758	34,301	33,543
phase	759	2,258	1,499
panorama	769	13,456	12,687
snowboard	772	17,864	17,092
journalist	777	2,111	1,334
poker	782	8,284	7,502
live	791	2,071	1,280
zombie	796	13,470	12,674
smartphone[a]	799		
elegant	807	3,973	3,166
echo	817	3,447	2,630
forum	820	4,749	3,929
finger	830	1,043	213
studio	831	1,520	689
golf	833	1,811	978
cowboy	838	5,100	4,262
baby	840	588	−252
karma	847	18,823	17,976
heroin	850	5,934	5,084
butter	862	2,418	1,556
troll	871	11,577	10,706
matrix	873	5,949	5,076
streaming	877	30,064	29,187
memo	882	5,183	4,301
airbag	885	20,359	19,474
solo	887	5,218	4,331
terrorist	893	2,858	1,965
hardware	895	4,050	3,155
spaghetti	896	9,386	8,490
isolation	904	4,313	3,409

superstar	905	7,120	6,215
panda	914	15,238	14,324
mentor	915	4,603	3,688
gladiator	917	23,987	23,070
pitbull	918	51,738	50,820
basketball	929	1,809	880
mineral	931	4,627	3,696
hammer	935	6,314	5,379
alphabet	953	9,387	8,434
motivation	954	3,145	2,191
softball	957	8,280	7,323
vitamin	962	3,743	2,781
national	963	231	−732
latex	987	14,244	13,257
simulator	988	13,337	12,349
tiger	1,004	6,863	5,859
block	1,014	1,318	304
general	1,017	2,804	1,787
hi	1,023	2,083	1,060
radar	1,068	4,825	3,757
status	1,077	1,217	140
toaster	1,091	15,535	14,444
mutation	1,092	8,786	7,694
aquarium	1,095	10,570	9,475
interview	1,113	945	−168
supermodel	1,123	18,678	17,555
jaguar	1,132	20,099	18,967
alternative	1,135	2,084	949
alligator	1,155	9,742	8,587
marathon	1,169	6,539	5,370
multimedia	1,178	7,483	6,305
tampon	1,179	25,597	24,418
cheeseburger	1,192	16,940	15,748
medium	1,194	3,262	2,068
jackpot	1,196	17,317	16,121
joystick	1,201	19,902	18,701

laser	1,202	3,926	2,724
nest	1,203	4,164	2,961
software	1,220	1,582	362
navigator	1,228	17,182	15,954
frustration	1,234	3,261	2,027
countdown	1,244	15,255	14,011
patriot	1,265	12,431	11,166
fantasy	1,282	2,983	1,701
explosion	1,285	3,042	1,757
layout	1,289	7,603	6,314
adoption	1,294	3,702	2,408
inspiration	1,296	4,090	2,794
instrument	1,300	1,616	316
cheerleader	1,301	10,507	9,206
freak	1,311	9,367	8,056
imperial	1,313	5,086	3,773
finalist	1,314	10,418	9,104
interface	1,349	6,264	4,915
sprint	1,350	12,187	10,837
muffin	1,352	8,726	7,374
okay	1,354	1,647	293
flamingo	1,364	22,488	21,124
patent	1,373	4,445	3,072
evolution	1,378	2,964	1,586
nylon	1,380	8,605	7,225
generator	1,385	5,911	4,526
insider	1,393	5,394	4,001
veteran	1,395	2,405	1,010
dimensional	1,397	19,609	18,212
designer	1,400	2,442	1,042
feminist	1,406	4,692	3,286
avatar	1,428	17,149	15,721
form	1,440	523	−917
portrait	1,444	2,671	1,227
inflation	1,451	3,218	1,767
olive	1,454	6,242	4,788

dock	1,462	4,960	3,498
grapefruit	1,471	12,395	10,924
integration	1,491	3,601	2,110
tunnel	1,508	3,377	1,869
vibrator	1,509	25,575	24,066
realist	1,536	10,175	8,639
franchise	1,540	4,396	2,856
skyline	1,542	9,724	8,182
installation	1,546	4,476	2,930
delegation	1,576	5,768	4,192
ensemble	1,610	5,279	3,669
transporter	1,613	22,043	20,430
karaoke	1,622	17,417	15,795
aspirin	1,631	7,976	6,345
diplomat	1,643	4,966	3,323
kiwi	1,703	23,419	21,716
bass	1,730	5,180	3,450
experiment	1,743	2,000	257
brutal	1,745	4,741	2,996
gorilla	1,759	9,570	7,811
plasma	1,781	8,412	6,631
illegal	1,786	2,082	296
deodorant	1,795	19,425	17,630
gospel	1,801	5,524	3,723
hunger	1,821	4,628	2,807
minimum	1,822	4,422	2,600
ninja	1,825	18,418	16,593
cupcake	1,843	17,235	15,392
magnesium	1,881	12,516	10,635
interpretation	1,907	2,395	488
investor	1,911	1,710	−201
pause	1,919	2,794	875
materialist	1,927	21,996	20,069
brownie	1,929	14,105	12,176
meditation	1,931	6,278	4,347
intuition	1,934	8,678	6,744

bitter	1,963	3,606	1,643
urgent	1,972	5,390	3,418
irrelevant	2,008	5,855	3,847
trainer	2,021	4,498	2,477
motivator	2,028	15,896	13,868
cocktail	2,033	5,275	3,242
navigation	2,041	8,389	6,348
collage	2,046	11,407	9,361
spoiler	2,098	21,421	19,323
setup	2,108	5,943	3,835
minimalist	2,109	16,228	14,119
filter	2,134	5,951	3,817
asteroid	2,170	6,263	4,093
single	2,191	5,905	3,714
absurd	2,196	5,977	3,781
parallel	2,220	5,915	3,695
major	2,234	4,579	2,345
neutral	2,239	4,256	2,017
leopard	2,243	12,250	10,007
altar	2,251	5,731	3,480
general	2,268	804	−1,464
opportunist	2,274	21,287	19,013
tolerant	2,302	9,361	7,059
deck	2,315	2,805	490
blocker	2,365	14,230	11,865
astronaut	2,367	5,726	3,359
mozzarella	2,450	15,056	12,606
dominant	2,492	3,194	702
shooter	2,509	6,803	4,294
fossil	2,519	5,095	2,576
intolerant	2,533	15,911	13,378
format	2,545	3,758	1,213
neutron	2,571	10,394	7,823
park	2,584	1,231	1,353
synonym	2,630	17,691	15,061
individualist	2,650	22,244	19,594

exhibitionist	2,759	32,059	29,300
analyst	2,787	1,678	−1,109
dna	2,807	2,846	39
algebra	2,817	13,191	10,374
skateboard	2,847	23,073	20,226
wolf	2,871	4,183	1,312
fundamentalist	2,872	9,435	6,563
minimal	2,927	4,351	1,424
website	2,949	4,998	2,049
desktop	3,010	6,930	3,920
minister	3,067	1,920	−1,147
variable	3,090	1,872	−1,218
improvisation	3,406	10,182	6,776
Israeli	3,419	3,910	491
mediation	3,443	8,471	5,028
lobbyist	3,587	5,377	1,790
manipulator	3,662	20,575	16,913
traditionalist	3,692	14,246	10,554
bronze	4,569	4,974	405
thermometer	4,623	9,867	5,244

a. No COCA frequency information was available.

APPENDIX 11

COMPARISON OF THE 114 WORDS KNOWN BY ALL RESPONDENTS IN BRYSBAERT ET AL. (2020) WITH KVL RESULTS

Word	KVL Spanish		KVL German		KVL Chinese	
	Facility value[a]	Knowledge rank	Facility value	Knowledge rank	Facility value	Knowledge rank
actor	.87	1,567	.93	1,550	.92	536
address	.89	1,507	.80	3,390	.73	2,426
airport	.88	1,245	.98	290	.84	1,461
amazing	.68	3,468	.53	5,726	.87	1,520
back	.96	418	.98	316	.95	383
bath	.90	1,261	.95	730	.83	1,887
believe	.92	977	.94	1,227	.91	856
best	.95	490	.99	71	.97	268
between	.95	429	.98	344	.93	768
big	.97	185	.99	116	.77	2,652
biology	.96	251	.96	598	.87	1,168
born	.90	1,002	.96	451	.90	974
broken	.91	888	.95	738	.79	2,122
check	.81	2,297	.79	3,260	.93	425
children	—[b]	—	—	—	—	—
chocolate	.92	695	.93	1,486	.78	2,293
city	1.00	3	.98	215	.98	89
cleaner	.92	839	.84	2,546	.89	1,118
coffee	.94	821	.95	819	.92	792
corner	.94	663	.94	1,280	.87	1,254
crying	.81	2,151	.97	609	.82	1,709
darkness	.53	4,314	.95	793	.82	1,450

day	.99	19	1.00	10	.97	110
do	–	–	–	–	–	–
document	.93	722	.90	1,867	.91	1,044
eat	.98	76	1.00	3	.97	126
expensive	.97	199	.92	1,741	.89	963
experiment	.92	797	.92	1,743	.81	2,026
find	.98	243	.87	2,212	.92	569
finish	.94	816	.97	665	.96	360
finished	.89	1,086	.90	1,751	.80	2,224
five	.98	82	.98	256	.98	54
foot	.80	1,712	.86	2,253	.87	1,355
full	.88	1,175	.97	298	.92	812
global	.84	1,779	.99	73	.81	2,009
group	.93	606	.98	351	.93	718
happy	.98	151	.97	403	.97	338
hate	.96	365	.97	334	.97	113
hello	.98	130	.87	2,183	.95	438
help	.98	79	.98	221	.93	623
historic	.91	912	.91	1,646	.65	3,975
history	.97	304	.98	293	.96	247
horse	.95	616	.97	691	.88	1,035
hospital	.92	1,011	.98	367	.93	655
hotel	.96	195	.98	190	.96	83
how	–	–	–	–	–	–
inside	.89	1,103	.85	2,560	.78	1,788
intelligence	.26	6,305	.86	2,472	.72	2,825
kids	.96	331	.98	182	.97	30
level	.98	166	.95	955	.94	468
magazine	.89	1,058	.90	1,823	.80	2,030
manager	.67	3,327	.82	3,134	.88	1,221
me	–	–	–	–	–	–
men	–	–	–	–	–	–
midnight	.88	1,254	.98	217	.92	659
milk	.98	53	.98	239	.95	312
motivation	.46	4,800	.95	954	.70	2,810
move	.96	239	.98	275	.96	292

music	.51	4,634	.96	710	.98	42
officially	.46	5,151	.90	1,763	.73	2,520
often	.89	1,232	.98	444	.89	1,141
online	.98	295	.98	160	.96	321
optimism	.37	5,601	.91	1,736	.60	4,505
oxygen	.44	4,997	.71	4,104	.75	2,906
party	.96	184	.94	857	.97	56
phone	.93	540	.96	853	.96	236
player	.95	374	.98	276	.71	3,276
popularity	.38	5,614	.74	4,088	.63	3,859
positive	.53	4,383	.36	6,298	.76	2,394
present	.96	321	.98	599	.62	4,250
problem	.60	3,980	.84	2,835	.95	371
promise	.67	3,573	.91	1,666	.84	1,741
radio	1.00	11	.93	1,326	.91	930
read	.95	688	.96	563	.96	124
right	.93	744	.98	273	.82	1,682
room	.95	390	.98	383	.95	430
rule	.96	220	.94	1,137	.92	755
said	–	–	–	–	–	–
save	.53	4,378	.77	3,542	.94	316
secretary	.91	1,008	.83	2,423	.60	4,167
service	.36	5,716	.80	3,273	.86	1,333
seventeen	–	–	–	–	–	–
sexy	.82	1,932	.78	3,249	.92	841
shirt	.92	1,013	.90	1,882	.83	1,874
sky	.94	609	.97	705	.97	202
smile	.91	986	.99	121	.93	590
snow-boarding	.60	4,179	.76	3,564	.21	7,006
somebody	.85	1,678	.83	2,859	.79	2,104
someone	.92	1,019	.94	965	.95	390
song	.92	741	.98	44	.92	725
soon	.95	532	.98	425	.88	1,177
sport	.98	97	.93	1,453	.96	319
start	.86	1,437	.98	142	.94	629

subject	.66	3,195	.76	4,008	.55	4,375
sugar	.96	396	.98	365	.78	2,380
sun	.94	6	1.00	9	.97	95
surviving	.19	6,650	.76	3,748	.34	6,269
technology	.87	1,413	.85	2,882	.81	2,059
telephone	.97	138	.94	1,142	.92	633
think	.93	708	.72	3,705	.94	589
this	–	–	–	–	–	–
tomorrow	.96	302	.97	688	.89	1,068
toy	.96	264	.98	304	.96	155
two	.99	10	.98	241	.98	37
uncle	.95	314	.96	771	.97	151
us	–	–	–	–	–	–
verb	.89	1,527	.79	2,961	.85	1,516
vocabulary	.93	876	.90	1,835	.79	2,256
walk	.94	552	.99	84	.93	443
water	.98	236	.99	40	.95	129
who	–	–	–	–	–	–
woman	.90	1,026	.91	1,572	.89	1,384
yellow	.97	277	.96	732	.97	176
you	–	–	–	–	–	–
Minimum	.19	3	.36	3	.21	30
Maximum	1.00	6,650	1.00	6,298	.99	7,006
Mean	.85	1,391	.92	1,347	.86	1,314
(sd)	(.18)	(1,652)	(.099)	(1,328)	(.129)	(1,332)
Median	.93	797	.95	793	.91	856

a. Facility value is simply the proportion of items answered correctly on a test. For example, .870 (or 87%) of all the answers on the KVL test for *actor* were correct. Brybaert et al. facility values for all lemmas on this table are 1.00 (100%).

b. Eleven Brysbaert et al. words were not on the KVL due to the KVL not including function words, and inflections being included in the baseword lemma (e.g., *children→child*). Thus, the total analysed was 103 lemmas.

APPENDIX 12

BEST-KNOWN 30 LEMMAS ON THE SPANISH-KVL

The complete KVL for Spanish learners of English is available on the British Council KVL website (**www.britishcouncil.org/exam/aptis/ aptis-expertise/knowledge-based-vocabulary-lists-kvl**).

This is an illustrative sample of *KVL-Spanish Version 1.0* showing the best-known 30 lemmas. It includes columns for the name of the lemma, its word class, its KVL knowledge rank, and its frequency rank according to COCA corpus frequency data, plus a column to indicate lemmas with an uncertain ranking [uncertainty indicated by (–)].

ID	Lemma	Word class	KVL knowledge rank	Frequency rank	Uncertain KVL ranking
31686	dance	verb	1	1,974	NA
33677	jet	noun	2	3,163	(–)
31110	city	noun	3	290	NA
37677	zoo	noun	4	6,371	NA
34665	orange	noun	5	3,296	NA
36635	sun	noun	6	1,237	NA
32902	german	adjective	7	1,833	NA
30720	book	noun	8	241	NA
34626	one	noun	9	837	NA
37146	two	number	10	80	NA
35390	radio	noun	11	905	(–)
34506	no	misc	12	93	(–)
33271	human	adjective	13	399	NA
33258	hour	noun	14	272	NA
37588	winner	noun	15	1,926	NA
31012	change	noun	16	356	NA
33161	hero	noun	17	1,922	NA

32532	family	noun	18	147	NA
31705	day	noun	19	90	NA
30064	acid	noun	20	3,259	NA
30663	black	adjective	21	253	NA
30423	atomic	adjective	22	5,498	NA
30757	boy	noun	23	382	NA
32578	federal	adjective	24	493	(–)
34395	my	misc	25	44	NA
36089	shoe	noun	26	1,427	NA
30562	beach	noun	27	1,947	NA
34002	love	noun	28	579	NA
33301	ice	noun	29	1,234	NA
33724	key	noun	30	1,468	NA

APPENDIX 13

BEST-KNOWN 30 LEMMAS ON THE GERMAN-KVL

The complete KVL for German learners of English is available on the British Council KVL website (**www.britishcouncil.org/exam/aptis/ aptis-expertise/knowledge-based-vocabulary-lists-kvl**).

This is an illustrative sample of *KVL-German Version 1.0* showing the best-known 30 lemmas. It includes columns for the name of the lemma, its word class, its KVL knowledge rank, and its frequency rank according to COCA corpus frequency data, plus a column to indicate lemmas with an uncertain ranking [uncertainty indicated by (–)].

ID	Lemma	Word class	KVL knowledge rank	Frequency rank	Uncertain KVL ranking
20714	bomb	noun	1	2,002	NA
22284	English	adjective	2	1,792	NA
22151	eat	verb	3	543	NA
23279	hungry	adjective	4	3,202	NA
23747	kiss	noun	5	4,007	NA
23301	ice	noun	6	1,234	NA
21686	dance	verb	7	1,974	NA
22654	fit	adjective	8	3,423	(–)
26635	sun	noun	9	1,237	NA
21705	day	noun	10	90	NA
20849	burger	noun	11	7,385	(–)
20618	better	adjective	12	452	NA
24531	not	not-no	13	28	NA
20690	blog	noun	14	7,885	(–)
27581	wind	noun	15	1,093	NA
20958	cat	noun	16	1,785	NA
20893	camel	noun	17	7,059	NA

27546	west	noun	18	665	NA
22220	elite	noun	19	2,752	(–)
23673	jeans	noun	20	3,444	NA
23765	Korean	adjective	21	3,546	NA
23319	idol	noun	22	9,584	(–)
22100	drive	verb	23	490	NA
24664	orange	adjective	24	3,164	NA
22878	generation	noun	25	1,027	(–)
21716	dear	adjective	26	3,359	NA
23745	king	noun	27	2,353	NA
23748	kiss	verb	28	2,316	NA
20517	ball	noun	29	913	(–)
26446	star	noun	30	538	NA

APPENDIX 14

BEST-KNOWN 30 LEMMAS ON THE CHINESE-KVL

The complete KVL for Spanish learners of English is available on the British Council KVL website (**www.britishcouncil.org/exam/aptis/ aptis-expertise/knowledge-based-vocabulary-lists-kvl**).

This is an illustrative sample of *KVL-Chinese Version 1.0* showing the best-known 30 lemmas. It includes columns for the name of the lemma, its word class, its KVL knowledge rank, and its frequency rank according to COCA corpus frequency data, plus a column to indicate lemmas with an uncertain ranking [uncertainty indicated by (–)].

ID	Lemma	Word class	KVL knowledge rank	Frequency rank	Uncertain KVL ranking
10923	car	noun	1	289	NA
10958	cat	noun	2	1,785	NA
13711	just	adverb	3	66	NA
10757	boy	noun	4	382	NA
14635	open	verb	5	355	NA
10740	both	adverb	6	375	NA
12082	dream	verb	7	2,609	NA
16516	story	noun	8	233	NA
13748	kiss	verb	9	2,316	NA
13747	kiss	noun	10	4,007	NA
12705	food	noun	11	366	NA
14506	no	misc	12	93	NA
16937	time	noun	13	52	NA
12032	dog	noun	14	753	NA
13720	keep	verb	15	156	NA
17074	tree	noun	16	596	NA
14983	plan	verb	17	691	NA

13169	hi	misc	18	2,083	NA
13132	heart	noun	19	460	NA
13203	home	adverb	20	406	NA
14407	name	noun	21	298	NA
12649	fish	noun	22	948	NA
14526	north	noun	23	578	NA
11635	cry	verb	24	1,355	NA
14390	must	verb	25	223	NA
14746	page	noun	26	708	NA
12541	far	adjective	27	975	NA
14634	open	adjective	28	581	NA
14083	map	noun	29	1,547	NA
13731	kid	noun	30	312	NA

APPENDIX 15

SAMPLE OF THE KVL-SPANISH-TECHNICAL SPREADSHEET

The complete technical KVL document for Spanish, German, and Chinese learners of English is available on the British Council KVL website (**www.britishcouncil.org/exam/aptis/aptis-expertise/knowledge-based-vocabulary-lists-kvl**).

This is an illustrative sample of *KVL-Spanish-Technical 1.0* showing the best-known 20 lemmas. It has columns for a range of data for each lemma, including the name of the lemma, its word class, its facility value, GLMM intercept value, standard deviation of the conditional mode estimate, uncertainty of ranking indicated by (−), KVL knowledge rank, its frequency rank according to COCA corpus frequency data, the translation on the *Vocabulary Challenge*, and the example sentence.

ID	Lemma	Part of speech	Count	Correct	Facility value	GLMM intercept	Conditional modes sd	Uncertain ranking	Knowledge rank	Frequency rank	Translation	Test prompt example sentence	Highlight
31686	dance	verb	171	171	1.00	5.14	0.81	NA	1	1974	bailar	Me encanta bailar y voy a clases de ballet todas las semanas.	bailar
33677	jet	noun	167	167	1.00	4.97	0.81	(–)	2	3163	jet	El accidente ocurrió en el momento en el que despegaba el jet, no hubo sobrevivientes	jet
31110	city	noun	172	172	1.00	4.85	0.82	NA	3	290	ciudad	Londres es una ciudad grandísima que ofrece de todo al visitante.	ciudad
37677	zoo	noun	178	178	1.00	4.76	0.82	NA	4	6371	zoológico	A los niños les suele gustar ir al zoológico	zoológico
34665	orange	noun	177	176	0.99	4.66	0.69	NA	5	3296	naranja	Me encanta tomar zumo de naranja por la mañana para desayunar.	naranja
36635	sun	noun	167	166	0.99	4.57	0.66	NA	6	1237	sol	El sol brilló durante todo el día.	sol

32902	German	adjective	162	161	0.99	4.56	0.66	NA	7	1833	alemán	Mi mejor amigo es alemán y vive en Berlín.	alemán
30720	book	noun	160	159	0.99	4.54	0.67	NA	8	241	libro	¿Has leído el último libro de Pedro Madurga?	libro
34626	one	noun	167	166	0.99	4.49	0.66	NA	9	837	uno	Sydney es uno de las ciudades más interesantes del mundo.	uno
37146	two	number	167	166	0.99	4.48	0.66	NA	10	80	dos	Tengo dos hermanos mayores y uno pequeño.	dos
35390	radio	noun	185	184	0.99	4.47	0.66	(–)	11	905	radio	Bájale el volumen a la radio que no puedo escuchar lo que me estas diciendo	radio
34506	no	misc	161	160	0.99	4.47	0.66	(–)	12	93	no	¿Te gustó la película? ¡No!	no
33271	human	adjective	170	167	0.98	4.43	0.53	NA	13	399	humano	El cuerpo humano es un organismo muy complicado.	humano
33258	hour	noun	164	163	0.99	4.37	0.66	NA	14	272	hora	Las medicinas deben tomarse cada dos horas o después de las comidas	horas

37588	winner	noun	166	165	0.99	4.32	0.66	NA	15	1926	ganador	El ganador del partido recibirá un trofeo.	ganador
31012	change	noun	166	165	0.99	4.32	0.66	NA	16	356	cambio	Quiero hacer un cambio en el guión. No sé si te va a gustar.	cambio
33161	hero	noun	174	173	0.99	4.29	0.66	NA	17	1922	héroe	A su vuelta le dieron una bienvenida digna de un héroe nacional	héroe
32532	family	noun	166	164	0.99	4.25	0.60	NA	18	147	familia	Nos vamos a reunir en familia para celebrar la navidad.	familia
31705	day	noun	172	170	0.99	4.23	0.59	NA	19	90	día	Hoy es un día muy especial para mí. Es mi cumpleaños.	día
30064	acid	noun	162	158	0.98	4.18	0.50	NA	20	3259	ácido	El ácido sulfúrico es el compuesto quimico mas común	ácido

REFERENCES

Abdi, H. (2007). The Kendall rank correlation coefficient. In N. Salkind (Ed.), *Encyclopedia of measurement and statistics*. Sage.

Alderson, J. C. (2005). *Diagnosing foreign language proficiency*. Continuum.

Baayen, R. H., Davidson, D. J., & Bates, D. M. (2008). Mixed-effects modeling with crossed random effects for subjects and items. *Journal of Memory and Language, 59*(4), 390–412. https://doi.org/10.1016/j.jml.2007.12.005

Banta, F. G. (1981). Teaching German vocabulary: The use of English cognates and common loan words. *Modern Language Journal, 65*, 129–136. https://doi.org/10.1111/j.1540-4781.1981.tb00962.x

Bao, Z., & Xu, X. (2022). Evaluating word lists against word frequency, lexical age-of-acquisition and concreteness. *Lingua, 278*, 103417. https://doi.org/10.1016/j.lingua.2022.103417

Bates, D. M. (2010). A simple, linear, mixed-effects model. In *Lme4: Mixed-effects modeling with R* (pp. 1–26). Springer.

Bates, D. M., Mächler, M., Bolker, B., & Walker, S. (2015). Fitting linear mixed-effects models using lme4. *Journal of Statistical Software, 67*, 1–48. https://doi.org/10.18637/jss.v067.i01

Bauer, L., & Nation, I. S. P. (1993). Word families. *International Journal of Lexicography, 6*, 253–279. https://doi.org/10.1093/ijl/6.4.253

Benigno, V., & de Jong, J. (2017). *Developing the GSE Vocabulary*. Pearson Global Scale of English Research Series. www.pearson.com/english/about/gse/research.html

BNC Consortium (2007). The British National Corpus, XML Edition, 2007. Oxford Text Archive. http://hdl.handle.net/20.500.12024/2554

Bravo, M. A., Hiebert, E. H., & Pearson, P. D. (2006). Tapping the linguistic resources of Spanish–English bilinguals: The role of cognates in science. In R. K. Wagner, A. E. Muse, & K. R. Tannenbaum (Eds.), *Vocabulary acquisition: Implications for reading comprehension* (pp. 140–156). Guilford Press.

Brezina, V., & Gablasova, D. (2015). Is there a core general vocabulary? Introducing the New General Service List. *Applied Linguistics*, *36*(1), 1–22. https://doi.org/10.1093/applin/amt018

Brown, D. (2018). Examining the word family through word lists. *Vocabulary Learning and Instruction*, *7*, 51–65. https://doi.org/10.7820/vli.v07.1.brown

Brown, D., Stoeckel, T., McLean, S., & Stewart, J. (2020). The most appropriate lexical unit for L2 vocabulary research and pedagogy: A brief review of the evidence. *Applied Linguistics*, 1–7. https://doi.org/10.1093/applin/amaa061

Brysbaert, M., Keuleers, E., & Mandera, P. (2020). Which words do English non-native speakers know? New supernational levels based on yes/no decision. *Second Language Research*, 1–25. https://doi.org/10.1177/0267658320934526

Brysbaert, M., & New, B. (2009). Moving beyond Kucera and Francis: A critical evaluation of current word frequency norms and the introduction of a new and improved word frequency measure for American English. *Behavior Research Methods*, *41*(4), 977–990. https://doi.org/10.3758/BRM.41.4.977

Brysbaert, M., Stevens, M., Mandera, P., & Keuleers, F. (2016a). How many words do we know? Practical estimates of vocabulary size dependent on word definition, the degree of language input and the participant's age. *Frontiers in Psychology*, *7*, 1116. https://doi.org/10.3389/fpsyg.2016.01116

Brysbaert, M., Stevens, M., Mandera, P., & Keuleers, F. (2016b). The impact of word prevalence on lexical decision times: Evidence from the Dutch Lexicon Project 2. *Journal of Experimental Psychology – Human Perception and Performance*, *42*(3), 441–458. https://doi.org/10.1037/xhp0000159

Cameirão, M. L., & Vicente, S. G. (2010). Age-of-acquisition norms for a set of 1,749 Portuguese words. *Behavior Research Methods*, *42*, 474–480. https://doi.org/10.3758/BRM.42.2.474

Coxhead, A. (2000). A new academic word list. *TESOL Quarterly*, *34*, 213–238. https://doi.org/10.2307/3587951

Cumming, G., & Finch, S. (2005). Inference by eye: Confidence intervals and how to read pictures of data. *American Psychologist*, *60*(2), 170–180. https://doi.org/10.1037/0003-066X.60.2.170

Dale, E., & O'Rourke, J. (1981). *The living word vocabulary*. World Book – Childcraft International.

Dang, T. N. Y., & Webb, S. (2016). Evaluating lists of high-frequency words. *ITL-International Journal of Applied Linguistics, 167*(2), 132–158. https://doi.org/10.1075/itl.167.2.02dan

Dang, T. N. Y., Webb, S., & Coxhead, A. (2022). Evaluating lists of high-frequency words: Teachers' and learners' perspectives. *Language Teaching Research, 26*(4), 617–641. https://doi.org/10.1177/1362168820911189

Davies, M. (2008–). The Corpus of Contemporary American English (COCA): 560 million words, 1990–present. www.english-corpora.org/coca/

Davies, M. (2017). 60K COCA lemma list. www.wordfrequency.info/purchase.asp

Davies, M. (2021). The TV and movies corpora: Design, construction, and use. *International Journal of Corpus Linguistics, 26*(1), 10–37. https://doi.org/10.1075/ijcl.00035.dav

Davies, M., & Gardner, D. (2013). *A frequency dictionary of contemporary American English: Word sketches, collocates and thematic lists.* Routledge.

de Ayala, R. J. (2009). *The theory and practice of Item Response Theory.* Guilford Press.

De Boeck, P. (2008). Random item IRT models. *Psychometrika, 73*(4), 533–559. https://doi.org/10.1007/s11336-008-9092-x

De Boeck, P., Bakker, M., Zwitser, R., Nivard, M., Hofman, A., Tuerlinckx, F., & Partchev, I. (2011). The estimation of item response models with the lmer function from the lme4 package in R. *Journal of Statistical Software, 39*(12). www.jstatsoft.org/v39/i12/. https://doi.org/10.18637/jss.v039.i12

de Groot, A. M. B. (2006). Effects of stimulus characteristics and background music on foreign language vocabulary learning and forgetting. *Language Learning, 56*(3), 463–506. https://doi.org/10.1111/j.1467-9922.2006.00374.x

de Groot, A. M. B., & Keijzer, R. (2000). What is hard to learn is easy to forget: The roles of word concreteness, cognate status, and word frequency in foreign language learning and forgetting. *Language Learning, 50*, 1–56. https://doi.org/10.1111/0023-8333.00110

de Groot, A. M. B., & van Hell, J. G. (2005). The learning of foreign language vocabulary. In J. F. Kroll & A. M. B. de Groot (Eds.), *Handbook of bilingualism.* Oxford University Press.

Dressler, C., Carlo, M. S., Snow, C. E., August, D., & White, C. E. (2011). Spanish-speaking students' use of cognate knowledge to infer the meaning of English words. *Bilingualism: Language and Cognition, 14*(2), 243–255. https://doi.org/10.1017/S1366728910000519

Dunn, K. J. (2014). What makes L2 words difficult to know? Using Explanatory Item Response Theory to model the difficulty of vocabulary test items for learners of English as a second language. Unpublished doctoral dissertation, Lancaster University. Retrieved September 2021 from: https://ethos.bl.uk/OrderDetails.do?uin=uk.bl.ethos.653089

Ellis, N. C. (2002). Frequency effects in language processing: A review with implications for theories of implicit and explicit language acquisition. *Studies in Second Language Acquisition, 24*, 143–188. https://doi.org/10.1017/S0272263102002024

Ellis, N. C. (2006). Language acquisition as rational contingency learning. *Applied Linguistics, 27*(1), 1–24. https://doi.org/10.1093/applin/ami038

Fan, M. (2000). How big is the gap and how to narrow it? An investigation into the active and passive vocabulary knowledge of L2 learners. *RELC Journal, 31*(2), 105–119. https://doi.org/10.1177/003368820003100205

Fang, Z., & Schleppegrell, M. J. (2008). *Reading in secondary content areas: A language-based pedagogy.* University of Michigan.

García, G. E. (1991). Factors influencing the English reading test performance of Spanish-speaking Hispanic children. *Reading Research Quarterly, 26*, 371–392. https://doi.org/10.2307/747894

Gardner, D. (2013). *Exploring vocabulary: Language in action.* Routledge.

Gardner, D., & Davies, M. (2014). A new academic vocabulary list. *Applied Linguistics, 35*(3), 305–327. https://doi.org/10.1093/applin/amt015

Goldstein, H., & Healy, M. (1995). The graphical presentation of a collection of means. *Journal of the Royal Statistical Society Series A 158*, Part 1, 175–177. https://doi.org/10.2307/2983411

González-Fernández, B., & Schmitt, N. (2019). Word knowledge: Exploring the relationships and order of acquisition of vocabulary knowledge components. *Applied Linguistics, 41*(4), 481–505. https://doi.org/10.1093/applin/amy057

Gyllstad, H., Vilkaitė, L., & Schmitt, N. (2015). Assessing vocabulary size through multiple-choice formats: Issues with guessing and sampling rates. *ITL International Journal of Applied Linguistics, 166*, 276–303. https://doi.org/10.1075/itl.166.2.04gyl

Hall, C. J. (2002). The automatic cognate form assumption: Evidence for the Parasitic Model of vocabulary development. *International Review of Applied Linguistics*, *40*, 69–87. https://doi.org/10.1515/iral.2002.008

He, X., & Godfroid, A. (2019). Choosing words to teach: A novel method for vocabulary selection and its practical application. *TESOL Quarterly*, *53*(2), 348–371. https://doi.org/10.1002/tesq.483

Helms-Park, R., & Deonjic, V. (2013). Cognates. In C. A. Chapelle (Ed.), *The encyclopedia of applied linguistics*. Blackwell.

Howatt, A. P. R. (2004). *A history of English language teaching* (2nd ed.). Oxford University Press.

Ishikawa, K., & Rubrecht, B. G. (2008). English loanword use on Japanese television. In K. Bradford Watts, T. Muller, & M. Swanson (Eds.), *JALT2007 conference proceedings*. JALT. http://jalt-publications.org/archive/proceedings/2007/E007.pdf

Iwaizumi, E., & Webb, S. (2022). Measuring L1 and L2 productive derivational knowledge: How many derivatives can L1 and L2 learners with differing vocabulary levels produce? *TESOL Quarterly*, *56*(1), 100–129. https://doi.org/10.1002/tesq.3035

Janssen, R., Schepers, J., & Peres, D. (2004). Models with item and item group predictors. In P. De Boeck & M. Wilson (Eds.), *Explanatory Item Response models: A generalized linear and nonlinear approach* (pp. 189–212). Springer-Verlag.

Kendall, M. G. (1955). *Rank correlation methods*. Hafner Publishing Co.

Kremmel, B. (2016). Word families and frequency bands in vocabulary tests: Challenging conventions. *TESOL Quarterly*, *50*(4), 976–987. https://doi.org/10.1002/tesq.329

Kremmel, B. (2017). Development and initial validation of a diagnostic computer-adaptive profiler of vocabulary knowledge. Unpublished doctoral dissertation, University of Nottingham.

Kuperman, V., Stadthagen-Gonzalez, H., & Brysbaert, M. (2012). Age-of-acquisition ratings for 30,000 English words. *Behavior Research Methods*, *44*, 978–990. https://doi.org/10.3758/s13428-012-0210-4

Kuppens, A. H. (2010). Incidental foreign language acquisition from media exposure. *Learning, Media and Technology*, *35*(1), 65–85. https://doi.org/10.1080/17439880903561876

Laufer, B. (1989). What percentage of text-lexis is essential for comprehension? In C. Lauren & M. Nordman (Eds.), *Special language: From humans thinking to thinking machines* (pp. 316–323). Multilingual Matters.

Laufer, B. (2000). Task effect on instructed vocabulary learning: The hypothesis of 'involvement'. In *Selected papers from AILA '99 Tokyo* (pp. 47–62). Waseda University Press.

Laufer, B. (2005). Focus on form in second language vocabulary learning. *EUROSLA Yearbook, 5,* 223–250. https://doi.org/10.1075/eurosla.5.11lau

Laufer, B., & Cobb, T. (2019). How much knowledge of derived words is needed for reading? *Applied Linguistics,* 1–29. https://doi.org/10.1093/applin/amz051

Laufer, B., Elder, C., Hill, K., & Congdon, P. (2004). Size and strength: Do we need both to measure vocabulary knowledge? *Language Testing, 21*(2), 202–226. https://doi.org/10.1191/0265532204lt277oa

Laufer, B., & Goldstein, Z. (2004). Testing vocabulary knowledge: Size, strength, and computer adaptiveness. *Language Learning, 54*(3), 399–436. https://doi.org/10.1111/j.0023-8333.2004.00260.x

Laufer, B., & Paribakht, T. S. (1998). The relationship between passive and active vocabularies: Effects of language learning context. *Language Learning, 48*(3), 365–391. https://doi.org/10.1111/0023-8333.00046

Laufer, B., & Ravenhorst-Kalovski, G. C. (2010). Lexical threshold revisited: Lexical text coverage, learners' vocabulary size and reading comprehension. *Reading in a Foreign Language, 22*(1), 15–30.

Levitzky-Aviad, T., & Laufer, B. (2013). Lexical properties in the writing of foreign language learners over eight years of study: Single words and collocations. *EUROSLA Monographs, 2,* 127–148.

Lotto, L., & de Groot, A. M. B. (1998). Effects of learning method and word type on acquiring vocabulary in an unfamiliar language. *Language Learning, 48,* 31–69. https://doi.org/10.1111/1467-9922.00032

Łuniewska, M., Haman, E., Armon-Lotem, S., Etenkowski, B., Southwood, F., Anđelković, D., Blom, W. B. T., Boerma, T., Chiat, S., Engel de Abreu, P., Gagarina, N., Gavarró, A., Håkansson, G., Hickey, T. M., Jensen de López, K., Marinis, T., Popović, M. D., Thordardottir, E., Blažienė, A., Cantú-Sánchez, M., et al. (2016). Ratings of age of acquisition of 299 words across 25 languages: Is there a cross-linguistic order of words? *Behavior Research Methods, 48,* 1154–1177. https://doi.org/10.3758/s13428-015-0636-6

McLean, S. (2018). Evidence for the adoption of the flemma as an appropriate word counting unit. *Applied Linguistics, 39*(6), 823–845. https://doi.org/10.1093/applin/amw050

Melka, F. (1997). Receptive vs. productive aspects of vocabulary. In N. Schmitt & M. McCarthy (Eds.), *Vocabulary: Description, acquisition, and pedagogy.* Cambridge University Press.

Montelongo, J. A., Hernandez, A. C., Herter, R. J., & Hernandez, C. (2010). Vocabulary/Vocabulario: The transparency and morphology of Spanish–English nouns. *The California Reader*, *43*, 5–10.

Nagy, W. E., García, G. E., Durgunoglu, A., & Hancin-Bhatt, B. (1993). Spanish–English bilingual children's use and recognition of cognates in English reading. *Journal of Reading Behavior*, *25*, 241–259. https://doi.org/10.1080/10862969009547816

Nation, I. S. P. (1990). *Teaching and learning vocabulary*. Newbury House.

Nation, I. S. P. (2006). How large a vocabulary is needed for reading and listening? *Canadian Modern Language Review*, *63*(1), 59–82. https://doi.org/10.3138/cmlr.63.1.59

Nation, I. S. P. (2013). *Learning vocabulary in another language*. Cambridge University Press.

Nation, I. S. P. (2016). *Making and using word lists for language learning and testing*. John Benjamins.

Nation, P., & Crabbe, D. (1991). A survival language learning syllabus for foreign travel. *System*, *19*(3), 191–201. https://doi.org/10.1016/0346-251X(91)90044-P

O'Sullivan, B. (2020). *The comprehensive learning system*. British Council. Retrieved 14 September 2021 from: www.britishcouncil.org/sites/default/files/the_comprehensive_learning_system_new_layout.pdf

Otwinowska, A., & Szewczyk, J. M. (2017). The more similar the better? Factors in learning cognates, false cognates and non-cognate words. *International Journal of Bilingual Education and Bilingualism*. https://doi.org/10.1080/13670050.2017.1325834

Palmer, H. E., West, M. P., & Faucett, L. (1936). *Interim report on vocabulary selection for the teaching of English as a foreign language*. Report of the Carnegie Conference, New York 1934, and London 1935. P. S. King and Son.

Paquot, M. (2010). *Academic vocabulary in learner writing: From extraction to analysis*. Continuum.

Paribakht, T. S., & Wesche, M. (1997). Vocabulary enhancement activities and reading for meaning in second language vocabulary acquisition. In J. Coady & T. Huckin (Eds.), *Second language vocabulary acquisition* (pp. 174–200). Cambridge University Press.

Pellicer-Sánchez, A., & Schmitt, N. (2012). Scoring Yes–No vocabulary tests: Reaction time vs. nonword approaches. *Language Testing*, *29*(4), 489–509. https://doi.org/10.1177/0265532212438053

Perhan, Z. (2008). Enhancing English vocabulary knowledge through instruction on Ukrainian–English cognates in a Ukrainian undergraduate program. Master's thesis, available from ProQuest Dissertation and Theses database.

Peters, E. (2018). The effect of out-of-class exposure to English language media on learners' vocabulary knowledge. *ITL International Journal of Applied Linguistics, 169*(1), 141–167. https://doi.org/10.1075/itl.00010.pet

Pinchbeck, G. G., Brown, D., McLean, S., & Kramer, B. (2022). Validating word lists that represent learner knowledge in EFL contexts: The impact of the definition of word and the choice of source corpora. *System, 106*, 102771. https://doi.org/10.1016/j.system.2022.102771

Pinchbeck, G. G., & Schmitt, N. (2018). Word list development and validation. Presentation at AAAL 2018, Chicago, USA.

R Core Team. (2020). *R: A language and environment for statistical computing.* www.R-project.org

Rasch, G. (1960). *Studies in mathematical psychology: I. Probabilistic models for some intelligence and attainment tests.* Nielsen & Lydiche.

Read, J. (2000). *Assessing vocabulary.* Cambridge University Press.

Rijmen, F., Tuerlinckx, F., De Boeck, P., & Kuppens, P. (2003). A nonlinear mixed model framework for item response theory. *Psychological Methods, 8*(2), 185–205. https://doi.org/10.1037/1082-989X.8.2.185

Rodgers, M. P. H., & Webb, S. (2011). Narrow viewing: The vocabulary in related television programs. *TESOL Quarterly, 45*(4), 689–717. https://doi.org/10.5054/tq.2011.268062

Rogers, J., Webb, S., & Nakata, T. (2015). Do the cognacy characteristics of loanwords make them more easily learned than noncognates? *Language Teaching Research, 19*(1), 9–27. https://doi.org/10.1177/1362168814541752

Schepens, J., Dijkstra, T., Grootjen, F., & van Heuven, W. J. B. (2013). Cross-language distributions of high frequency and phonetically similar cognates. *PLOS ONE, 8*(5), e63006. https://doi.org/10.1371/journal.pone.0063006

Schmitt, N. (2010). *Researching vocabulary.* Palgrave Macmillan.

Schmitt, N. (2019). Understanding vocabulary acquisition, instruction, and assessment: A research agenda. *Language Teaching, 52*(2), 261–274. https://doi.org/10.1017/S0261444819000053

Schmitt, N., Jiang, X., & Grabe, W. (2011). The percentage of words known in a text and reading comprehension. *Modern Language Journal, 95*(1), 26–43. https://doi.org/10.1111/j.1540-4781.2011.01146.x

Schmitt, N., Nation, P., & Kremmel, B. (2019). Moving the field of vocabulary assessment forward: The need for more rigorous test development and validation. *Language Teaching, 53*(1), 109–120. https://doi.org/10.1017/S0261444819000326

Schmitt, N., & Schmitt, D. (2014). A reassessment of frequency and vocabulary size in L2 vocabulary teaching. *Language Teaching, 47*(4), 484–503. https://doi.org/10.1017/S0261444812000018

Schmitt, N., & Schmitt, D. (2020). *Vocabulary in language teaching* (2nd ed.). Cambridge University Press.

Schmitt, N., Schmitt, D., & Clapham, C. (2001). Developing and exploring the behaviour of two new versions of the Vocabulary Levels Test. *Language Testing, 18*(1), 55–88. https://doi.org/10.1177/026553220101800103

Schmitt, N., & Zimmerman, C. B. (2002). Derivative word forms: What do learners know? *TESOL Quarterly, 36*(2), 145–171. https://doi.org/10.2307/3588328

Schonell, F. J., Meddleton, I. G., & Shaw, B. A. (1956). *A study of the oral vocabulary of adults*. University of Queensland Press.

Seidlhofer, B. (2005). English as a lingua franca. *English Language Teaching Journal, 59*(4), 339–341. https://doi.org/10.1093/elt/cci064

Shiotsu, T. (2011). Producing an index of word difficulty through learner self-assessment data: An application of Rasch modelling. In B. O'Sullivan (Ed.), *Language testing: Theories and practices*. Palgrave Macmillan.

Simpson-Vlach, R., & Ellis, N. C. (2010). An academic formulas list: New methods in phraseology research. *Applied Linguistics, 31*(4), 487–512. https://doi.org/10.1093/applin/amp058

Smolík, F., & Filip, M. (2022). Corpus-based age of word acquisition: Does it support the validity of adult age-of-acquisition ratings? *Plos One, 17*(5), e0268504. https://doi.org/10.1371/journal.pone.0268504

Sorrell, C. J. (2012). Zipf's law and vocabulary. In C. A. Chapelle (Ed.), *Encyclopedia of applied linguistics*. Wiley-Blackwell.

Stadthagen-Gonzalez, H., & Davis, C. J. (2006). The Bristol norms for age of acquisition, imageability, and familiarity. *Behavior Research Methods, 38*, 598–605. https://doi.org/10.3758/BF03193891

Sylvén, L. K., & Sundqvist, P. (2012). Gaming as extramural English L2 learning and L2 proficiency among young learners. *ReCALL, 24*(3), 302–321. https://doi.org/10.1017/S095834401200016X

Thorndike, E. L., & Lorge, I. (1944). *The teacher's word book of 30,000 words*. Teachers College, Columbia University.

Tonzar, C., Lotto, L., & Job, R. (2009). L2 vocabulary acquisition in children: Effects of learning method and cognate status. *Language Learning, 59*, 623–646. https://doi.org/10.1111/j.1467-9922.2009.00519.x

Tréville, M. C. (1996). Lexical learning and reading in L2 at the beginner level: The advantage of cognates. *Canadian Modern Language Review, 53,* 173–190. https://doi.org/10.3138/cmlr.53.1.173

van den Berg, R. G. (2019, 26 December). Kendall's tau – Simple introduction. Retrieved 6 March 2021 from: www.spss-tutorials.com/kendalls-tau/

van Zeeland, H., & Schmitt, N. (2013). Lexical coverage in L1 and L2 listening comprehension: The same or different from reading comprehension? *Applied Linguistics, 34,* 457–479. https://doi.org/10.1093/applin/ams074

Wang, J., & Chen, B. (2020). A database of Chinese–English bilingual speakers: Ratings of the age of acquisition and familiarity. *Frontiers in Psychology, 11,* Article 554785. https://doi.org/10.3389/fpsyg.2020.554785

Wang, J., Liang, S.-L., & Ge, G.-C. (2008). Establishment of a medical academic word list. *English for Specific Purposes, 27,* 442–458. https://doi.org/10.1016/j.esp.2008.05.003

Ward, J. (1999). How large a vocabulary do EAP engineering students need? *Reading in a Foreign Language, 12*(2), 309–324.

Ward, J., & Chuenjundaeng, J. (2009). Suffix knowledge: Acquisition and applications. *System, 37,* 461–469. https://doi.org/10.1016/j.system.2009.01.004

Webb, S., &. Rodgers, P. H. M. (2009a). Vocabulary demands of television programs. *Language Learning, 59*(2), 335–366. https://doi.org/10.1111/j.1467-9922.2009.00509.x

Webb, S., & Rodgers, P. H. M. (2009b). The lexical coverage of movies. *Applied Linguistics, 30*(3), 407–427. https://doi.org/10.1093/applin/amp010

Wesche, M., & Paribakht, T. S. (1996). Assessing L2 vocabulary knowledge: Depth versus breadth. *The Canadian Modern Language Review, 53*(1), 13–40. https://doi.org/10.3138/cmlr.53.1.13

West, M. (1953). *A General Service List of English words.* Longman, Green & Co.

Zhu, K. (2011). On Chinese–English language contact through loanwords. *English Language and Literature Studies, 19*(2), 100–105. https://doi.org/10.5539/ells.v1n2p100

Zimmerman, C. B. (1997). Historical trends in second language vocabulary instruction. In J. Coady & T. Huckin (Eds.), *Second language vocabulary acquisition.* Cambridge University Press.

Authors